YOUNG AT HEART

The Good Years

A Memoir: Traveling, Living and Loving

Sandra Pelanne

DAWNING DAY PUBLISHERS

Delray Beach

Cover Image: pixabay.com

Cover Design: Lily Pelanne

ISBN 978-1-7325430-0-3

Dawning Day Publishers
7749 Doubleton Drive
Delray Beach, FL 33446

Printed in the United States of America

Dedicated to my mother, Ruth "Golda" Cohen Stadtlander,

for saving my letters and making this memoir possible.

"I've never tried to block out the memories of the past, even though some are painful. I don't understand people who hide from their past. Everything you live through helps to make you the person you are now."

—Sophia Loren

ACKNOWLEDGMENTS

In writing this memoir I received encouragement from disparate places and would like to express my thanks to several special individuals. Foremost would be my husband, Claude, who helped me by offering his thoughts and support all along the way while dealing with a sensitive time in my life, and our two daughters Lily and Mimi for their patience. Lily took the extra time needed to help design the book cover. Her expertise was greatly appreciated.

Thanks also to my dear friends Ina Mazer, Jane Finn and my cousins Sally and Chuck Pehr who read my memoir in its entirety and made constructive and sometimes critical editing comments. Emily Wolpers helped with research and Caroline and John Bliss encouraged me to continue writing as did The Writers Colony, and my teacher and editor, Barbara Cronie of Editing Par Excellence.

CONTENTS

CONTENTS

1

High School and My Family

When I was in my early twenties in the mid-1960s, it was a particularly tumultuous and rebellious time in American history. There was the Vietnam War, the Civil Rights Movement, Women's Liberation, and political assassinations of Robert Kennedy and Martin Luther King, Jr., just for starters. My escapades during those years were life-altering ones that began the messy, painful process of moving from the impossible notion of invincibility in youth to acquiring a few nuggets of wisdom along the path to responsible adulthood. And so, with my mind still intact, it's important to capture those moments before they are lost to me forever. But it's best if I start with high school, that's where my dream of traveling started.

Watching the clock above Mr. Maloney's head, waiting for the bell to ring in algebra class, then hurrying out to the wall for a quick smoke, I always tried to avoid the popular girls who congregated to one side of the wall while the cool guys huddled nearby with smoke wafting above their heads in ring-like halos. My best friend Susan and I exchange comments about the day as the morning rituals begin. We plot our next Saturday afternoon outing to the *Encore,* a bar in Shadyside in a district of Pittsburgh, Pennsylvania known for live music.

Susan and I had disengaged from high school in the eleventh grade, almost like graduating before it was time. We remained only in body, our spirits lay elsewhere. When we hit the ripe old age of sixteen and seventeen, we were dating the college crowd at the University of Pittsburgh or "Pitt" as it was affectionately known. Our Saturday afternoons were spent at the *Encore Cocktail Lounge* listening to the Harold Betters Jazz Quartet. Harold was a masterful trombonist and a well-known musician on the Pittsburgh music scene. When the quartet played "Moanin'" made famous by Art Blakey's Jazz Messengers, it was impossible to keep your hands or feet from tapping out the rhythm on the bar or floor. What could be better than listening to stirring, soulful jazz while chugging down mugs of cold, frothy beer? Somehow we were able to get admitted using fake ID cards provided by older siblings, or simply daringly forged on our own. Susan was my link to obtaining a fake ID. Her older sister, Kay, was the go-to person for anything remotely illegal. She never failed us.

"You need a new identity card? Done. You need a six-pack? Done."

We were never denied entry. Susan, with her flawless, blonde pageboy and big, blue mascara- laden eyes, attracted the college jocks like the quarterback getting rushed at the two-yard line. Usually the overflow of sweaty, swaying hunks would eventually move in my direction, although my short brown pixie wasn't nearly the draw. We would stand in the crowded space undulating to the music, bodies brushing against one another, listening to the rhythmic beat of the band all for the price of a beer. The room filled with smoke and a general haze enveloped it like a dense fog. When I opened my mouth to speak over the din, the acrid taste entered my lungs and practically burned a hole in my throat. The music was deafening.

"Susan, can you hear me? Harold's on a roll! The trombone has to be the most amazing instrument ever invented! Isn't he the best?" The smoke was so heavy I could hardly breathe. I managed to choke out the words in raspy gasps.

"I can barely make you out," she laughed. "Yeah, he's totally awesome. Makes the smoke and slippery floors worth it." She gingerly danced a few steps in my direction avoiding the puddles of beer.

There was never any thought given to the possibility of getting caught or whether my father would be disappointed in me or worse, punish me if he discovered where I spent my Saturday afternoons. My brothers, Sid and David seven and five years older than I was, never had restrictions placed on them like I did. They had cars and had the freedom to come and go at will. Then they went off to college where they did what they wanted when they wanted. My father enforced strict curfews, and I resented having my life ruled by him. He was brought up by a stern disciplinarian, my *Opa* (grandfather) who resorted to using a leather belt to keep his sons in line.

My father used the same tactics on my brothers when they were younger. He never hit me. His angry voice was enough to make me comply as I retreated to my room to sulk. My admiration and love for him never wavered, and if I did anything to displease him, his anger was enough punishment. My mother the quiet, repressed house *frau,* was much more lenient and overlooked some of my lesser infractions. On occasion she hurled a dirty dish rag from the kitchen sink in my direction, splattering coffee grounds and potato peels all over the wall. She always seemed to miss.

My mother's relationship with my father was a constant source of interest. She was born in Poland and arrived in Ellis Island in 1920 when she was twelve years old. Her golden brown hair as a child led to her nickname, "Golda." Her flawless, fair complexion and green eyes were in contrast to my father's dark hair, ruddy complexion, and brooding countenance—plus he was a German Jew. My mother was convinced that German Jews had nothing but scorn for their Polish counterparts. German Jews were well educated and had better economic opportunities than the poorer Polish Jews.

My father's sister Aunt Regie showed little respect for my mother, treating her like a peasant who was never good enough for her darling, younger brother whom she adored and affectionately called, "*Valush.*"

"Your father was so brave when he had his accident. It was before his Bar-Mitzvah. He never complained, even when he was in terrible pain. I cried for days when it happened. Your father was special, very special," she emphasized.

When my father was twelve years old in Cologne, Germany, he had been playing with molten lead that accidentally came into contact with cold water and exploded in his face. He never got proper medical treatment for severe facial burns.

"I took him everywhere with me like a mother hen protecting her chick. He suffered terribly. You know I taught him how to dance. We went to all the popular nightclubs and dance parlors together. He was my dance partner."

"That explains why he taught me to dance in the basement," I said. "While my friends were jitterbugging up a storm, we were gliding across the floor doing the tango." My dad would spend Sunday afternoons in our rec room teaching me to cha-cha, mambo, samba, and tango. My friends thought it was pretty cool that my father was my dance instructor. He had a graceful way of dancing with his right arm held high with my hand comfortably resting in his. He led me confidently around the room, steering me away from the furniture pushed to one side of the room. Those were afternoons I looked forward to since I had my father's undivided attention. The strains of Latin music would fill the room and vibrate off the walls of the enclosed, dimly lit room. He clearly delighted in teaching me to dance. Aunt Regie told me he once won a trophy at a South American dance contest. His seductive interpretation of the dances must have been hard to resist, particularly if the judges were women.

The room had pine paneled walls and a curved bar for serving drinks. I would quietly sneak down the stairs to the basement and steal the tiny bottles of enticing, forbidden liquors that were stored behind the bar and fill the bottles with water. This practice came to a grinding halt when Dolores, the maid, was fired. I was ashamed that I had contributed to her demise. Even though I was feeling less than honorable, I did not disclose that I was the Grand Marnier thief for fear of my father's wrath. We had many illicit parties in that room and had filled many bottles with water. At one such party, members of the Pitt football team stole kosher, frozen chickens from the basement freezer as a joke. My mother was not amused.

Some days I would come home from school to find my aunt sitting on my father's lap giggling with delight as they *kibbitzed* (kidding around) in German. Aunt Regie had a distinctive, joyful laugh that emanated from somewhere deep inside her petite body. She was very affectionate with all five of her siblings, although my father was clearly her favorite. It always seemed a bit off to me to see her on my father's lap since I never found my mother there, but I never questioned it. My mother would mutter her discontent under her breath. It was clear she was not happy, but confronting my father was *verboten* (forbidden). She never argued with my father in front of us. He intimidated her. He was the established king of the household, and no one dared challenge him. However, she used to mock him *sotto voce* (quiet voice) in English and Yiddish when he said something she totally disagreed with.

"Who does he think he is, some big *macher*? (big shot) He's talking nothing but *dreck* (crap)." These priceless comments were usually made as she was preparing one of my father's favorite recipes like sweet and sour meatballs. She figured she could manipulate him with food. Any self respecting wife or mother wouldn't hesitate to use her best weapon.

She wore her sense of humor like a shield of armor to protect herself from my aunt's onslaught and my father's indifference. My father developed a hearing loss later in life so he never heard what she said aloud to herself. Besides, he didn't have a sense of humor as far as I could tell except when he was with his siblings, and he clearly didn't appreciate my mother's humor—she could have written *The Joy of Yiddish.* When she got together with her sisters, each with a funny story to tell, the room would come alive with peels of laughter as they crossed their legs in unison to avoid a mishap.

There was only one time I ever saw my father laughing uncontrollably. He was standing in front of our hall mirror trying on various hats from the closet, and then peering intently at his reflection. He deemed this spectacle of himself to be raucously funny, laughing so hard that he was coughing to catch his breath. It was difficult for me not to laugh along with him since I had never seen this silly side of my otherwise reserved father.

How they had managed to stay married all those years was inexplicable to me. My father read incessantly, appreciated opera, fine art, antiques, and expensive clothes. He bought my mother exquisite diamond necklaces, other fine jewelry, and furs. My mother was not impressed with material things, and rarely wore any of his extravagant gifts. She enjoyed a simple life without the frills. She used cucumber juice on her face instead of exotic elixirs. She lit the candles on Friday night at sundown, reciting the Hebrew prayer as she swayed back and forth with a lace doily covering her head, her hands cupped over her eyes.

Her nickname, "Golda," seemed justified since she possessed a golden heart to match. My mother was a favorite aunt to many of my female cousins. She was a good listener, "*Nu . . . nu*, tell me what's bothering you," didn't judge them when they discussed problems with their *boychiks* (boy friends), and always gave sound advice. One of many important attributes she instilled in me was trustworthiness. She was everyone's confidante, but remained true to each one, never revealing information that was given to her in confidence.

As much as my father was admired, he was uncomfortable discussing relationships and feelings. He once remarked to me, "Why are you always trying to climb inside my head?"

"I'm just trying to get you to express your feelings. I know you have them."

"You've read too many books . . . Sigmund Freud maybe?" He visibly squirmed at my probing questions about whether he loved his children equally. I always felt he hadn't treated David and Sid the same although he denied it. The fact that Sid had chosen my father's profession selling iron and scrap, made it easier for him to be critical of him. My father had difficulty showing affection although I never doubted his love for me. My brothers couldn't approach him in this direct way, but being the youngest and the only daughter afforded some special privileges. Of course my brothers thought I was the chosen child. My analytical nature and the dynamics of interpersonal family relationships kept my mind in a constant state of flux. It was vital for me to better understand the mysterious, circuitous route of motives and actions in the name of familial love.

They were mismatched. She kept kosher, he didn't. She was a Democrat, he was a Republican. She spoke Yiddish, he spoke German. It was never clear to me whether they could speak each other's native language or just refused. My mother thought this was my father's way of showing his disdain for her Polish-Jewish background. It was beneath him to speak Yiddish. It was the language of the downtrodden, the dispossessed.

"When I met your father, it was at a friend's party. I don't know how to say it, but I couldn't take my eyes off him. At Donahue's (the donut shop where she worked), the *goyim* (non-Jews) and *alte kakers* (old farts) were always flirting with me, but he was different. When he asked me to dance, I almost fainted." They danced the night away. She mentioned the mere touch of his arm sent shivers down the entire length of her body—she was clearly smitten.

"He came to the United States in 1932 with just the clothes on his back. He had nothing. He spoke only German, but he was charming, handsome."

"How did you talk to him if he didn't speak English?" I asked.

"Who needs to talk? He was a wonderful dancer. Our courtship was short. His mother was dying in Germany and he wanted to go back to Cologne to take care of her. He didn't have enough money for a ticket."

"Don't tell me you gave him the money? You didn't even know him."

"Well, yes, I did. I gave him the money because I had faith in him. I believed he would pay me back." She had some savings from her job at the bakery. Two of her four sisters worked there with her. "Selma and Margaret thought I was crazy to lend him the money. They said I'd never see him again, that he was a *nishtikeit* (a nobody) and he would never amount to anything. I didn't listen to their *chazerei* (junk, trash)."

After three months passed and my mother hadn't heard from him, she began to question her decision. But he did return, eventually repaid the loan, and they were married in 1934. To the surprise of my mother's sisters, he became a well-respected businessman and entrepreneur, founded a large iron and scrap company, and became a leading philanthropist in the Jewish community. My mother never wavered in her belief that he would accomplish great things. She would tell me he was a *macher* (a big shot) and a *mensch* (honorable person) when she was feeling kindly toward him.

When my father was away traveling for business, it was a time for my mother to relax, and for me to make my move. "Susan, tonight's the night. My dad's going out of town on business again. I think Ohio. Time to sneak out of the house. Let's *par-tay*! I have to wait until my mom's asleep but I should be good to go at midnight. Where should we meet?"

"Beechwood and Fifth at 12:15. I'll bring the booze."

"Sounds like a plan. I'll grab a few bottles from the bar and bring flashlights." My teenage years were rebellious ones. I took an inordinate number of chances and never once got caught sneaking out of the house in the middle of the night.

Susan had an incurable crush on my father. She would drop over unexpectedly if I told her my father was home, usually over weekends. Susan was infatuated with his sophistication, his manicured nails, Hickey Freeman suits, his soft German accent, and twinkling blue eyes. And then there was the distinctive facial scar as an added attraction that lent an aura of mystique. He had a permanent, smooth, pink, hairless scar that pulled his lip down on one side of his mouth as though pinned there. In those days in Germany, there were no treatment options for severe burns, and he never received plastic surgery. Susan had romanticized this horrific accident.

"Can't you picture your dad a swashbuckler fighting off the bad guys? Suddenly one of them slashes his face with a saber. He valiantly survives with blood gushing down his face, permanently scarred." She dramatically waved her arms in a slashing motion.

"You mean like the Three Musketeers?" *Oh, brother. She has it bad.* To my mother's dismay, Susan was not the only woman enamored with my father. There had been many over the years plus rumors of a South American lover.

My father set the future stage for my traveling affinity in 1953 when I was eight years old. He took the family to Europe and Israel for the entire summer. He wanted to visit his brother Max who lived in Paris, and return to Cologne to see if his family home was still intact after World War II, surprisingly it was. The seeds were sown for a lifelong desire to travel. Even during the summer of 1962 after graduating high school, instead of preparing for college like my school mates, I took a cross-country trip by bus with a friend just to see the good old USA. Traveling was in my blood.

2

Stephens College 1963 and Harlem

I had painful memories of prejudice and discrimination from my freshman year of college in 1963 which was spent at Stephen's College, an all girls' liberal arts college in Columbia, Missouri. It was the school my Texan sister-in-law had attended and she had spoken highly of it, but I hadn't bothered to do my research. When I arrived at Stephen's, I discovered it wasn't integrated. This revelation weighed heavily on my mind and kept me awake at night. How could I speak of my belief in equal rights for all and attend a college that restricted admittance to a select, privileged, white segment of the population? If I was destined to remain there for the year, I would make it a productive one and take an activist role in bringing integration to the school. Most of the students were from the South, and I was in the distinct minority being a liberal Jew from the East.

My views on the subject were made clear to anyone who would listen to me. The southern atmosphere and downright prejudice of some of the student body put me on the firing line on a regular basis. A student from Alabama shared a particularly telling story about her black housekeeper who spent the night at her home to care for her ailing father and had taken a bath. After the housekeeper left, the bathtub was unceremoniously thrown out! It was my first hand experience with the weight of southern intolerance in the 1960s . . . not only was it directed toward blacks, it was also directed toward Jews.

22

One of the Southern belles accused me of stealing her watch, conjuring up the stereotypical portrayal of the money-grubbing Jew. My handful of loyal friends consisted of southerners, midwesterners, and an international free spirit from Sweden. They paid a visit to my accuser and told her to shut her trap and stop spreading lies, or she would regret it. My best friend Emma didn't tell me about the confrontation until months later. It was reassuring to know that I had a principled group of friends who were willing to defend me during that difficult year.

Mr. Hannigan, my favorite instructor who taught a course in religion and philosophy, was organizing a trip to Harlem for spring break and was looking for twelve volunteers. It was coordinated with the East Harlem Triangle Association, a social services organization. The students would be trained in surveying the inhabitants of a designated block of buildings targeted for demolition. A new public housing complex was scheduled for construction within a few years. In order to qualify for housing, the residents had to meet strict, new guidelines—no prior arrests, no drugs, no alcohol. The East Harlem Triangle Association was convinced that the surveys would provide proof that the current residents would not qualify for public housing and thousands would be left homeless if the buildings were razed.

"Emma, what do you think of joining me on this trip to New York? It's a worthy cause, a trip to remember and tell your future kids about." I encouraged her.

"You mean Harlem don't you? If I told my parents where I was going, they would flip out. There's no way they would let me go. I know you have a huge crush on Mr. Hannigan. Is that the real reason you want to go?"

"Okay, I admit I have a crush on him, but you know I believe in social justice. You've told me a thousand times that I'm a real pain in the ass about it. This is a chance to elevate talk into action and enjoy the company of Mr. Hannigan for a week. Hey, I'm not proud. I can kill two birds with one stone." She rolled her eyes at me and shook her head, swinging her silky blonde hair from side to side.

"I've never called you a pain in the ass. Dang it! I don't use vulgar language. Southern upbringing is more genteel than that."

"Is that so? Well you said it in your own genteel southern style. I got the message loud and clear," I jokingly replied.

Emma had to come with me. She was a pretty blonde with rosy cheeks, a freckled-face, and a priceless southern Missouri twang that made me smile every time she opened her mouth. She had grown up in a segregated community devoted to family and small town living. Her knowledge of blacks was mainly as domestic servants to the white population in Cape Girardeau. It took considerable prodding and encouragement before she asked her parents for permission to go. I assured them I would look after her. Surprisingly, they believed me.

Soon it was spring break. We were packed and ready to leave. It was Emma's first plane ride. She couldn't contain her excitement from the moment the plane took off and we climbed above the clouds. The flight would take us through Washington, D.C. with a connection to New York City.

We landed at Idlewild Airport at 4:00 a.m. Mr. Hannigan ushered the group to a bus going to the Westside Terminal in New York City. We arrived at our destination an hour later, tired but excited about the week to come. Reverend Clark was there to meet us. He gave us a quick overview before leaving us at the Memorial Chambers Baptist Church in Harlem. We were greeted by group leaders and sweet rolls. We were totally exhausted. They explained that it was too early to be taken to our host families so we could sleep in the church pews for a few hours. Later we were introduced to our hosts and were given the rest of the day to explore the city before our orientation meeting. We were on our own.

"We look like complete hags . . . hayseeds from Missouri . . . like we just fell off the turnip truck. My hair is all straight and stringy."

Emma's hair was definitely limp. We were hot, sweaty, and worn out before we realized, we had walked from 70th to 42nd street.

"My feet are worn down to stubs . . . they feel dead. I'm just plum tuckered out," Emma continued. We tried to be unobtrusive as we walked swiftly through the streets of Harlem, speaking softly trying not to draw attention. Our senses were bombarded with the sights, sounds, and smells as we passed people sitting on the stoops of buildings, smoking, talking and staring as we walked by. From open windows we caught the aroma of coffee intermingled with strange, pungent spices that we couldn't identify. Emma tried to conceal her blonde hair with a black scarf and wore dark sunglasses and a trench coat. Even so, some guy called out, "Hey, Blondie!" I thought Emma would jump out of her skin. She was visibly shaken. Our white faces stood out in an expansive profusion of brown ones. There was no hiding the fact that we were *crackers* (whites).

We attended an orientation meeting and listened to a spokesperson from the housing authority try to convince the people in the audience that they would be accepted into public housing without a problem. There was muffled whispering. No one was buying their little white lies. Our group leaders prepared us for the surveys. Emma was ecstatic to learn she could use her Spanish (it was her major) in many of the areas we would be surveying. The questions on the surveys were personal, intrusive about drug use, and past criminal offenses. We split up into small groups with Emma and me sometimes separated. I wondered how she would hold up without her sidekick there to reassure her everything would be all right.

We were eighteen years old with little experience with life and death situations. The stories we heard had common threads involving drugs, alcohol, illicit sex, arrests, and the complete breakdown of the family unit. Living conditions were appalling. Buildings reeked of urine, feces, mold, and dirty laundry. There were no phones, intermittent heat and hot water, or none at all. Mattresses and pillows were black, soiled beyond recognition, paint peeling off the walls in strips. Cockroaches scurried up and down the walls and floors helter-skelter like a scattering army in retreat.

We checked our beds nightly after finding cockroaches in our suitcases, one on Emma's toothbrush, and one on my pillow. "Boy, does this stink. I actually stepped in a human turd. I almost gagged but didn't want to offend anyone. Even had a cockroach run up my leg but didn't flinch," Emma said and then shuddered in disgust.

"I had the most incredible interview with a madame who ran a prostitution ring with underage girls. She went to jail for it. She asked me how old I was, and then told me her girls were younger than I was. I couldn't believe how honest she was. She'll never get into public housing."

"I actually had one funny interview. This woman said she had so many mice in her apartment that they came out to play at night and went 'squeak, squeak.' She said she gave them names and talked to them while she was in bed."

"Did you laugh?"

"At the time I did, but now that I think about it, she must have been loopy."

Emma and I went to a boarding house together to collect a few surveys. It was in deplorable condition with broken windows, rotting food, and empty liquor bottles lining the darkened hallway. It was like entering a House of Horrors at Kennywood Park outside Pittsburgh. There were four boys living in one room: nineteen through twenty-three. It was minimally furnished with two beds pushed into corners and a small dirty couch. There was trash littering the floor. Emma kept her foot propped in the door to keep it open while I conducted the interview . . . *smart move.* They told us no one else lived there with them, but we spotted black heels and hosiery under a bed and a woman's rumpled dress on the couch. We were certain they were high on dope. The stale air was heavy with the smell of marijuana. I managed to keep the interview on point and they answered all our questions without incident. As we left, we were afraid to turn around until we safely walked out into the street and breathed a sigh of relief—it was a scary afternoon.

During the week my father came into New York City on business. I wasn't sure whether he actually had work to do, or whether he was there to check up on me and report back to my mother that I was safe. Emma and I met him for dinner one night at a posh midtown restaurant decorated with crystal chandeliers and golden drapes. The patrons were in elegant dinner attire. We were miles and eons from daily life in Harlem.

"We look like piddlin' waifs. These uppity folk will think your dad picked us up off the street."

"Or they'll think he's our sugar daddy," I added. "It's unreal after Harlem. Though it'll be hard to beat shrimp Creole and sweet potato pie." My dad was clearly happy to see me. He greeted me with a big, exuberant hug. I was just as happy to see him. His eyes were especially blue and twinkling.

"So how's your trip so far?"

"Interesting. Meeting lots of nice people and learning about life in the Big Apple. New York is amazing." Emma and I had agreed to keep the conversation light on specifics or my dad might have yanked us out of Harlem. We enjoyed a good meal of sirloin steak and potatoes *au gratin*. He seemed satisfied with our report and put us in a taxi for our return ride.

On our way back we saw a woman run across Madison Avenue with blood streaming down her face. She was screaming and trying to get someone to stop. No one did. After the elegant dinner with my father, it was surreal.

"I interviewed a sixteen-year-old girl who was a member of one of the Puerto Rican gangs in East Harlem. She's been sleeping with men since she was eleven years old and knew every kind of contraceptive imaginable. I actually learned a few tricks," said Emma.

"That's interesting Emma, especially since you're still a virgin. Take notes for future reference," I said with a grin. But I remember thinking, it wasn't funny at all. She was only eleven years old when she started having sex? It was appalling, but I didn't want to upset Emma with one of my deeper, unsettling analyses until we had left New York City.

"I heard she's the toughest girl on the block. She told me she got mad at a storekeeper the other day and threw a key at him slicing off part of his ear. You think she was lying?"

"I don't know. Maybe trying to shock you. Either way, I sure don't want to mess with her."

During the week we went to see "The Blacks," a provocative off Broadway play by Jean Genet, the French playwright. We sat in the front row facing an all black cast wearing masks. They stared at us threateningly as they performed their roles depicting racial hatred and discrimination in our society. It was a powerful, emotional performance. We walked out of the theater in a daze.

The Neighborhood Triangle Association had informative talks about narcotics, social work, and Black Nationalism, an ominous black power organization in Harlem that was growing in strength. We attended a dance at the church and had no reservations dancing with partners, black, tan or somewhere in between. Emma was teased relentlessly for her accent. They were convinced she was from the Deep South. It was a great feeling to overcome fear and racial barriers along with a raw dose of reality in witnessing life's injustices, an education we would never have gotten if we hadn't volunteered for this project.

Before we left Harlem, we wanted to buy a gift for our hosts. We were told to go to 86th Street, but took the subway to Fifth Avenue instead and went to Saks. We decided to buy a solid white towel set with brown trim instead of one with a pattern since the walls were busy enough.

Emma scrubbed her black girdle with Ajax for the last time. We then reluctantly packed our suitcases, staying vigilant for marauding cockroaches trying to hitch a ride to Missouri, sad to be leaving our new found family of friends.

Toward the end of my freshman year, Stephens became integrated. I had the honor of hosting the first black student to the campus. Emma and I agreed she was the whitest black person we had ever seen. After considerable soul searching, I decided to transfer to Pennsylvania State University in State College, Pennsylvania to complete my education. I felt I could exert my freedom of expression there without persecution. The Stephen's College administration was happy to rid themselves of their resident rabble-rouser. After I transferred to Penn State, my father told me he received a letter from the college six months before, complaining about my activist activities. He said he was proud of me and what I was trying to achieve. My one regret was no longer hearing Emma's endearing twang. We never found out whether the information we compiled in Harlem ever had its desired effect.

In May of 1966 I graduated from Penn State with a BA in Social Welfare. It was finally time to put my plan into action, spread my wings and fly. If I had gone to Europe for my junior year abroad, I might never have come back to graduate. There was a plan that had been germinating for years waiting to be executed—I would go abroad after graduation.

3

Europe Here I Come!

Rather than go to a four-year college like the majority of our class, Susan my best bud had taken a different route. She attended a two-year program in New York City to become a retail fashion buyer and already had her first job. I warned her well in advance of my graduation that once I had my BA degree in hand, I would be embarking on a European adventure and I was counting on her to join me. She had been an integral part of my life since seventh grade, and this adventure would be one more chapter to add to our scintillating history together.

When I called her to tell her of my plan, she said without hesitation, "I'll quit my job! When do we leave?" No questions asked. That was the Susan I knew and loved; such was the impulsive nature of youth.

As a graduation gift, my father reluctantly gave me a thousand dollars for the trip, thinking I would only be gone for the summer, and once I ran out of money I would come home with only visions of graduate school dancing in my head.

"Remember, that check is all you're getting. Your mother and I still don't know why you have to go for the whole summer. You need to get ready for graduate school. That's the plan."

"But Dad, you know how I love to travel. It's like the whole world is out there waiting for me to discover it," my arms outstretched emphasizing the magnitude of my dream finally coming to life.

"Something like an explorer going into uncharted waters. It's exciting just thinking about it. Don't worry I haven't forgotten 'The Plan.'" I used two fingers from each hand to indicate quotation marks.

He needed some convincing before bidding me *bon voyage* since he could not fully understand my fascination with Europe. He had emigrated from Germany in 1932 before the war when he was twenty-four years old. He intended to visit an uncle living near Pittsburgh and make his life there. He appreciated the freedom and opportunity that America provided without persecution, and my plan of going back to Europe had little appeal.

"You can't trust those people. I had many friends in Germany who wouldn't have anything to do with me because I was Jewish. We grew up together, went out drinking together, went dancing together, but the Nazis changed all that. They turned their backs on me like they didn't even know who I was." He was haunted by this fact and never failed to remind me how his German friends shunned him once Hitler came onto the world stage. It was a cautionary tale and I understood his reservations. He never stopped to realize I was seeking an adventure just as he had when he decided to leave Germany for parts unknown.

My adventure began by embarking on the Cunard's *Queen Elizabeth* to Cherbourg, France, in May 1966, a six-day Atlantic crossing. Susan decided to fly since she needed to give adequate notice at her job. Our plan was to meet in Paris. We would stay with my Aunt Andrée and Uncle Max, who lived in a suburb of Paris. We were both twenty-two years old.

Standing on the deck of the ship with my parents before it set sail was both exhilarating and slightly daunting. My secure and predictable life would be gone forever once the ship set sail, and I thought my parents sensed that their independent daughter was about to sever the cord forever. Wearing a blue and white checked wool coat and a rakish beret, I waved goodbye with a flourish, blinking away tears. I had high hopes, a rapidly beating heart and thoughts of exciting exploits in my future as land slipped away from view. Never once did I worry about being a young, single woman traveling alone.

The ship proved to be my first learning experience. My ticket was in Cabin Class, similar to today's Business Class, so I was assigned to a dining table with stodgy English businessmen. Being twenty-two and the youngest passenger traveling alone, created quite a stir with my dining companions. The group was in disbelief that my parents had permitted me to travel alone without supervision. They collectively decided it was prudent to take me under their protective wings. Never having associated with men my father's age, particularly proper Englishmen, it was a little unnerving to become a subject of their melodrama.

The full force of class discrimination and stuffiness of English society descended upon me and brought the issue front and center. Walking the decks, speaking to deck hands and craving conversation with sailors my age was considered unconscionable and beneath my class. The lectures given on proper protocol for a young lady of my station were a daily subject of conversation at the dining table. Sitting there quietly, grinding my teeth while they bombarded me with their intolerance was enough to give me indigestion after an otherwise perfectly sublime meal.

"I say, you can't speak to seamen as you would to your family or university friends. They are working-class chaps. I dare say your father would not permit you to speak to a tram driver in *your* country would he?" It was all about appearances. Instead of getting into a pissing contest, I refrained from answering. The assumption they could summarily tell me to whom I could speak was insufferable.

Now that I was on my adventure to Europe, the stodgy old farts on the *Queen Elizabeth* could never alter my sense of equality for all that I had fought to preserve my freshman year in college. During the voyage, I managed to maintain a sense of decorum at the dining room table, although I was certain I had ground my teeth down to stumps.

France: The Art of Being A Francophile

My Uncle Max met me at the Gare du Nord train station. He drove a big, black Citroen. He always reminded me of a dashing George Raft, an actor from the 1940s, even to the same cigarette dangling out of the corner of his mouth. He was my father's oldest surviving sibling in a family of seven children; a quiet man with twinkling eyes when he smiled, much like my father's. I had always admired him. Stories of his escape from the Gestapo had become legendary within the family. He had been a successful nightclub owner and well-known boxing promoter in Germany. His fighters had become champions. Articles about them and Uncle Max appeared in all the sporting magazines of the time. Uncle Max was famous. The Nazis weren't happy with his celebrity. They were determined to either lock him up on trumped-up charges, or dispose of him altogether. He was too successful, too renowned, and Jewish—a wanted man.

It was never clear whether the story had been embellished over the years, but he managed to elude the Gestapo with the help of his German girlfriend. She had saved his life by being taken prisoner rather than disclosing his location. He escaped to Paris where he became a member of the French Resistance during World War II where he remained throughout the War.

Uncle Max visited us once in Pittsburgh. My father wanted him to live in the US like the rest of his siblings, but Uncle Max concluded that life in the US was harsh. He claimed my father worked too hard and had little time for enjoyment. He was accustomed to his stress free life in Paris where he had become a prosperous diamond merchant. My father expressed disappointment with his decision, but Uncle Max returned to France to live out his life.

We picked up Susan at the Orly Airport several days later. Staying with relatives, particularly a French aunt who talked incessantly in three languages (English, French, and German), was another revelation. Susan and I were used to showering every day. The water tank hanging above the bathtub was heated by electricity, and it was in continual operation. Aunt Andrée found this daily routine to be wasteful given the high cost of electricity and the frugal nature of the French. She vociferously complained to my uncle after each shower, in German and then French to emphasize the point, but he generally ignored her constant complaints. Instead of using soap and hot water, Aunt Andrée's personal hygiene consisted of masking her perspiration with a bottle of French perfume. The combination of body odor and perfume saturated the air of the close quarters of their house. It was enough to make you sick or force you outside to the tiny balcony for a breath of fresh air. Susan's take on the situation was that my Uncle Max was spending too much time ogling her and Aunt Andrée was jealous.

"Hey, I know when someone's flirting with me. Can't you see him staring at me and smiling? I caught him looking longingly at my boobs. He's got nothing but lust in those lecherous eyes."

"You must be doing something to encourage him."

"Well, I did smile back just to be polite," she meekly replied. "He reminds me of your father. He's sexy."

Aunt Andrée was twenty-five years younger than Uncle Max, and it was conceivable that she was jealous of Susan receiving so much attention. Susan may have had a legitimate point. I acknowledged Uncle Max did seem unduly solicitous to her. Whatever the reason, we were kicked out of the house after two weeks. Maybe it was just the impetus we needed to finally venture out on our own.

We were confident that we would be able to make our way through the streets of Paris even though we didn't speak French well. The French had a reputation for being rude to Americans and not speaking English even if they could. Instead, we were surprised to find them curious and helpful when we asked for information or directions.

Our first priority was finding an apartment that we could afford, so we headed to the *Alliance Française* on Boulevard Raspail, a central meeting place for international students. There was a large bulletin board in the main lobby covered with job notices, items for sale, and apartment rentals. An interesting advertisement caught our eye for a small two bedroom apartment on rue de Varenne, near the Rodin Museum. It sounded reasonable. We could afford it if we found a third roommate. Susan, always one to seek out opportunities, boldly walked up to a heavyset American girl who was also standing at the bulletin board.

"Hi, I notice you're looking at the same ads we are. Need a few roommates? The two Ss, Susan and Sandy—ready, willing, and able. In other words, we're available."

"Great! I was checking you out too and was about to ask you the same question. Name's Christine. Where are you from? I detect a midwestern twang."

"Well, you're not too far off. Western Pennsylvania, actually Pittsburgh."

"Neat! Official home of the Pirates. I'm a big fan of Maz (Bill Mazeroski). Will you ever forget the 9th inning in the 1960 World Series when Maz hit that home run to beat the Yankees? It was the best World Series game in the world! I'm from St. Louis. Love the Cardinals but my heart beats for the Pirates." *She's certainly an enthusiastic sports fan.* The decision was made to live together. We had something in common . . . baseball.

The apartment was on the third floor. There was a rickety two-person elevator and a crooked, well-worn staircase to the upper floors. Depending on the day and how courageous we were feeling, Susan would opt for the elevator. I usually preferred to walk up the three flights instead. When the door snapped shut inches from my nose, I felt like I had been locked into a slowly moving casket that was going up instead of down. It was an anxiety-provoking few minutes.

The Frenchness of the apartment was thoroughly charming with long windows that swung out to an interior courtyard. The ceilings were exceptionally high, and it was light and bright in keeping with the classic Haussmann architecture of the late nineteenth century. Georges-Eugene Haussmann had been commissioned by Napoleon III to renovate Paris and was instrumental in its superior restoration and design. The sloping, crosshatched, wooden floors creaked even if you stepped lightly on them. Not surprisingly, you could always hear Christine coming in advance of seeing her bulky body even if you were sleeping. A few weeks after she moved in with us, I found candy wrappers and empty food containers on the floor and under her bed on a regular basis, a good reason to explain her weight. In short, Susan and I thought she was a slob, but she was good-hearted and paid her share of the rent.

The electricity went off frequently, another reason to avoid the elevator. We were forced to take romantic baths with a silver candelabra sitting by the side of the tub, dripping candle wax on the floor. It was like a scene from the opera, *La bohème,* with Mimi's garret lit only with candlelight. Since we were on a limited budget, our culinary talents were restricted to mostly omelets with sautéed onions and potatoes. They were tasty and most importantly, cheap to make.

"Let's go to the Le Mans car race. I've heard it's sort of like the Daytona 500. Could be a fun scene watching the French enjoy their time off, swilling bottles of wine the whole time," I said.

"Great suggestion! I've never gone to a racetrack before, and that one is world famous. How do we get there?" Susan was on board.

"Already checked it out on my Metro map. We can take the train from Gare Montparnasse. It should take about an hour."

"Boy, aren't you the efficient one. I'd forgotten how you plan things right down to the tiniest detail. The world's greatest planner!"

"That's me. Efficient Ernestine. I don't like surprises. I prefer to anticipate problems before they happen. Remember the Girl Scout Motto—'Be prepared.'" *Of course, I never made it past the Brownies.*

"Well, you're living up to your name now." Susan always complimented me on time well spent in planning.

Wanting to immerse ourselves in as much French iconic culture as possible, the twenty-four hour sports car race held on June 18-19, 1966, would be an exciting excursion. In our naiveté and having attended only baseball and football games, we were entirely unprepared for the throngs of enthusiastic French fans who were jostling and pushing to get inside the narrow entrance to the track. The event was sold out and everyone wanted to make it through the gate. It was our first realization that the French were not always polite or civil when it came to their beloved sports. We were sucked into a human riptide from which there was no escape, as each wave of the crowd was thrust violently forward through the gate. We feared that we might be crushed or trampled to death as we surged onto the field, belched out in a stream of humanity.

We crammed into the stands under a heavy, gray sky anticipating rain at any moment. There was electricity in the air. It almost made your hair stand on end. The tension was palpable. The boisterous crowds were chattering away in French and other mostly unidentifiable foreign languages. Some of the patrons hung over the railings with fancy silk scarves waving in the breeze trying to get a better look at the fifty-five racing cars lined up beside the pit stops. A band marched down the track playing "The Star Spangled Banner" followed by "God Save the Queen" (the British National Anthem). The band played eight different national anthems in all with flag bearers carrying flags representing each country. There were colorful signs surrounding the track for Cinzano, Esso, Firestone, and Renault. The public address system blasted out instructions to the drivers and fans. Although Susan and I were unable to distinguish the words, we sensed the race was about to start. A helicopter hovered overhead adding to the cacophony of noise as it flew low, back and forth over the crowds.

Then there was a rush of activity. The mechanics rapidly changed the tires on the waiting cars, and drivers ran to their cars, jumped in, revving the engines to a roar, quickly navigating the cars away from the pack, and taking off down the track in a cloud of dust.

Ferrari had dominated the last eight races, winning seven consecutively. This time Henry Ford II, who was at the race, was determined to turn the tables on Ferrari. He entered eight MK IIs and five GT 40s, all Ford produced cars. It was fascinating to watch the race cars come in for their pit stops and see the mechanics' precision in fueling the cars and changing tires in a matter of nanoseconds.

While wandering around the track we met two American guys who were also taking in the scene for the first time. They told us they had come to the race in a car. "It might be a good idea to latch onto them. Remember, this race is an overnighter," Susan suggested.

"Yeah, Susan. We can always crash in their car for a few z's." Hours later we all retreated to their beat-up Peugeot for a short nap. As she nodded off, the guy in the back seat with Susan kept trying to make out with her. It got to be too much of a hassle. "Okay, bozo I've reached my point of no return." She pushed him away for the last time. We hopped out of the car and returned to the grandstand.

With the first rain drop, Susan and I decided to leave. After the unpleasant experience entering the track, we did not relish the thought of staying to see the finish, fearful we would be subjected to another human tsunami.

"Can't say that was particularly enjoyable. We were lucky to get out alive. I was seriously afraid of falling and having sweaty, smelly Frenchmen pile on and crush me to death. And adding rain to the mix—it would've been a big, muddy mess." Susan adjusted her crisp, white, cotton top that had gotten smudged with dirt in the initial fray. She was all about fashion and looking her best. Even during moments of duress, she never forgot her appearance and her public persona. It was of utmost importance to her.

"But it was so exciting hearing those revving engines and then seeing them come down the track at breakneck speed. They were really bookin' it. I loved it! It's amazing that they're racing for twenty-four hours. At least we can say we were there." We found out later that we had missed the best part. It was the first time in history that America's Ford placed first, second, and third in the race. Ferrari's record had been dashed by the mighty Americans.

"I need a drink." Susan was ready for refreshments after leaving the racetrack.

"Let's try *Harry's American Bar*," I said, feeling the need to seek out fellow Americans for a bit of camaraderie after our harrowing day.

Instead of Americans, I met my first Frenchman. Jean-Michel was diminutive in size, had wavy, sandy-colored hair, and a determined, self-confident air. He was very French-looking with sunken cheekbones like the famous singer Charles Aznavour. He was facing the door with one elbow resting on the bar. His stance struck me as being posed for effect like one of those jockey lawn statues I used to see in our Pittsburgh neighborhood, except he was white. Willie Shoemaker came to mind, but without his jockey's cap.

As I stood inside the entrance adjusting my eyesight to the dimly lit room, he approached me with a swagger like he had rehearsed this maneuver many times before. I was charmed by his French, the melodic, sultry language of Edith Piaf. He didn't speak a word of English. My high school French was put to the test—Madame Dubois would have been proud.

"*Parlez-vous anglais?*" (Do you speak English?) My accent was pure American.

"*Non*," he replied. "*Parlez-vous français?*" (Do you speak French?)

"*Je parle français un peu.*" (I speak a little French)

"*Voulez-vous un verre?*" (Do you want a drink?) he asked, gesturing toward the bar. "*Je vais t'apprendre le français.*" (I'll teach you French) Susan and I hung out with Jean-Michel until late into the night. He was effervescent and chatty.

Our conversations were fairly basic for our first few encounters. We then started dating regularly and managed to communicate using various methods: my trusty English/French dictionary, hand gestures, and general body language. When we saw each other, he would automatically kiss me on both cheeks, the customary French greeting, taking care not to ruffle his clothes or hair. He took great pride in being immaculately dressed and coiffed. This French salutation always seemed peculiar to me when a simple handshake would do.

"Don't you think it's odd the way Jean-Michel kisses both your cheeks? He really doesn't even touch them. He puckers up and then kisses the air. Does he think you have cooties?"

"That's an excellent point. The French don't seem to be self-conscious about practically screwing in public after they semi-kiss cheeks. Go figure. It's like dogs sniffing each other's butts before they hump each other. It's weird."

After barely more than a couple of weeks going out with him, he started writing me poetry. His poems were about love and longing. He could have copied them verbatim out of a French book of poetry, and I never would have been wiser. He professed his undying love, *"Je t'aime, mon amour. Épouse-moi."* (I love you, sweetheart. Marry me.) He wrote with a flourish using a black ink pen. It resembled calligraphy.

Even in my frivolous youth, I knew it was American citizenship he sought. He made it clear we would marry and then move to the United States. He provided male companionship which I savored, but I was not looking for a husband. We walked all over Paris together, usually ending a splendid afternoon at one of the spectacular public parks. We frequented the Tuileries and Luxembourg Gardens, where he gave me my first French kiss after he perfunctorily kissed both cheeks. After kissing the air, he had no qualms displaying his amorous tendencies. He stuck his tongue halfway down my throat. I almost gagged.

At times I felt like I was watching a porn peep show while at other times I became an active participant. Children sailed their miniature boats on the pond while we whittled the day away sitting in the cafés on the Left Bank, museum hopping, and visiting the zoo. I don't remember him ever having a job. Maybe he could get a job embossing wedding invitations.

Courses at the *Alliance Française* helped sharpen my conversational language skills since Jean-Michel was forever correcting my high school French, and it was getting annoying.

"*Non, non, non, ce n'est pas correct, cherie!*" (No, no, no, that isn't correct, sweetheart!) Jean-Michel wanted to impress his young, American girlfriend by demonstrating his eloquent French language usage. His pronouncements of love seemed disingenuous and calculating after our short time of togetherness. Knowing his ulterior motive to use me as his conduit to the United States kept me from having substantive feelings for him. Not to be callous, but he was serving a purpose by teaching me French and providing some diversion while I was living in Paris, nothing more. Once I left Paris, I knew he would soon be forgotten.

One day we had lunch at one of the myriad cafes lining the avenue along the Seine. Jean-Michel became impatient when he couldn't get the attention of the waiter, so he abruptly stood up and left without paying the bill. I sheepishly followed him. I kept turning around to see if the waiter was galloping toward us with a *gendarme* (policeman) waving a gun. Another time a waiter accidentally dumped his tray of food down Jean-Michel's back, defiling his newly pressed suit and scarlet ascot. It was not a pretty scene with a seething Jean-Michel lambasting the waiter for his clumsiness.

"*Merde! Vous pourriez faire attention!*" (Shit! Be careful!) He demanded the waiter pick up his cleaning tab in his prissiest, most condescending tone. He was unequivocally pissed! *I was secretly amused.*

He was also responsible for introducing me to my first artichoke. He ordered it for me and then attentively watched as I fidgeted in my seat. I had no clue what to do with it. *It seems inconceivable that you use a knife and fork to cut it.*

"*Qu'est-ce qu'il y a, cherie?*" (What's wrong, sweetheart?) It was clear from his question that he was teasing me. After an agonizing few minutes of embarrassment and viewing it from every angle, he offered to show me how to dissect it. He dipped the ends of the leaves in the delicious garlic infused mayonnaise until he eventually exposed the artichoke heart. It seemed like a laborious undertaking for such a paltry reward, but he relished every delectable morsel.

Jean-Michel had a tiny studio apartment with a single sink in the middle of the room where he took sponge baths and a water closet (toilet room) in the common hallway. The toilet known as a Turkish toilet, was a virtual pit in the floor with two non-skid strips on either side one for each foot to keep from slipping into the abyss, as you strategically poised your butt over the hole in hopes of making a direct hit. This type of toilet—I'm being generous to call it that—was found in many of the bars and restaurants around Paris during the 1960s, but it seemed incongruous finding it in a residential apartment building where residents used it on a regular basis. It certainly kept potty time down to a minimum—no reading *Tin Tin,* the French weekly comic book while sitting on the throne. There was a long chain dangling from the wall tank to flush. The toilet paper was either a waxy-coated paper or ripped up newspaper squares, both equally unsatisfactory. It was a primitive excuse for a toilet. How do you adequately wipe yourself with wax-like paper while squatting or standing upright? The first time I flushed, I failed to jump out of the way, as the water swirled around my feet thoroughly soaking my shoes.

"*C'est très drôle!*" (That's very funny!) He practically collapsed on the floor doubled over with laughter when I relayed what had happened. *What a schmuck!*

He seemed to enjoy belittling me so he could demonstrate his total command and control of the situation. There was something arrogant about him, and I was at his mercy since I didn't speak fluent French. But I suffered through these humiliating episodes for a purpose . . . he provided a valuable service as tour guide to the City of Lights, and he had perfected the French kiss. I finally got up the courage to ask him where he showered. After living with my aunt and uncle, I wasn't surprised when he told me he went to a public bathhouse once a week. Remember the joke about the French—the safest place to hide your money is under a bar of soap.

Finding a job was equally as important as finding companionship and becoming immersed in French culture. Again, we were drawn to the *Alliance* and the bulletin board. Susan started selling *The International Herald Tribune*. She lasted two days. Then she got a job as a maid working for some weirdo who told her never to wake him up or face dismissal. I found a job as a waitress and kitchen helper at a small café in Porte d' Orleans. It meant taking either the bus or Metro on a daily basis. Madame LaFontaine, the matron, ran her tiny restaurant of ten tables like a platoon sergeant. It was a family affair consisting of her husband and two young children, and I followed her lead as she commandeered the troops.

The walls of the restaurant dining room were covered with quaint country scenes from Provence where the owner's family vacationed every summer. They added a touch of coziness to the tiny restaurant and its stark, whitewashed walls. There were ten small, wooden tables with white linen tablecloths and matching cloth napkins. The same customers came in daily for lunch. They brought personalized napkin holders which they left on the tables with their used napkins at the end of the meal. The napkins would be reused for several days. This was a curious custom, but saved on daily laundering. Restaurants only used cloth napkins. When lunch was over, I stacked them on a shelf of a buffet each with an identifying napkin holder. Once the napkins became unduly soiled, they were handed to me. Madame LaFontaine would take them to the laundromat to be washed and ironed.

There wasn't any set menu. It was at the whim of Madame LaFontaine. The clientele appeared faithfully between 12:00 p.m. and 2:00 p.m. to partake of her delicious home-cooked, simply prepared meals. My favorite was her veal stew with a salad of sliced tomatoes topped with raw garlic and homemade vinaigrette. I watched and later assisted, as she prepared the daily meals, delivering them to anxiously waiting customers, and finally completing my chores by washing the dishes by hand at the end of the day.

She kept the ripe Camembert cheese, a staple in the last course of the meal, in a drawer instead of the refrigerator. The strong, pungent cheese would almost overpower the sweet aroma of sauteing onions, leeks and other assorted vegetables, sizzling in the pan as she prepared the day's succulent meal. It was here that I learned to cook. The only downside to my job was taking the overcrowded buses or Metro crammed with people reeking of garlic, Gauloises (strong, unfiltered French cigarettes), BO, and the ever-present perfume on my homeward trek.

Working in a French café was a thrilling opportunity. It conjured up images of great chefs getting started in the kitchen, doing menial work before climbing the ladder of success. Maybe I would follow the same path to fame as Julia Child. My only other job had been a part-time housekeeper for a faculty member in my senior year of college. There was no comparison.

Madame LaFontaine gave me leftovers to supplement my meager salary. Susan eagerly awaited her inspired cooking, always beating Christine to the door of our apartment. "Hey, what delectable yummies do you have for me today?" She hungrily eyed my backpack. "Let's eat fast. Christine won't be back for half an hour."

"Don't you feel even a tiny bit guilty? She is our roommate after all." This maneuver to outsmart Christine always made me uneasy.

"No, why should I? Does she offer to share her candy bars or chocolate eclairs? Besides, who said we had to be fair? Life isn't fair." Her blunt comments were unforgiving. She was visibly disappointed if I showed up empty-handed, it meant eating omelets. Learning by observation and practicing what I observe made me feel confident that I was making a contribution to the French labor force while lining my pockets with a few disposable *francs*.

One regular patron took a fancy to me, the *charmante* (charming) young American. He was a slimy-looking cartoonish character with polished, black hair and a hunched over body that formed the letter "C." He sat alone at the same table every day and tried repeatedly to bump or touch me when I walked by his table. He smelled of perspiration and musty old clothes, probably not showering for days or even weeks given Jean-Michel's personal hygiene. *What a ghastly thought!* He occasionally stuck out a twisted leg to try and trip me. It made me increasingly cautious of every step I took when I navigated around his table. There was no way to avoid him since the café was minuscule in size, and I was the only waitress. I considered dumping a plate of food on him like the waiter had done to Jean-Michel, but I was worried Madame LaFontaine might fire me. Trying to explain the situation to her in my rudimentary French would have strained my working knowledge of the language, so I suffered in silence.

Susan made a few cogent suggestions. "Why don't you just tell him to buzz off. Or tell him he's a piece of *merde* and he reminds you of Dick Dastardly. Better yet, report him to the *gendarme* for *touchant* (touching) an under-aged virgin."

"Very funny. I'll give it some thought. You're lucky you don't have to deal with this smelly jerk."

"You should take pity on *me*," she said emphatically. "The crazy guy I work for must be running a drug ring or something. What if I accidentally wake him up? He'll probably shoot me."

At the end of July, Madame LaFontaine announced that the restaurant was closing in mid-August. The French considered the vacation month of August sacrosanct. Everyone exited Paris simultaneously, like a mass migration of geese heading south, leaving the deserted city behind to the intrepid tourists. Madame LaFontaine had become very fond of her *petite Americaine,* and invited me to join her family on their holiday in Provence. This announcement was the final curtain call on my job. As flattered as I was by the offer, I declined. Susan and I had other plans. We decided to leave the city and join our French compatriots on holiday.

Beware of Deux Chevaux Citröens

Making the decision to leave Paris, seemed easy enough. The difficult part was calculating how to pull it off with limited funds and no contacts anywhere in Europe except for Uncle Max. After thinking about it for several days, I concluded the only way to accomplish our goal was to hitchhike. It would require little to no money for travel expenses, and we could consolidate our finances for food and shelter. It sounded like the perfect solution.

I said my goodbyes to Jean-Michel and told him I would return by summer's end. We packed one suitcase each. We figured we would wash things as we went along to save on weight. On the day of our departure we gave Christine the September rent in advance and assured her we would be back. After consulting the Metro map, we took the Metro to its farthest point south with anticipation of adventures ahead. From there we were on our own—destination unknown.

Two young women, one with long, blonde hair, were an easy pickup. My dark brown, curly hair didn't conjure up the same fantasies as Susan's golden locks, but in the beginning we were able to flag down an infinite number of cars. For some odd reason getting into a car with a total stranger didn't seem to be a problem. We didn't give it a second thought. We decided to avoid cars with two men which might prove problematic, but that was the only reservation we discussed.

Initially, there was an abundance of friendly, curious drivers who stopped to give us a lift. Two slim, attractive, young women standing by the side of the road in mini dresses with arms outstretched, thumbs thrust skyward, and suitcases by their sides, presented an endless stream of choices. We soon became selective by shunning cars that seemed too small or pedestrian in preference for large, roomy, black

Mercedes or Citroens. The lowly Deux Chevaux, resembling a bug-eyed beetle with a rollback canvas roof, was an instant reject.

The drivers, mostly men, could not believe we were hitchhiking. They were right to be astonished. We were an oddity, but being foreigners we were quickly forgiven for the impropriety. Unlike the permissive 1960s era in America, provincial French societal norms were not accustomed to women hitchhiking. Most French young women of our age lived at home, worked, and waited to be married.

On our first day we managed to make it as far as the outskirts of Tours after a succession of uneventful rides. We were dropped off by the side of a country road lined with a canopy of *platane* trees (a type of Sycamore). It was a long, deserted road with fields of sunflowers on either side. The steady stream of passing cars had ceased soon after we left the environs of Chartres as we headed toward the southwest. There were slim pickings from that point onward, and we deposited our weary bodies on our suitcases and waited. Toward the end of the day, a dilapidated Deux Chevaux with bulging headlights ambled down the road.

"Do you think we should bite the dust and flag him down? We've been waiting in the same spot for hours."

"You mean you're ready to swallow your pride? I'm shocked."

"No one will see us if we hop in and slump down in our seat. Besides, I'm tired of waiting for a Mercedes to come along. Just as long as he isn't an ax murderer." Susan was definitely a snob when it came to the Deux Chevaux. She was a sophisticated party girl and had always gravitated toward the monied crowd of Thunderbirds and Corvettes. Was she ready to concede defeat?

"Okay, I agree. Time to bite the dust," I said. It was an opportunity to move our adventure further along, so we stretched out our arms with thumbs aflutter to catch his attention. The car slowed and came to a halt alongside us. Susan climbed into the back with our suitcases, and I sat in the front with the driver. She slouched out of sight immediately as soon as the car lurched forward. Driving in a

Deux Chevaux was like sitting on bouncing lawn chairs. When the car went over a bump, my head hit the canvas roof. At first glance the driver seemed innocuous enough, a typical thirty-something Frenchman dressed in blue workman's duds. We spoke little, and I stared out the window at the passing fields dotted with stone farmhouses, feeling relaxed and confident that we would make it to Bordeaux before nightfall. He turned his head frequently in my direction with a curious half smirk. *Is that a friendly gesture?* I couldn't be sure. Susan fell asleep.

It wasn't long before I noticed out of the corner of my eye, that the driver had unzipped his pants and was unabashedly masturbating! All he needed to complete the picture was the French flag waving from the summit! How could he drive with one hand while the other one was vigorously pumping his penis? And then to my alarm, he grabbed my hand and tried to place it on his flagpole! I was horrified, screaming to Susan to throw our suitcases out the door and jump.

"What do you mean jump?" She awoke abruptly startled by my shrill, frantic outburst.

"There isn't any time to explain, just *jump!*"

As I opened the passenger door, the driver realized I intended to jump out so he slowed down long enough for us to tumble out the door following our thrown suitcases. Miraculously, we managed to stay upright even though the car was still rolling, as we landed on the edge of the pavement with our bodies poised for an immediate sprint. It paid to be in shape.

My biggest fear was that he would stop the car and come after us. Running with a heavy suitcase was not in our plan book. Besides, there was nowhere to run. There was only a solitary road and deserted farmland on both sides. I filled Susan in on the sordid details as we hurriedly collected our suitcases and watched the dirty little Deux Chevaux come to a halt farther down the road. The driver got out and walked into the field, apparently to finish off the job.

"Now what were you saying about an ax murderer? Why didn't you consider the possibility of a fucking pervert?" My heart rate was racing as though I had just finished the ninety-yard dash.

As we nervously contemplated what to do before he returned to his car, we noticed another car approaching in the distance. Susan, pumped with adrenaline, began doing jumping jacks in the middle of the road to get the driver's attention.

"There's a pervert jerking off in the sunflowers! Stop! Stop the car!" she shouted.

"Do you really think we should flag him down?" My voice trembled in fear.

"Hell yes! What's the chance of a serial killer or another sexual deviant? Nil, zero, start jumping!"

I hope Susan's right. I'm not totally convinced. I began jumping high off the ground defying gravity like an acrobat on a trampoline. My legs began to shake violently on the verge of collapse, after witnessing the unexpected spectacle of a fully erect *schlong*. Why had we decided to hitchhike? It was all my fault. We were doomed. The driver slowed down from what seemed like a cruising speed of one hundred miles per hour in a huge, black Mercedes. We blocked the narrow two-lane road standing side by side, frantically waving our arms. He had no choice but to stop or run us over. There was panic in my voice as a stream of French words spilled out of my mouth.

"*Monsieur, si vous plaît, aidez-nous! La situation est dangereuse!*" (Sir, please help us! The situation is dangerous!) as I pointed to the parked Deux Chevaux down the road. He looked perplexed as though we just escaped from an insane asylum, shaking his head looking at us and then at the parked Deux Chevaux. My high school French vocabulary drew a blank when I needed descriptive terms like masturbation and erection, so I resorted to an X-rated version of Marcel Marceau, the famous French mime pantomiming what had happened.

"*Je comprends maintenant, mademoiselle.*" (I understand now, Miss.) His reddened face and embarrassed tone indicated he finally got the picture. He understood something terrible had happened. He connected the dots. We hesitantly climbed into the luxurious car with a sense of relief, but with a heightened sense of wariness. My hand gripped the car handle just in case, ready to flee at a moment's notice. The man in the black Mercedes safely delivered us to Bordeaux, our final destination of the day. He obviously had taken pity on us since he gave us money for a hotel, proving that not all men are evil. As the sun set on our first day, we were still alive and kicking, but for how long?

4

Spain: Do Blondes Really Have More Fun?

"I really want to see Spain, Portugal, and Italy, and our funds will only get us so far," I said. "Realistically, how can we do all this if we throw in the towel now? Bad things can happen in a flash. We know that, but are we willing to play Russian roulette?"

"We can beat the odds. I feel it in my bones. I'm convinced of it." Susan placed her hand over her heart for added emphasis. Our reality check was over. We never remained anywhere for longer than a day or two. Of course our itinerary depended on where the drivers were headed, so we remained flexible and fluid in order to change direction at any point. Our travels took us to Provence, then Biarritz on the west coast of France, through St. Jean de Luz, a charming seaside resort on the border of France, to San Sebastian our first Spanish destination.

Entering Spain presented new, unexpected problems. Spanish men were immediately drawn to Susan and her blonde hair. It was as though she were the Pied Piper using a blonde wig to round up the rats instead of a magic flute. They followed us down the street in droves like hound dogs pursuing their prey, occasionally having the nerve to touch or stroke her hair or worse, grabbing her between the legs.

"Should I wear a scarf or a brown paper bag over my head to get them to leave me alone?"

"I can pretend I'm leading you to the gallows (just kidding). A scarf will never do it. A bottle of black hair dye might do the trick," I teased.

"You know I'm not a natural blonde. I could go back to mousy brown."

"Let's try the scarf first before doing anything drastic. Covering your head might make you less conspicuous and reduce your chances of being a target." It was worth a try.

Hitchhiking through Spain was a challenge. In rural areas there were few cars and we spent hours, even days waiting for a ride to come along, wilting in the sun. It forced us to spend an inordinate amount of time in uninteresting, provincial villages where we were a novelty and where no one spoke English. People stared and pointed at us, particularly the elderly women dressed in black. They must have thought we had been banished from our families for some unthinkable act, or worse . . . prostitutes.

These towns reeked of olive oil no matter where we went. The nauseating smell hung in the heavy, dense air, tickling my nose hairs and creeping silently into my suitcase like the green slime from the 1958 science fiction movie *The Blob*. It was difficult to find anything to eat that wasn't swimming in a pool of EVOO. After a few days, I gagged whenever a strong whiff would blow my way.

"Susan, how can you stand it? Every town we've come to smells like rancid olive oil. It really makes me want to throw up. Do you think they would take it personally if I held my nose or got a surgical mask at the pharmacy? I'll tell them I have leprosy."

"Yeah, they'd probably be highly insulted. Then the next thing you know, there'd be a mob of women in black, throwing buckets of olive oil at us as they chased us out of town."

"If we died from the heat, they'd probably pick our bones clean like hyenas or vultures," I said.

"What a disgusting thought. You've seen too many Greek movies. But you're probably right." Susan grimaced. "I don't want to test that theory so don't die on me."

Our diet consisted mainly of paella, gazpacho, *tortilla de patatas* which reminded us of our comfort food in Paris (an omelet with potatoes and onions), and of course sangria. These select items were the only dishes we could find that did not have olive oil as its main ingredient. The other issue we struggled with was waiting until 10:00 p.m. or later to eat dinner. No one served food before that ungodly hour of the night. Even with Susan and her blonde locks, feigning famine and fatigue, the restaurant managers would not serve us. I often wondered how Spain's economy fared when most of their labor force was hungover every morning after their late-night dinners.

We slowly zigzagged our way to Bilbao in the Spanish Basque region, where we went to our first bullfight. Susan and I are devout animal lovers. Seeing the innocent bull who had no idea that his life was about to end tragically, being abused by *picadores* stabbing him with lances, was too cruel for words. Then the *banderillas* planted barbed sticks in his neck muscle. It was gruesome. Not only was it abusive to the bull, but the *picadores* came out riding heavily padded horses that were gored by the enraged bull. We left soon after this brutal display.

"I wonder how Ernest Hemingway and his fellow aficionados would have enjoyed their bull fights inside the ring instead of outside as spectators?" Susan nodded in agreement.

"It's hard to believe anyone could enjoy seeing animals suffer that way, but the crowd was really getting it on," I said. "It's like the more blood and gore, the more excited they got. Are we missing something?"

"I don't know. But whatever it is, I swear I'm never going to another bullfight."

"Neither am I."

The pageantry of the matador in his gold and silver embroidered costume strutting around the arena to the sound of trumpets, and the march-like music of the *pasodoble* would have been enough. It was our last bullfight.

From Bilbao we headed south to the interior, stopping in Toledo along the way to visit El Greco's house, and eventually arrived in Madrid after many days of travel. My minor in college had been art history, so I was anxious to visit as many famous museums as possible along the way. Having already spent days or perhaps weeks exploring the Louvre and the Orangerie in Paris, I was excited to add the Prado to my list, which housed the paintings of masters like El Greco, Goya, and Valázquez.

Unmitigated Chutzpah

In Madrid we were again confronted with the problem of men. While walking down the street, it was like an obstacle course trying to avoid them. They unashamedly tried to grab or grope us. We were not prepared for their lurid stares and blatant attempts to touch us. I considered buying a bat or umbrella and swatting them to keep them at bay like pesky flies.

"This is ridiculous. American men would never behave like sex-depraved animals. We should report them to the police." Susan had had enough.

"Do you really think we could trust the police to do anything? They'd probably throw us to these wolves like bait without a second glance."

"Wish we had a slingshot. I'd aim it right between their legs. Then we'd see some great balls of fire. Can't you picture them howling and hopping around grabbing their precious jewels?" We both broke out laughing.

"Well, we have to figure out something or we're never going to enjoy ourselves in this hateful country," I said. We continued fighting off legions of men everywhere. It dawned on us that the pervasive nature of this unpleasantness could mushroom into something more toxic. We felt unprotected and vulnerable. It was time to take action.

"What if we find someone to run interference? He could provide protective cover."

"What do you mean?" I said.

"Not sure, but preferably a guy, a humongous guy. Someone who knows Madrid and can show us around. Someone we can trust."

"You aren't going to find a big guy in Spain. They're all short. I'm taller than most of them."

"Okay, so he'll be a little guy but commanding like Napoleon. Size isn't as important as being aggressive, fearless. Maybe Al Capone-ish with a machine gun."

First we found a small hostel with a room so confining that the twin beds each touched a wall and each other. It was like a prison cell with paint peeling off the walls and bars on the windows. The only option for exiting the room was to jump from the bed to the door. It was unbearably hot, humid, and airless . . . but it was cheap.

Since appearances were everything, we put on makeup even though it was soon dripping down our cheeks in rivulets, and our most alluring dresses, well-wrinkled from limited laundry access. We made a speedy exit from our steam room to find our savior.

Our most productive encounter was with an older taxi driver, Hector. "Do you speak English?" I asked.

"Yes. *un poco.*"

"How would you like to protect us uh . . . *proteger?*" (after I consulted the Spanish dictionary) He looked at us askance, with a furrowed brow.

"*Guardaespaldas.*" I referred him to the dictionary pointing to the word for "bodyguard" since I couldn't even begin to pronounce it.

"*Sí,* yes!" A light bulb seemed to go on, and he immediately understood and smiled. He worked as a tour guide when he wasn't driving a taxi, and he seemed intrigued with the prospect of showing two young, attractive American women around the city in which he was born. He never asked for money or any favors in return, so we befriended him.

He drove us everywhere including outside the city where the arid, unforgiving landscape was populated only with boulders, to see the world-renowned *El Escorial,* the palace and monastery built by King Philip II. Construction of this historically significant site started in 1563 and took twenty-one years to complete. It was filled with Renaissance paintings and sculptures. We wandered through the formal gardens sweltering in the sun.

We then went to *Valle de los Caidos* (The Valley of the Fallen) eight miles north of *El Escorial.* It was built by prisoners to commemorate the countrymen who died in the Spanish Civil War in 1936. A cross 492 feet high was erected at the site, considered the largest one in the world. Controversy surrounded its construction. Francisco Franco, Spain's Fascist dictator, was instrumental in getting it built and he viewed it as a tribute to himself instead of to the Spaniards who had perished in the war. He's buried in a tomb in the basilica which is carved into the rocky mountainside underneath it. Regardless of this controversy, it is an imposing memorial site with the Sierra de Guadarrama Mountains serving as a lofty backdrop. We appreciated Hector's decision to take us there.

Hector and his friends introduced us to Flamenco music and dancing. We were taken to *tablaos,* which were smoke-filled cafés featuring popular dance troupes. The women dancers who appeared to be older and more mature, wore beautiful, ruffled dresses exposing their legs. As they stamped their feet in high-heeled pumps with precision and intensity to the Flamenco guitar, they swirled their dresses, shawls and fans to the seductive music. They played castanets as they danced from one end of the stage to the other.

"Get a load of those tight pants. You can see everything . . . I mean *everything.*" Susan couldn't take her eyes off the dancing men. She was practically drooling.

"Sexy, very sexy. They have amazing bodies. This must be like manna to these repressed housewives. Look at those bulges. Whew! Is it getting hot in here or is it me?" I fanned my face in mock amusement.

"Yeah, definitely more fun for women than men," she said. The men wore revealing tight, black pants and bolero jackets, exposing their chests and other body parts that left little to the imagination, while holding their bodies in an upright, stylized manner. Their boots forcefully stamped staccato-like steps as they clapped their hands to the rhythm of their heels. I was mesmerized by the passionate sensuality of the dance.

Heat Stroke and Sheer Stupidity

We spent more time in Madrid than planned, since Susan succumbed to the heat. The room was stifling. She was dizzy and nauseated, probably suffering from dehydration, and I worried about her health in a strange and unfamiliar country. She lay in bed unable to get up or open her eyes.

"Take me away . . . anywhere cold like Antarctica. Let's leave this fucking country to the bedbugs and the olive oil. This is the pits."

"I know you're delirious but you're making perfect sense. The temperature in this room must be 125 degrees. Close your eyes and meditate. Picture yourself on an iceberg sitting in the lotus position with a freezing butt."

"Okay . . . I'm visualizing. Polar bears, ice floes . . . now go get me some ice cold water. I could kill for a few ice cubes."

"Aye, aye, Capitano. I'll be right back." I gave her a military salute. "Going on a mission to find ice and bottled water, not an easy task." The temperature outside must have been over 100 degrees Fahrenheit, but in that muggy, airless room it was intolerable. Being young and strong, and having me as her nursemaid, Susan improved after several days and she felt well enough to venture out into the street. It was definitely a reason to celebrate.

Soon we were out on the town again. This time we decided to try our luck at a classy hotel bar. Susan's blonde hair was nectar to honey bees. Before long we snagged two handsome, dark-haired, older Spaniards. They both spoke impeccable English with British accents. We concluded, after reconnoitering in the ladies room, that they were well educated and well-heeled.

"They look like a safe bet. They're wearing fancy-schmancy Italian suits, and did you see those expensive Bruno Magli shoes?" Susan offered her immediate assessment based solely on their sartorial preferences. Her fashion sense was certainly more developed than mine. I couldn't tell a Bruno Magli from a common Oxford. "The taller guy is flashing a diamond ring on his pinky. Imagine that?" She was definitely impressed. *My father wears a blue sapphire on his pinky. Maybe she's drawing a comparison, and he definitely wears expensive suits.*

"Okay. You've convinced me. They'll show us the nightlife we've missed. People will think they're our sugar daddies, but what the hell. It's not like we're going to run into someone we know. Do you think they're married?"

"It's only one night of bar hopping and disco dancing. Nothing wrong with that. Who cares if they're married?" she said. We returned from our bathroom powwow psyched for the evening's festivities.

After a few drinks they invited us to their apartment, not to a nightclub. Susan and I stole glances at each other, trying to decide if that was a wise thing to do, but in the end we threw common sense out the window as we climbed into the interior of another huge, black Mercedes (obviously the car of choice for successful businessmen).

They drove us to an apartment building in a high-end neighborhood of Madrid, and we took the elevator to the penthouse floor. The apartment was furnished in elegant Louis XV gilded antiques with thick oriental rugs and oil paintings that I had only studied in my art history classes. We walked through the heavily gold draped living room as I admired the period furniture and priceless art collection. *OMG! It's like a museum. Is that a Monet above the mantle and a*

Renoir in the dining room? From the terrace that extended the full-length of the apartment, there was a breathtaking, panoramic view of the city skyline.

Before long, we were plied with several glasses of Moet & Chandon champagne—*nothing but the best for these guys.* We had hit pay dirt.

"Your apartment is beautiful," I said. "You definitely have an appreciation for the Impressionists." *How wealthy is this guy?*

"Yes, my family has collected art for years. Please, have another glass of champagne." He politely handed me my third glass with a broad self-assured smile. But my optimism was short-lived. They soon began to make advances, and we were clearly feeling a bit tipsy. The taller of the two men moved closer to me. *He's invading my personal space. He's trying to make me drunk? Duh, beware of tall, dark strangers.* He pushed himself against me and kissed me forcibly. Susan was busy fending off the other guy. We were caught off guard by their fresh assaults.

"No, get away from me. I don't want to kiss you. I don't even know you." I was getting upset.

"I like a feisty woman who puts up a fight." He came toward me aggressively again and grabbed me around the waist.

"I said, No, and I mean No!" Realizing we made a terrible mistake, I shook him off and ran to the other side of the room. It was time to survey our surroundings and prepare an emergency exit strategy. My attention was drawn to a plaque on the wall. It was a diploma from the University of Cairo. Another plaque indicated we were dealing with an Egyptian diplomat. Our suitors were not Spaniards! *Oh God, how did we make such a disastrous mistake? They're Arabs!*

My antennae were in full flight mode, like a grasshopper about to be gobbled up by an ugly toad—news flash, I'm Jewish! We were in imminent danger. We had to take immediate action to vacate the premises *tout de suite* (right away). The Egyptian had arms like an octopus trying to stick them in every crevice.

"Get your hands out of there! Who do you think you are?" He practically ripped the front of my dress trying to liberate my boobs. I was feeling desperate, my knees were weak.

As their advances escalated, and our pleas of "No!" remained unheeded, I pushed the diplomat aside with both arms as hard as I could. He stumbled against the wall hitting it with his elbow as I made a mad dash out the door to the elevator with Susan close behind. She slammed the door shut behind her. The hallway was in total darkness. *I should have remembered from Paris. Hallway lights are turned off to save electricity costs, and lights are activated by pushing a button on the wall.*

"Where the hell is the button?" I yelled.

"I don't know! I can't find it either. Shit! I think I squished a bug or something on the wall. Should we scream fire? Think, think . . . we have to get out of here before we're raped!" Susan turned around facing the apartment door when she heard it flung open. She stood her ground ready to do battle.

The two Middle Eastern diplomats were in hot pursuit grappling for us in the dark. We stayed out of the line of fire formed by the stream of light coming from the apartment. With my voice shaking and my back against the wall, I stammered, "If you don't turn on the lights, you're going to cause an international incident."

That declaration seemed to bring some clarity to possible consequences of their actions. *But what if they have diplomatic immunity? Then we're screwed.* Suddenly the light came on.

"Drive us back to our hotel *now*," I said emphatically. "We said, 'No' a thousand times. We made it clear we didn't come here for sex."

"What did you think you were coming here for, a game of blow football?" *I'm not sure what kind of game that is, and I don't want to speculate.* You're old enough to know why we brought you here." I had to admit he had a legitimate point. The tall Egyptian angrily clipped his words with lips curled. He resembled a wanton killer from a D-rated horror movie.

"Well, you got the wrong idea. If you don't take us home now, I'm going to scream so loud they'll hear me at the American Embassy." I tried to sound in control, but inside I was in a knotted state of panic. I was scared sober, even after three glasses of champagne.

After some diplomatic negotiating, they agreed to drive us back to our room. We thought this was a prudent plan since we had no idea where we were, or how we would have flagged down a taxi in the middle of the night. *What if they wrestle us to the ground? Get ready to kick him in the balls.*

We walked to the car. Susan sat in the back seat and I sat in front with the University of Cairo alumnus. I was in a heightened state of anxiety. My body was shaking. The Egyptian kept both hands on the steering wheel instead of groping me. *Lucky me, but unlucky Susan in the back seat. Who knows whether he's really driving us to our hotel?* He was talking to his friend in Arabic. *What if they're planning a surprise attack on a lonely road somewhere? How would we fight them off? There's no way I'll submit even though that's what you're supposed to do. Kick him where the sun don't shine.* I would go down fighting.

If we were forced to jump out, this time we were unencumbered by suitcases. It was rapidly becoming our *modus operandi* (method of operation).

"Hey, I said get your frigging hands off me! Don't you understand English?" I could hear Susan in the back seat lambasting her assailant to cease and desist. It didn't seem to be working. As I turned around to see if she was okay, she yelled, "Don't touch me, I'm Jewish!" in a steely-toned voice.

If I hadn't swung around in my seat at that moment, I would not have believed my eyes. He physically recoiled like a cobra. She had metamorphosed from a sexy, blonde young woman into an "Untouchable," the subhuman lowest of the low. He looked at her with wild eyes like he was expecting her to grow horns. It worked like a charm—Susan wasn't even Jewish. We were summarily dropped off in front of our humble lodgings thankful we had averted another catastrophe, but our self-confidence had been seriously sullied.

How Much Dumber Can You Get?

After that traumatic experience, we decided it was time to leave the heat and occupational hazards of Spain and head for Portugal. The thought of another encounter like the Middle Eastern diplomats was too scary to contemplate. It should have triggered a reevaluation of our entire mode of travel and how to better gauge the character of total strangers. But for some unfathomable reason, we were blind to anything that required revising our original plan to travel around Europe without using our precious cache of funds. We had spent nearly a month traveling in Spain, and we were tired of the food, the men, and the relentless heat. Getting out of Spain was almost a mission impossible. Cars were scarce, and we were beginning to feel exposed and defenseless standing in the open for interminable hours.

Our journey slowly inched forward in the direction of Portugal. Each day we would wait endlessly for a ride to come along. We were usually picked up by local farmers who were headed only a few miles down the road to purchase seed or provisions at the local marketplace. They were friendly and made helpful suggestions on where to stand to avoid the searing heat of the midday sun. We would be thoughtfully deposited under a tree or near a building complex that offered some shade. Sometimes we stayed rooted to the same spot for days feeling like squatters, only leaving it to find a room to rent for the night. It became tedious and frustrating, since we desperately wanted to get out of Spain at all cost.

It gave us time to discuss our plans and revise them in scope, once we realized the difficulty of getting from Point A to Point B on any kind of schedule.

"Maybe we should consider renting bicycles," Susan offered.

"How do we carry our suitcases on bicycles? Not only would these peasants think we were crazy, they'd think we just escaped from the circus." We had mainly packed skirts and dresses. *Susan, on a bicycle wearing a mini skirt, while trying to keep her legs together, and balancing a suitcase on her head* . . . made me double over with laughter. I was possessed by my famous laughing fit. It must be the heat—I was slaphappy.

"Remember the drinking parties at the Pitt frat house? There were more kegs of beer then I'd ever seen before, and everyone was drunk as skunks," Susan said. "*You* even got drunk, which was a first. You were a control freak so I wasn't sure how you'd handle it."

"Locking myself in the bathroom and throwing up all night made quite an impression on me. I got it out of my system early. I never drank more than one or two beers at a time in college. I learned my lesson."

Susan continued to reminisce. "The best times were double dating, and remember the night we walked to Beto's in a blinding snowstorm to get pizza with extra pepperoni? We couldn't find our way home."

"Yep, I remember that storm. The snow was three feet deep. I also remember a guy trying to grab you outside Beto's, and I slapped him in the face."

"You were Fearless Fosdick. You didn't miss a beat. He was so stunned he turned around and left . . . his ego totally deflated along with his dick." We laughed. There were also the years apart in college, recapping our relationships with men along the way, and how each one had soured at the end for one reason or another. We both liked to keep our options open when it came to men—no settling down for us.

She was enjoying the excitement of living in Manhattan when I tapped her for my traveling buddy, and I wondered now if she regretted leaving it all behind given our current circumstances. Not wanting to feel guilty—a Jewish affliction—I refrained from asking her. Manhattan sounded positively intoxicating, even living in a teeny, tiny apartment with a window air-conditioner. An air-conditioner set to its lowest temperature sounded divine. At least the sun wouldn't be relentlessly beating down on our heads like it was now. *Close your eyes. Meditate. Breathe in, breathe out . . . visualize that air-conditioned room. You're almost there.*

Toward the end of the day we were confronted with a dilemma. We were offered a ride at dusk by two young men in their twenties, after another full day of waiting by the roadside. Up to that point, we had avoided accepting rides from two men. Our desperation to get on the move again and leave Spain in the dust, overrode rational thought. Spain was not about to loosen its grasp on us just yet.

We soon established that we were all heading to Portugal by pointing and referring to our Spanish dictionary, making mindless chit-chat in our pigeon Spanish. As soon as one of the guys got into the back seat with Susan, I should have known things were about to go downhill even though we were headed uphill.

"Susan, did you just notice that road sign pointing to Portugal? They just turned in the opposite direction. We're going up into the mountains, and it's getting dark. Could it be a shortcut?" *Am I kidding myself?*

"I can't believe it. Don't tell me we did it again." Susan sounded scared. "Think fast. What should we do?" She grabbed my shoulder from the back seat.

"I'd say, get ready to jump at a moment's notice. Right now, all I feel is panic taking over my body and ratcheting up into flight mode. Time to pack it in. Think Wonder Woman!"

"Jesus. This isn't funny!"

It didn't feel right from the get-go. Why hadn't I listened to my trusty inner voice again to consider the perils of getting into a car with two guys? My skin began to tingle, like when you accidentally stick your finger into an electric socket. My curly hair began to unfurl when they parked the car on the side of the road. Without so much as a howdy-do, they lunged at us like apes in heat. *The optimum word of the day . . . Vamos!* (Let's go!)

"Jump, Susan, jump!" My words were simple and direct, like primers in first grade when I was learning to read. This time civility was left by the wayside as we desperately fought them off. Elbowing the driver with as much strength as I could muster, I jumped out of the car. Susan stumbled out of the back door. *At least this time the car is standing still!* With a full rising moon lighting our way, we ran at warp speed up the steep mountain road leaving our suitcases behind. We glanced back briefly to make sure they weren't sprinting toward us and saw them dump our suitcases out the door, turn the car around, and take off into the night.

"Susan, they must have decided we weren't worth the effort. The sheer stupidity of getting into that car . . . what's wrong with us?" I was hyperventilating.

"Well, we survived another day. Thank the Gods!"

5

Portugal: The Promised Land

We retrieved our damaged suitcases and clothes strewn along the road and hillside, sat down on a rocky outcropping, crying, trembling, and realizing we had just averted being raped, again! We wondered how we could have been so incredibly stupid, so gullible, and whether we had a death wish that we hadn't realized, when a lone van appeared around a bend in the road going down the mountain in the opposite direction. It stopped in front of us.

"Need a ride?"

It was like an archangel speaking from on high. *Had we died and gone to heaven?* Amazingly, the van was carrying an American couple, the Millers, who were headed to Portugal on vacation. Simultaneously laughing and crying at such stupendous luck, we climbed into the back seat with a huge sigh of relief. Maybe there was a hitchhiking God after all. It was our long awaited salvation.

We finally crossed the border into Portugal. We considered getting out of the car and kissing the ground like the Pope had done on TV. Spain had finally released us from its stranglehold. It had left an incredibly negative impression, one that would remain for decades. We felt as though the country had held us hostage and we had barely managed to escape.

"Girls, be sensible. Use some common sense. Hitchhiking is a really bad idea. Why don't you take the train?" Mrs. Miller tried to talk some sense into us.

"I'll admit we've had some close calls, but ninety-five percent of the time it's been fine."

"You're really hedging your bets. Remember, there are a lot of predators out there, and it takes only one maniac to change your lives permanently," she proffered.

"Too bad you aren't driving to Rome. We'd love to come with you and keep you entertained the whole way," I said.

"Sorry, we only have one week left in Portugal, then back to the good ol' USA." We spent several enjoyable days with the Millers before reaching Lisbon.

"Bye you two. It's been great fun. Think about what I said. Good luck!" Mrs. Miller smiled and gave each of us a hug before getting back into the van. Her husband gave us a thumbs up and waved from the car window.

We found ourselves near Rossio Square, the most popular meeting place in the heart of Lisbon. The Column of Dom Pedro IV, the King of Portugal, held a prominent position in the center of the square. There were two baroque fountains at either end of the square encircled by neoclassical buildings, porticoes, and galleries with outdoor cafés, shops and restaurants. People were milling around enjoying the day, and we surveyed our surroundings with new found optimism.

Lisbon was an attractive port city built along the Tagus River which spilled out into the Atlantic Ocean. We welcomed the sea breeze after the stifling heat of Madrid, and we were convinced our luck had changed. Even the smells and sounds of the city beckoned us. The mouthwatering smell of baking Portuguese bread, *caldo verde*, a traditional potato soup with kale and spicy *chourico*, grilled meats and sardines drifted through the air. The heavy, stagnant smell of unrefined olive oil that hung on every breath of air was gone. After an arduous month in Spain, we felt we had reached the promised land.

Our plan was to explore Lisbon first and then head north to Porto and Madeira to get the full flavor of the country. Unlike Spain, many of the people we met in Lisbon spoke several languages including English. We concluded, based on our chance meetings, that the urban populous appeared educated and economically better off than the Spaniards. The public squares were filled with international students as well as native residents.

Lisbon was built on hills like San Francisco with St. George's Castle, an ancient fortification, commanding a panoramic view of the city. It didn't take us long to become fascinated with the historic quarter of Alfama, teeming with vendors and small neighborhood bars and restaurants. It was a labyrinth of narrow, winding cobblestone passages and stairways with unexpected curiosities around every corner. We watched residents cheerfully greet neighbors while carrying out their daily chores washing laundry, cleaning vegetables, and scaling fish right outside their doorways. The facades of many of the buildings were covered with colorful ceramic tiles depicting scenes from ancient times. We were told they were used to reduce the need for annual painting. In the process they created enduring works of art.

Old fashion trolleys traversed the city center as the primary means of transportation. You could hop on and off at strategic points. The Millers had warned us to beware of pickpockets on the tram lines since they were always overflowing with people. We used them with caution usually at the end of a day after miles of walking. We marveled at smiling old women walking up and down the stairs carrying baskets of produce. They waved at us and were bemused by our obvious fatigue in negotiating the stairs. The stairs were the killers.

There were several observation points in the area which afforded magnificent views of the city's red tiled roofs and busy harbor. It was a chance to sit and enjoy a cold drink or a glass of port while taking in the scene below us. We fell in love with Lisbon and the Portuguese.

The people were exceedingly friendly, and we were no longer targets of the local male population. What a sense of relief.

Mrs. Miller had advised us to take the local train to Porto one day to explore the countryside. We decided to do just that, but as the landscape became more rural and sparsely populated as the train left the coastline, we were reminded of the desolation and oppressive heat of parts of Spain.

"I'm feeling a bit nauseous. All of a sudden just looking out the window reminds me too much of Sp-Spain," I sputtered. "And the heat is getting to me. What if we get off the train and I smell olive oil? It will be the end of the line for me."

Susan nodded vigorously. "I totally agree. It's so hot you can see waves of heat rising from the ground. Let's go back." Our clothes were soaked through with sweat. We took the next train back to Lisbon.

After a few days of frequenting a variety of lively cafés around Rossio Square and Praca do Commercio, we met two attractive young men, Fabio and Eduardo. There was instant chemistry, plus they spoke excellent English. Fabio was adorable. His long, bushy, arching eyebrows danced when he smiled.

"So what do you think of Portugal?" he asked.

"It isn't Spain, and it's getting better by the minute." *Am I flirting?*

"Um, care to elaborate? Are you saying you didn't like Spain?" Fabio flashed an arched eyebrow at me. He had sexy bedroom eyes with drooping eyelids.

"Do you have a month? It might take that long."

"Let's get a drink and you can tell me all about it." Fabio's eyebrows seemed to wink at me in a come hither sort of way. I was more than willing to follow.

We spent the rest of our time in Portugal with our new beaus and their friends, going out for dinner, drinking port, laughing and dancing to Frank Sinatra's "Strangers in the Night," a particular favorite at the dance clubs. The Portuguese had a keen appreciation for Sinatra.

In keeping with my expanding cultural education, Fabio introduced me to *fado*, the traditional music of Portugal. I repeatedly asked him to take me to taverns and nightclubs in Alfama just to hear the haunting, melancholy tunes. A female singer or *fadista* dressed in black with a deep, stirring vibrato, sang about love, death and despair, accompanied by the dramatic strains of a classical guitar. I lamented the fact that I could not fully appreciate the heart and soul of the music without understanding the nuances of Portuguese. It sounded like a passionate, emotive language.

One of the highlights of my stay in Portugal was a day trip with Fabio to magical, romantic Sintra. Pena Palace, located on a prominent hill in the Sintra Mountains, was built on ruins dating back to the Middle Ages. It was extensively restored and expanded in the 19th century by King Ferdinand II with a rambling collection of Moorish spires, arches, and battlements painted in strikingly vibrant colors. It looked like a bizarre distortion of Disneyland's Sleeping Beauty castle on steroids. Standing on one of the parapets, you could catch the perfumed breezes from the nearby hilltops ablaze with purple fuchsia, orchids, and giant tree ferns with Lisbon visible on the horizon.

There were an infinite number of gardens, flower filled pathways, moss covered rocks, and numerous ponds and waterfalls, reminiscent of a fairytale kingdom. Fabio and I walked along, his arm slung over my shoulders, breathing in the fresh air and enjoying the sunny day. Each breath was totally satisfying. At that moment I could have stayed in Lisbon for the foreseeable future in the arms of my delightful bushy-browed male companion. This is what life abroad was all about. I wanted the day to freeze in time. Enjoyment this fulfilling was fleeting, and soon it would be over never to be recaptured in the same way.

"It's too bad we ended up getting stuck in Spain for a month. I would have definitely preferred the month here with you in Portugal." We sat down under the shade of an ancient cork tree shielded from the harsh noonday sun. Its gnarled branches reached low over our heads, as though in a protective embrace.

"Summers in Lisbon can be rather lazy. I go to the beach regularly and spend my nights going to clubs dancing and drinking," he said.

"It sounds perfect to me. Hitchhiking has gotten to be a real drag. I'd like to just sit on a beach soaking up some rays, hanging loose."

"Never heard that expression. Is that American slang?"

"Guess so. It just means to sunbathe, doing nothing, relaxing." We feasted on a picnic lunch of cold gazpacho, a large hunk of creamy Portuguese cheese that we slathered over crusty bread, accompanied with spicy slices of *chourico,* and a bottle of port to wash it all down. It was a glorious day. Fabio stretched out on the grass resting his head on my legs. He pulled me down for a kiss. I stretched out on my back next to him, looking up at the sky.

"See the cloud formations? It's fun figuring out what they look like . . . that one looks like a mountain peak in the Alps." I raised my arm and pointed to the cloud.

"Yes, I see what you mean. What about that big one over there? Doesn't it look like a crouching cat?" He pointed to the west.

"Wow, it really does!" Finally, I had found someone who could playfully enjoy a favorite childhood game with me. Most men I had known refused to indulge me. They would never acknowledge what I saw in the clouds and had no interest in trying, telling me it was a total waste of time. They had no imagination, no curiosity. For me, it was like the Rorschach psychological test. What did the images resemble? What did they say about my psychological health? Fabio told me he had thoroughly enjoyed his introduction into cloud gazing—he was a definite keeper.

The surrounding countryside of Sintra was interspersed with magnificent manors, castles, and estates partially hidden by forests and lush vegetation. Fabio and I felt like the prince and princess of our storybook fiefdom. My knight in shining armor had gallantly rescued me from the Spanish Inquisition in the most exquisite way.

"I *really* like Fabio. Things have gotten kind of heated. I'm debating if I should sleep with him. If I do, I might not want to leave. Maybe it's time to say *Ciao*, baby."

"Me too with Eduardo. They're terrific guys, but if we don't leave soon we'll never make it to Italy before summer is over." Susan put the finishing touches on her eye makeup.

"It's too bad we didn't get here sooner. Spain was a total waste, a real bummer," I said.

"Everything has been better here. I wish we could just close our eyes and open them in Rome." Susan's wistful thinking gave me pause. *Going back through Spain on our way to Italy gives me the heebie-jeebies.*

After two weeks, Susan and I decided it was time to leave our idyllic situation in Lisbon before we became too attached to our boyfriends and too involved in our relationships. Eduardo and Fabio expressed their deep disappointment in our decision. Fabio asked that I do one parting favor for him.

"You're an American so this may be hard to understand, but I've been promised to a young girl from a wealthy family near my village. My parents arranged it and they insist I marry her. She's never been out of Portugal. She's a country girl . . . not independent like you."

"I get the picture. You're right. Americans would never go for that. It sounds so 18th century."

"I don't want to marry her . . . I don't love her. You would be doing me a big favor. Would you help me?"

"How?"

"It's all about humiliation. If her family sees us kissing in a public place, they'll be disgraced."

"Just for kissing? In the movies you have to be found in bed with someone. Uh . . . sure if you think it'll work." He looked at me and smiled, then grabbed me for a bear hug. He was definitely relieved. It sounded fairly simple to me, and I could chalk it up to another adventure.

Fabio asked me to accompany him to a local café that was frequented by the young woman's relatives. He was convinced our scandalous behavior would quickly reach his fiancée's village. Her family would be shamed, and they would be forced to cancel the nuptials. He knew I wouldn't suffer a backlash since I was an American from an entirely different culture. Besides, I was soon leaving the country behind. It was the least I could do to get him out of his predicament.

A few days later we entered the bustling café. All eyes turned in our direction. The din of voices suddenly dropped to a whisper. It was positively titillating, knowing that our every move was being watched. We sat in the rear of the café at a small table. Fabio ordered drinks. The stage was set.

"Okay, this is it. Are you ready for the performance? It has to be convincing."

"This is exciting. I feel like Scarlett O'Hara in *Gone with the Wind*."

Fabio laughed. "I'm really going to miss you. Are you sure you want to go to Italy? I promise to take you to the beach every day to catch rays and hang out."

"I'd love to take you up on your offer, but Susan really wants to leave." And then when he knew all eyes were fixated on us, he leaned into me and planted a sizzling, juicy kiss squarely on my mouth while wrapping both arms around me. It was a real turn on being in a public place. *Maybe I'll reconsider leaving. Boy, he should get an Oscar for his performance! He's really throwing himself into his role. Bravo! A round of applause please!* We canoodled unabashedly for about thirty minutes putting as much gusto as possible into each passionate kiss. *Maybe this is what porn films are like? I was ready to start ripping off his clothes. Would we get arrested for lewd behavior?* Fabio wanted to make sure he didn't leave a single doubt in anyone's mind about what they witnessed. It was a memorable scene worthy of one of the best Spanish *telenovelas*.

Fabio restored my faith in the opposite sex after my previous grueling month in Spain. I had thoroughly enjoyed his company and *joie de vivre.* Would I regret leaving him? Time would only tell. He would not be forgotten—Portugal had not disappointed. A few months later I called him to check in. He informed me that the ploy, had worked flawlessly. He was a free agent.

6

Spain and France: Redux and Regret

Because it was our only route to Italy, we reluctantly started our journey back through Spain reinstituting our method of madness. Since everything had gone so well in Portugal, we just pushed the dangerous aspects of hitchhiking out of our minds. It was illogical and ill-conceived, but it was thumbs up as we made our way to Algeciras where we were planning to take a side trip to Tangiers, Morocco, for a little exotic color. The last frightening encounter with the two Spaniards on the mountain road seemed to have faded from conscious memory. We opted for risk over rational thought.

A small, red Alfa Romeo convertible sports car stopped to pick us up. Susan sat in the front bucket seat, and I squeezed into the minute jump seat with my suitcase resting on my lap. The driver was British, talkative, and as it turned out, reckless. He drove like a race car driver without the expertise needed to make it to the finish line. He kept his right hand on the steering wheel while flourishing his left arm into space. We didn't have the luxury of seat belts. It was soon our undoing, as he was unable to negotiate a sharp curve in the road, lost control of the car, and went down over an embankment. I watched my life flash before my eyes.

We came to an abrupt stop, as the car plowed into the ground with flying dirt and weeds raining down on us. The car tipped over on its side, and the three of us spilled out in all directions like downed bowling pins. There weren't any broken bones, but I injured my back. It took us awhile to right the car and get it back on the road with help from some passing drivers. As we haltingly drove along at a reduced speed to Algeciras, I was in acute pain. So now not only were we dealing with the danger of predatory men, we were dealing with the possibility of accidental death.

"My back is killing me . . . not sure I can walk. We need to talk." Susan watched me writhing in my seat. The rebirth of common sense was beginning to replace spontaneous combustion. We were slowly coming face to face with the real threat to our continued well-being. Reaching the ripe old age of twenty-three was seriously in doubt.

By the time we arrived in Algeciras, the last ferry had already departed. We spent the night outside the ferry terminal waiting until morning. I was unable to sit so I lay down on the ground in excruciating pain. It was a painfully long night, and I wondered how I would make it to Tangiers and still continue our journey. When we finally boarded the ferry, my condition had not improved so I remained prone on the deck until arrival

Our first impressions of Tangiers reminded us of the old 1940s Hollywood sets of North Africa as scenic backdrops with crowded, covered marketplaces or *souks*. The Moroccans wore traditional *djellabas* (loose fitting gowns with sleeves and hoods) and *fez* hats, and dirty, barefoot children ran around in packs begging for money. Their enterprising scrappiness required learning at least five different languages in order to capture the attention of an unsuspecting tourist. They tried each language out until they got a flicker of recognition. Their spunk and ingenuity were commendable.

It soon became apparent to them that we were not the rich Americans they had hoped for, and a few of them latched onto us as our sidekicks, even asking if I needed a doctor when they noticed I was limping. They took us through a labyrinth of *souks* selling copperware, pottery, trinkets, clothes, and other handicrafts. It was a fascinating few hours. We decided to bargain for *djellabas* with intricately embellished jeweled belts. Our sidekicks helped negotiate the prices for us.

"Now that we have new disguises, let's knock them dead at the local café," I said.

"You really think those Arabs won't figure out we're frauds? All they need to do is look into our baby blues. It's a sure giveaway." Susan was skeptical.

"At any rate, it might be funny to see their reaction." I was determined to masquerade as an Arab. It felt like Halloween and just another way to defy convention.

"What if they don't think it's funny? They might stone us to death. I hear they throw women in pits and torture them."

"Come on. You can't be serious? Just for wearing a *djellaba*? I'll take my chances. Are you in or not?" Susan reluctantly slipped on the *djellaba* and veil. We had one of the young urchin boys take our picture before we proceeded to the outdoor café frequented only by men. It was a silly attempt at trying to look like typical Moroccan residents instead of tourists. But the men sat around leisurely smoking cigarettes and drinking mint tea with honey, seemingly unaware of us or the bees buzzing around the rims of their glasses. Either we had succeeded brilliantly, or the men decided to ignore our antics.

As many tourists had done before us, we made the climb to the Casbah to view the Sultan's Palace overlooking the Straits of Gibraltar. After a day of sightseeing, we left for Gibraltar to continue our northward trek up the Costa del Sol to Barcelona. Outside Barcelona we were picked up by an older Spanish gentleman in a large, luxury car. He was charming. We told him about our experiences with men in Spain and how wary we had become of Spaniards. He assured us that most Spaniards had the utmost respect for women. He must have felt sorry for us because when he dropped us off in St. Tropez, he stuffed money into our hands before driving off. He wanted us to have a lasting memory of at least one honorable Spanish man. Since he was able to take us as far as St. Tropez, we did not have to linger in Spain longer than necessary.

From St. Tropez we took the train along the Riviera to Cannes with Italy in our sights. We intended to buy train tickets to Rome in Cannes since it was still painful for me to walk. Carrying a suitcase was agony. Italy would be the last country we planned to visit before returning to Paris. For once we used common sense.

The Côte d'Azur: Topless

Cannes, the home of the annual Film Festival, European jet setters, and global celebrities was an excellent choice along *Le Côte d'Azur*. We walked along *La Croisette*, the main avenue in Cannes lined with palm trees and formal gardens on one side, and the Mediterranean and narrow sandy beach on the other.

We were so intrigued with the beach scene that we ended up walking onto the sand and plunking down our suitcases. There was a profusion of colorful umbrellas, cabanas, and skimpy bikinis worn by both men and women. Many of the women were topless, and our eyes became riveted on their naked breasts.

"Wow! That's about all I can say. Wow! Can you imagine sitting on the beach like that?" Susan was in a state of shock scanning the scene in front of her.

"Well, one thing I notice is that French women have small, almost non-existent boobs. If I took off my top, it would cause a volcanic eruption heard round the world," I laughed.

"If I took my top off, no one would bat an eyelash." Susan was self-effacing about her tiny breasts.

We continued to gasp at this public display of nudity as we looked around. It was definitely a staggering scene given our prudish American background. The men seemed oblivious to the casually seated, nearly naked women flaunting their wares. Age obviously had nothing to do with it since there were elderly women equally unclad, revealing unattractive rolls of wrinkles and cellulite. *How revolting! I can't picture my mother sitting on the beach practically naked! It makes me shudder.*

We noted that some of the sunbathers changed into their bikinis behind a handheld towel wrapped around their bodies rather than in the privacy of a cabana. They seemed very adept at this maneuver, obviously practicing it for years until they could master it flawlessly in a matter of seconds. Could we accomplish this feat without uncovering more body parts than necessary?

"We shouldn't spend our money on a cabana. We need to save our infusion of cash from Carlos (the Spanish gentleman). It's all we have left. But we have our trusty towels in our suitcases. Why can't we change just like they did? They make it look easy—besides, no one cares." Susan said.

"It's a risk, but hell, yes. Let's go for it. You're probably right, no one will blink if a nipple gets full exposure since we're sitting in a sea of them." I headed to a nearby date palm. It could partially shield us although the trunk of the tree wasn't wide enough to conceal us. We tried to expertly hold the towel while we changed, trying to avoid a slippage.

Our clumsy attempts to perform this feat with aplomb reminded me of children trying to tap their heads and rub their stomachs at the same time. It caught the attention of a group of young men sitting on the beach nearby who were staring at us. We both turned bright red in embarrassment, but continued to persevere, finally wriggling into our bikinis, tops and bottoms. Susan's towel slipped away momentarily which caused a loud guffaw from the group. Susan turned as red as an apple.

We then plopped ourselves down on our towels as nonchalantly as possible and stretched out to catch some rays. A few men sauntered over to us and began speaking English. It was obvious to them that we were not French.

"So where are you from and where are you going?" asked one of them with a thick French accent. "Why do you have suitcases at the beach?" *Hmm. He has a great body and long, muscular legs, quite a hunk.*

"We're Americans. Just got here from Spain . . . headed to Italy. We wanted to spend a few hours on the beach and then look for a hotel room," I said.

Two of the men introduced themselves as Henri and Gilles, nice specimens in minute, taut bikinis. "We can help you with a hotel room, but it won't be a four-star rating," Gilles said.

"What do you mean?" We both asked in unison.

"We work in a local restaurant across *La Croisette* as apprentices." Henri pointed to the green awning of a building on the opposite side of the street. "We're in training to become waiters and get free room and board. Our room is above the restaurant."

Susan asked the obvious question. "Isn't there a policy against having women in your room?"

"You don't have to worry about that. We can get you in after dark without too much trouble," said Henri. Susan and I both got the impression it wasn't the first time they had done this. We thought it was worth a try if we could pull it off without getting caught and save money in the process.

After most of the beachgoers left, we hung around waiting for dusk. We decided to get something to eat at one of the small seaside restaurants farther down the avenue, but not too far since we were carrying our suitcases. We concluded that Cannes was everything we had read about with casinos, fancy hotels, yachts, and posh boutiques, none of which we could afford.

We walked into the lobby of the historic Carlton Hotel, a splendid turn of the century hotel, and pretended to be hotel guests. The lobby was busy with the hustle and bustle of hotel patrons checking in. We sat down enjoying the ambiance until a bellboy came over and asked if we wanted him to take our suitcases to our room. We politely declined and headed for the exit.

Gilles and Henri asked us to meet them at a rendezvous point near their restaurant at 9:00 p.m. They were there waiting for us. They picked up our suitcases and planned to deposit them in their room, and then come back to get us.

"Don't you think they've been gone long enough. It's been at least a half hour or more." Susan was concerned.

"Yeah, I was wondering the same thing. Do you think we did something stupid again?" Just as we were about to conclude that we had been snookered, they appeared out of the darkness. We spent the rest of the night with our two French good Samaritans.

"You and Susan can sleep in my bed," said Gilles. "I'll sleep on the floor on a pile of pillows. Not exactly the Carlton, but it's better than a park bench."

"That's very decent of you," I said. "Quite the gentleman. Are all Frenchmen like you?" Gilles shook his head and smiled.

"Well, then we're lucky we found you," Susan added.

"Actually, we found *you*," he said. He got another pillow from the closet and put it on the bed. They were perfectly content with the sleeping arrangements. It was refreshing to know they didn't expect anything in return. The room was clean and quiet. Maybe they were more respectful since we were foreigners, and they didn't want to leave the impression that Frenchmen couldn't be trusted. We noted that our instincts had been correct for once.

In late morning they left for the restaurant and told us to stay put until dark. They would bring us food when they got the chance. They also mentioned that a maid would be coming by, and we had to hide from her otherwise she would report their infraction to the *maître d'hôtel*. We were slightly confused since there weren't too many places to hide.

"Susan, the only places to hide are under the bed and in the closet. I'm not even sure I could fit under the bed."

"Ah, oh . . . I hear someone coming down the hall. It must be the maid." Susan quickly glanced around the room deciding where to hide. We heard chattering in French, and it was getting closer.

"Quick, we have to hide! Shit! Maybe *you* can squeeze under the bed. I'll take the closet." We sprang into immediate action. Susan barely squeezed herself under the bed, her nighty got caught on the edge of the bed momentarily bringing her to an abrupt halt. I headed for the solitary closet. Neither one of us had time to dress. I was praying I would not have one of my laughing attacks. It was at times like this I could not be depended upon to stay calm, cool and collected. I was known for my infectious peals of laughter that would quickly spread like wildfire to anyone within hearing distance. In this case, it would have gotten Susan cackling, our cover would be blown, and we would have been immediately ejected from our cozy accommodations.

I tried to focus on something other than our current predicament to keep things under control, and I was instantly transported back to high school. One day I cut school to hang out at my boyfriend's house while his parents were at work. Suddenly we heard the front door open. His father came home unexpectedly, and we were occupying the master bedroom on the second floor. He shoved me into a closet and threw my shoes in after me. His father actually came up the stairs and walked into the room. I thought I would just die if he opened the closet door and found me. What could I possibly have said, "Fancy meeting you here?" Duh, I don't think so. Fortunately, he had only forgotten some papers for work and was soon on his way after rummaging around in a drawer. This was the second closet I had hidden in, but probably not the last, given my track record.

The maid came into the room, appeared to tidy it up quickly, cleaned the small sink which was in the room and left within a few minutes. We came out of hiding and muffled our laughter until we were sure she was far enough away not to hear. We went back to sleep, and as promised, Henri brought us baguettes with *pâté* in the afternoon.

"We need to get out of this room." I was tired of staring at four walls. "We've been cooped up here all day. Cannes is waiting."

"As soon as it gets dark, let's go for a walk until we meet up with Henri and Gilles." Susan said. She was as stir crazy as I was.

That evening after dark, we left the room to walk the streets until we were joined by our Frenchmen at a local dive for dancing and drinking. We danced until the wee hours of the morning.

"It's been fun. So glad we got off the train in Cannes. It was *bonne chance* (good luck) meeting you. Thank-you for taking care of us," I said.

"*De rien*. (You're welcome.) We were glad to help damsels in distress. Send a postcard from Rome so we know you made it there," Gilles said. They both had been extremely kind, wining and dining us.

"If we ever come to the US, we'll look you up," Henri said.

"You can count on it! We'd love it. We'll leave our addresses. Hope you make it into the Michelin Guide one day. We'll tell everyone we knew you when you were just mere busboys," Susan said. We were on our way by dawn. We didn't fancy remaining captive another day and testing providence by hiding from the maids. All in all our two nights on the Côte d'Azur had paid off.

The train was decidedly more comfortable, reliable and faster. My back got a chance to rest. We were finished tempting fate, and we wanted to play it safe for the remainder of our trip. It was a refreshing development. Maybe we had learned something after all.

Our foray into parts unknown during our summer hitchhiking spree, facing almost constant danger of one sort or another, provided the glue that bound Susan and me together in lasting friendship. If we hadn't faced each day together as one impenetrable force, our travels might have had a very different ending. We could chalk up our summer experiences as a gripping survival story to tell our children when we were old and gray. It would demonstrate beyond a shadow of a doubt, that some young women take undo chances with their lives without recognizing the sheer folly of their reckless behavior. Susan and I were very lucky. It only took one sexual deviant or one daredevil driver to bring us back to life's starkest realities.

7

Italy: The Glory of Rome – The Eternal City

Our first introduction into Italian life was a sneak attack from the rear. In Spain, the men made direct frontal assaults, but in Italy it was a surreptitious pinch in the butt in the midst of a crowded bus or sidewalk that caught you completely off guard. It was disconcerting since you never saw it coming and by the time you turned around, the culprit had managed to melt into the crowd.

Our travels ended in Rome. Our funds had nearly run dry, making our return trip to Paris untenable. Susan was given the task of calling Christine to tell her we would not be returning to Paris as planned. The waning months of summer cast a golden glow over the Roman Forum. We were observers of archaeological wonders thousands of years old in a city of antiquity. It was enthralling to see unearthed Roman ruins below street level, jutting out and cordoned off in the middle of a bustling metropolis. It was no wonder Italians were unable to construct a mass transportation system underneath Rome with such a treasure trove of ancient ruins waiting to be discovered. I was awestruck. Rome made an immediate impression on me as no other city had. My passion for architecture and archaeology was given new life. This was a city to cherish.

A tour of the most famous tourist sights left us at Trevi Fountain, the supreme gathering place for students, and a prime hunting ground for all young Romans seeking female companionship. The immense Baroque fountain in all its splendor overwhelmed the small cobblestone piazza. It commanded a position of dominance surrounded by ancient ochre-colored buildings on three sides. It was here at this venerable old fountain made famous in the 1950s romantic comedy, *Three Coins in a Fountain,* that I fell in love just as Maria had, after throwing her coin in the fountain. My travels around Europe and surviving all the adventures were just the prelude for what was to become one of the most life-changing encounters of my life. It was as though I had been waiting for this exact moment since I reached the age of consent.

Amore Mio

It was Gianni Rossellini, with whom I fell madly, passionately in love. The first time I saw him he was standing in front of Trevi Fountain with his best friend Giacomo, checking out the plethora of newly arrived *ragazzi* (girls). Gianni was about six feet tall, lanky and extremely handsome. He had a noble Roman nose, dark silky hair that fell down over one eyebrow, and an impish smile . . . the epitome of a sexy Italian male . . . confident in himself and exuding charm from every pore. He was the most beautiful man I had ever seen. He resembled the aristocratic Roman statues in The Louvre. Our eyes met and he winked at me. My heart started pounding so hard I was sure he could hear it. He made his way toward me through the crowd. Since I spoke no Italian and Gianni did not speak English, the challenge was on to learn Italian ASAP.

"*Ciao bella. Come si chiama?*" (Hi, beautiful. What's your name?) I quickly consulted my dictionary and said, "*Mi chiama, Sandy.*"

From the moment he uttered the words *Ciao bella* accompanied by a wide grin filled with seductive allure, I was hooked. He could have picked me up right there and flung me over his shoulder and taken me to his cave. If only he knew, those two words had left me completely defenseless.

Dante Alighieri was a local Italian language school, and I enrolled in class the very next day. Being in a total immersion program with Gianni, I was determined to learn enough conversational Italian to communicate. It was my new number one priority. French was soon forgotten. The Italian language and Gianni had catapulted into first place.

"You're all over Gianni. I've never seen anything like it. You usually hold back until you've decided the guy isn't a sex maniac. What gives?" Susan was mystified.

"He really turns me on. Besides, I could say the same thing about you and Giacomo."

"You're right about that. Giacomo and I have the same chemistry."

"You can also talk to him in English . . . a huge advantage. Gianni doesn't speak a word. Do you think Giacomo could help out until I'm up and running?"

"He won't mind being your interpreter for awhile, but you better get up to speed quick. Do you really want to spend the rest of your cash on an Italian course when we still have to find a place to stay?"

"I'll give up food if I have to," I gushed. Susan and I spent every day together with Gianni and Giacomo. They found a cheap, *pensione* for us and they took us to all their favorite haunts that only Romans would know. At lunch time every day, Susan went home with Giacomo, and I went home with Gianni.

"*Namo a casa per pranzo.*" (Let's go home for lunch).

If Gianni lived in Mogadishu or Mozambique instead of Rome, I'm not sure it would have made a difference. It was all about him. I would have followed him anywhere. I ached for him when he was out of sight even for a few moments—I had it bad.

His friendliness was disarmingly sincere. I found him irresistible. My camera was always ready to capture the profile of his high bridged Roman nose from every conceivable angle. It was a perfect complement to his handsome face. He would indulge me with a laugh, obviously amused as I set up each frame. My favorite picture was his profile against a white wall with a bowl of oranges placed strategically on the window sill behind him. I ordered him to look to the side with his hands on his hips so I could get the full impact of his nose. I shot it in black and white for effect.

Gianni was very close to his parents. Family was important to him. Signora Giulia and Signor Arturo Rossellini accepted me into their home with genuine concern for my well-being, as though I was just a long lost family member who needed to be fed and nurtured. Gianni's sister Carla and her husband Enzo, who lived in the same building as Gianni, regularly ate their meals at the Rossellini's. Their acceptance of a total stranger into their family unit without reservation was touching. My own parents reserved their generosity mainly for their extended families.

Unlike the French who were constantly correcting my speech, the Rossellinis smiled affectionately at my faltering Italian and encouraged me to speak. Never once did they correct my grammar. We spent countless hours talking and eating together, and gradually my fluency improved with each conversation. Gianni, Carla, Enzo, and I traded stories about the US and Italy. They were fascinated with my stories of America. There was always something to talk about . . . the impact strikes had on Rome's inhabitants or how a government official had created the latest sex scandal by hiring prostitutes to entertain constituents. The more we talked, the more we concluded that Italian and American politicians were not so different, maybe only by degree in their more outlandish antics.

When I first met Gianni, his family lived in a dim, dank, ground level apartment on Via Gaetano Moroni where Signora Giulia was the *portiera* (concierge). Gianni didn't look like either one of his parents. His mother was a round, little woman with dark eyes, rosy cheeks, and a pug nose who always had a kind, encouraging word for me. Gianni's father was short and stocky with a straight, pencil-thin mustache above a perpetual smile. He sold bottled water for *Egeria Acqua Santa Di Roma* which he distributed to various locales in Rome. His precarious looking three-wheel, top-heavy delivery truck could have been blown over with one puff of wind, scattering bottles everywhere.

When he returned from deliveries, his arrival was announced in advance with the jangling of bottles as he drove to the rear of the apartment building. It was a signal to Signora Giulia's command post, her kitchen, to start cooking. I would stand near her taking notes since she could never tell me exact measurements for her fresh pasta or other recipes, not unlike my own mother. My days in the Parisian café, learning French cuisine, had whetted my appetite for learning Italian cooking now. Her *carciofi alla Romana* (cauliflower Roman style), *pollo alla Romana* (chicken Roman style), and *abbacchio alla Romana* (roast lamb Roman style) were delicious examples of some of her memorable masterpieces, and her spaghetti sauces received nothing but accolades.

Gianni was treated with reverence, but it didn't seem to faze Signor Arturo, the head of the household. He accepted his wife's love for Gianni without reservation; it was apparent he shared that same love. There was good-humored joking all around and they were always kind and thoughtful to him. I never once heard them argue.

At lunch Signora Giulia served all of us a set portion of pasta from a huge overflowing pasta bowl, and then refilled it to the brim and set it in front of Gianni, as though she were presenting an offering to a noble prince. Gianni emptied the bowl of pasta leaving it spotless. He could qualify for *The Guinness Book of World Records* for consuming the most prodigious amounts of pasta in record time.

When he was finished, he winked in my direction with a satisfied grin on his face, his hunger satiated. My Italian lover was a bottomless pit when it came to his mother's cooking. It reminded me of all the times I sat at my own family table when I was young, being warned I couldn't leave the table until I ate everything on my plate, and not to forget all the starving children in China. I never bought into my mother's scenario. The spinach remained heaped on my plate until it dried out in shiny layers. Even Popeye would have rejected it. If it had been pasta, it might have been a different story.

After the dishes were washed and the kitchen was tidied up, we sat in the living room to talk about the day's events. Gianni put his arm around me and gave me a squeeze, gently caressing my shoulders. He kissed me affectionately. We couldn't sit on the couch without touching each other. His parents and sister watched us closely. It must have been obvious to them that we were falling in love.

We ate dinners in the dimly lit kitchen until the Rossellini family moved into a beautifully decorated, sunny apartment with sparkling terrazzo floors on the second floor. Enzo, Gianni's brother-in-law, was a successful interior decorator who specialized in decorating residential apartments and villas for affluent Italians. He could turn a dungeon into a Ducal palace even when the subject property had limited living space. He had a creative touch and soon the Rossellini's apartment looked like something from *Architectural Digest* or *House Beautiful* furnished with the finest fabrics and antique furniture. Gianni slept in the living room on a daybed. The room doubled as a living room and dining room by day and a bedroom by night. There were long French doors opening to a balcony overlooking the street and a round antique dining table in the corner. Gianni never complained about not having a bedroom. It was the accepted way of life for a working-class family. Gianni made his living as a plumber. He contributed a portion of his earnings to his family's living expenses as did most dutiful, working-class Italian sons, all who lived at home with their families until they married.

Susan and I began living a life dependent on the kindness of our respective Italian families. She had Giacomo and the Roccas and I had Gianni and the Rossellinis.

"Let's go to the beach. We don't have plans today until tonight. Remember Giacomo and Gianni are working late," Susan reminded me.

"Yeah, why not? We haven't been to the beach since the Riviera. As long as we're back by late afternoon. I want to wash my hair and make myself beautiful before Gianni gets here." The beach was an hour's bus ride to Ostia. We put on our bikinis and mini dresses and set off for the day.

After getting off the bus, we were accosted by a carload of young, Italian men slowly following alongside us catcalling. "*Ciao bambola.*" (Hi doll.) We learned from Gianni and Giacomo early on how to react when Italian men became raucous and overzealous in their driven compulsion to pick up young women. We gave them a quick flick of the arm (an obscene Italian gesture), and shouted, "*Vattene!*" (Get lost!) and continued on our merry way.

As we walked along we noticed the traffic suddenly came to a standstill, but the car driving beside us didn't stop. The occupants were fixated on us, hanging out the windows, whistling instead of paying attention to the traffic in front of them. There was an enormous crash of metal upon metal as their car buckled into an accordion after plowing into the car in front of them. The drivers jumped out of their cars causing a major traffic jam, hurling insults like *vaffanculo* (go fuck yourself), *stronzo* (shit) and the blasphemous *li mortacci tua* (cursing dead relatives). Even though there was wild gesticulating, it never came to physical blows. Fender benders were common in Rome, as were the obscene gestures and barrage of profanities. However, this time we felt we had contributed to the crunch job, and it was more than a minor accident, so we made a hasty retreat to the beach, giggling all the way.

8

Parents: The Lap of Luxury

After a few months of *pensione* living, Susan and I were virtually broke. It was time to make Rome our temporary home, find jobs, and an affordable apartment. It was shortly after we made this decision that my parents decided I should pack my bags and return to Pittsburgh.

"Summer is over. Remember our agreement?" my father reminded me. Of course I had never agreed to anything. I had not figured on falling in love. I had no intention of leaving Gianni or Rome.

"We're coming to get you." My father sounded very sure of himself. "We'll take a trip around the world. David wants us to visit him." *Knowing my weakness for traveling, my father is trying to bribe me.* My brother David was in the Air Force, stationed in Japan, and my father thought I could easily be swayed by dangling a carrot in front of my nose like a rabbit. Then I would return to Pittsburgh and enroll in graduate school. His plan was obvious.

When I refused his offer, he decided to resort to Plan B. "We'll come to Europe anyway. I'd like to see Max (my uncle). You could meet us in Paris. How about it? Then we can travel around Europe and go to Israel just like we did in 1953. I'll send you the money."

My father thought he could convince me to leave Rome if we were face-to-face. He wasn't very adept at hiding his true intent. But I agreed to meet them. He sent me enough money for a one-way ticket to Paris.

94

Having lived in cheap *pensiones* crawling with bed bugs for a few months, I figured my parents would provide a brief respite by traveling in style. I gave Susan my remaining funds so she could find a place to live while she hunted for a job, and I told her and Gianni that I would be back.

It was on the train ride from Rome to Paris that I first faced the stark opposition to the Vietnam War which was in full swing in the fall of 1966. There was a group of Canadian students on the train who verbally pummeled me for America's stance in the war. It was common knowledge that young American men were avoiding the draft by fleeing to Canada where they were accepted with open arms. One of the Canadians became enraged when I failed to respond to his barrage, in my weak attempt to defuse the situation. It had the opposite effect. His face filled with blood like a balloon about to explode.

"You Americans have no business being in Vietnam! When are you going to stop the bombing, stop dropping napalm and killing innocent people? President Johnson is a murderer! Don't you watch the news? Don't you see all those dead Vietnamese? Your country is a shitty excuse for a democracy!" He was shouting.

"The South Vietnamese need our help to defeat Communism. They want to remain a free country. You're entitled to your opinion, but President Johnson is doing this *for* democracy." Instead of soaring rhetoric, my words dropped to the floor of the train like paper planes. He knew his subject matter well. He continued his tirade drowning me out. He was winning the argument. I was unable to wage an effective counteroffensive.

It was the first time I found myself defending my country in the war effort even though I was personally opposed to it. The Canadians must have realized my heart wasn't in it. It was one thing to have a difference of opinion with fellow Americans, but quite another when subjected to blistering attacks from combative non-Americans. My idyllic life of traipsing around the European continent without a care in the world seemed irreverent and irrelevant when thinking of young

American soldiers dying in Southeast Asia. My feet were no longer floating above the ground but came crashing down to a solid, unforgiving earth.

My parents were overjoyed to see me and I realized how much I had missed them. After the emotionally draining train ride, I was relieved to be in the loving arms of my parents. We spent time with my uncle and aunt. They seemed happy to see me again, particularly without Susan. Then we began our trip which included traveling to Belgium, Switzerland, and Germany, where my father was born. The hotels were first class all the way. In Interlaken, Switzerland, I slept soundly in a sumptuous bed with a featherlight comforter that calmed my weary, luxury deprived body. It was heavenly. I even considered accepting my father's offer. The Vietnam War and the Canadians who had badgered me on the train, began to recede from my memory far removed from the comfort and security of my luxurious hotel bed.

Our trip included stops in Pisa, Milan, Venice, Florence, and Rome. We were fortunate to reach Florence before the massive flooding that hit parts of northern Italy on November 4, 1966. We saw the renowned bronze doors by Lorenzo Ghiberti, the incomparable statue of David by Michelangelo, the Uffizi Gallery with notable works of art, and the Ponte Vecchio, a covered bridge spanning the Arno River where we shopped for jewelry and leather goods. We had gotten to see all the museums and artwork before disaster struck. The November flooding of Florence from the overflowing Arno caused major damage to parts of the city, particularly in the historic area and cultural center where irreplaceable masterpieces and manuscripts were housed. Thankfully, we had gotten to see all the museums and artwork before disaster struck.

In Venice we stayed at the Hotel Gritti Palace overlooking the Grand Canal. It was a swanky hotel with gold inlays and pastel ceiling frescoes. In Rome we stayed at the equally distinguished Excelsior Hotel on Via Veneto. It certainly was a drastic change from the *pensiones* Susan and I had frequented. Joining my parents for a worldly trip seemed worthy of consideration until we got to Rome and I was reunited with Gianni. There were no promises of material wealth or trips circumnavigating the globe that could persuade me to leave him. I was committed.

My parents seemed enchanted by Gianni. He had an engaging personality and it was easy to succumb to his charms. He acted as our tour guide, driving us around Rome pointing out all the highlights and maneuvering the car through narrow cobblestone streets as only a Roman can do. They never complained about being jammed into the tiny, little car. It was a surprise since my father was accustomed to roomy Cadillacs and Lincolns.

"Tell Gianni he's an extraordinary driver. This little car is taking us places I would never think possible except on foot. And the way he parks it anywhere, perpendicular to the curb and at any angle is quite remarkable. Won't the police tag him?"

"Dad, I don't think I've ever seen the Italian *polizia* issue parking tickets. It's like a free-for-all. No one stops at red lights. They just slow down."

"I'm going to be afraid to cross the street." My mother was a timid law-abiding citizen.

"Just be careful. Remember when you taught me to look both ways? In Rome it means life or death. Cars will weave around you," I warned her.

My mother was totally captivated with Gianni, the little Fiat 500, and his finesse driving the car. As much as they may have enjoyed his company, their position remained unchanged.

"Look, he's a nice person. In fact, he's a charming fellow. But, that doesn't mean we want you to stay in Italy, and God forbid make it permanent. He could never provide for you the way you're used to. Don't forget that." My father still held out hope I would marry a nice Jewish man of substantial means. Gianni did not fit the profile.

"Your parents are *molto gentile*, (very nice) and your mother is very funny. Do you think they like me?"

"*Certamente, amore*." (Certainly, love.) We spent several days in Rome before leaving for Israel. I assured Gianni I would return.

My recollection of Israel in the fall of 1966 was feeling insecure and frightened. You could physically sense the tension in the air and see the consternation in the faces of the Israeli people as they went about their daily lives. Our two-week stay gave me a better understanding of the Israeli psyche. My father's friends and relatives were resigned to a coming war. For Israelis, it was a simple matter of survival. Their tiny democracy was surrounded by mortal enemies who threatened their very existence. At night my sleep was continually interrupted by the sound of rapid gun fire in the distance. It was alarming to be awakened by a sound that meant death or destruction to someone lost in the darkness. Israelis were forced to endure living under these horrendous conditions. How could they keep their children safe and reassure them that all would be well? There was the uneasiness of knowing that the circumstances were worsening by the day. It was the prelude to the "Six Day War" in June of 1967.

"Being in Israel has only reinforced my decision to go back to Rome. It's too scary thinking life can end with a single bullet. I'm having too much fun. I'm not ready to die."

"You're making a big mistake. You belong at home. I'm not financing your stay." My father was adamant.

"I'll manage. I always do."

My mother was tearful; my father angry. Not being a man of many words, he glared at me with his proud, steel blue eyes. He didn't have to say how he felt; it was very clear. I had disappointed him again. My life seemed to hinge on how my father perceived me. I wanted him to be proud of me like he was of my brothers, but I always marched to a different drummer. If he told me to go left, I would go right. It was an act of defiance. Why did I continue to flex my liberated loins? Maybe because I could.

9

Via Francesco Amici: Dormitory Style

After leaving the financial security my parents provided during our tour of Europe, I was thrust back into the real world . . . how would I support myself? When I returned to Rome, I was elated to learn that Susan had found an apartment and another roommate, Molly, from Boston. She had a typical Boston accent . . . "Pahk the cah in Hahvahd Yahd." She was a dark-haired beauty with a gorgeous smile and long eyelashes that she batted repeatedly while lowering her head and smiling up at me. She always seemed to be flirting whether it was with a male or female. It was part of her persona.

"We rented an apartment on Via Francesco Amici," Susan said. "Molly helped me get a job at a glove store on Via Condotti. She's the best thing that's happened to us in a long time." Via Condotti was a celebrated street with some of Rome's finest boutiques.

"Do you think she can put in a good word for me? I'll make up some story about having retail experience. They'll never check my references." The apartment was sparsely furnished—just beds, dressers, no rugs, no curtains, no wall hangings. The kitchen had a modicum of usable pots and flatware, barely enough for all of us. Even so it was far better than any *pensione*.

Susan had met Molly and her boyfriend through Giacomo. Molly was working at the glove store and she suggested Susan apply for a job there. Susan not only secured a job for herself but assured Mario the owner, who was desperate for English-speaking salesgirls, that I could be added to the coterie once I returned from my trip. Mario didn't require work permits even though it was against the law. The only downside was the pay . . . a measly hundred dollars for a month's work. We would definitely have to pool our money together to pay rent and utilities.

That first winter of 1966 was bleak. The temperature, although it never got as cold as Pittsburgh, dipped into the thirties and was penetrating in its dampness.

"Why won't the landlady turn on the heat until late November? We'll be a frozen block before then." Molly crossed her arms in a hug and shivered.

"Can't we complain? I never heard of paying for heat that we never get. My fingertips, toes, and nose are blue." Molly and I seemed to suffer the most from the cold. Molly's boyfriend, the resident musician, frequently serenaded Molly on his guitar, but was unable to play because his fingers were too stiff to strum the strings. We dressed in several layers looking like quilt people from some obscure Eskimo tribe in Alaska.

Once the heat was turned on, it was intermittent. Either we sweltered to death, throwing all the windows open and disrobing, or we froze to death with all three of us sleeping together under multiple layers of clothes and blankets. Molly had not planned on spending the winter in Europe so she didn't even have a coat. When I wasn't wearing my coat, I gave it to her for much needed wooly warmth. We shared all our belongings during that miserable first winter.

The apartment became more of a coed dormitory with all our visiting boyfriends. The atmosphere bordered on sheer madness with a myriad of characters coming and going at random hours of the day or night. Not only did we share clothes, cosmetics, and accessories, we also shared the space with men—it was hard to lay claim to anything. Privacy was a precious commodity. When a couple wanted it for obvious reasons, the rest of us respectfully retreated to another room.

It seemed to work well enough, although there were times when squabbles would erupt, particularly involving Gianni and Giacomo, who were the most frequent visitors.

Giacomo was very possessive of Susan. It worried me that he seemed intent on alienating her from me. In my overly analytical mind, I concluded he was jealous that I had taken Gianni, his best friend, away from him and was wreaking his revenge. We managed to keep the peace most of the time, but there was an underlying tension developing between us. He had grown up in South Africa. His English was excellent, his voice curt, direct and dripping with sarcasm.

"Why don't you and Gianni leave us alone? We have every right to be in the bedroom more than you do. We found the apartment, not you. You didn't do anything. We *deserve* our privacy!"

They would shut the door to the bedroom and I could hear their muffled laughter. Giacomo made me feel like I was beneath an earthworm. He was self-centered and spiteful. It was difficult withstanding his snide verbal attacks without counterpunching, but I thought it would only escalate an already tense situation.

Gianni ignored Giacomo's sniping. "*E niente. Non ti preoccupare.*" (It's nothing. Don't let it bother you.) But it did bother me and made me increasingly angry.

If we got home from work to find the guitar missing from the apartment, we knew Molly had another fight with her boyfriend. "So what happened this time? It seems like you fight more than you make up," I asked.

"Yeah, it does seem that way doesn't it? I'm beginning to think we just weren't meant to be. He's so annoying."

"Are you sure it isn't the other way around? I know it's hard for you to believe, but you are definitely high-maintenance." Molly seemed to take my comment in stride. Instead of a verbal barrage, she threw a pillow at me. This frequent bickering between her and her boyfriend relieved some of the pressure on the rest of us who were always fighting for a bedroom.

Molly also became a target of Giacomo's wrath, but instead of meeting silence she lobbed zingers with precision, cutting him off at the knees. It was a brilliant power play. She was a master at hurling retaliatory salvos for his biting remarks. She had the survivor instinct. He met his match in Molly. These encounters lodged a permanent wedge between her and Susan that never recovered.

When the landlord's son came to collect the money for the utility bill, we would all scatter and pretend not to be home when he knocked on the door. It became a ritual since we rarely had enough cash on hand. Besides, we felt we had a legitimate case for withholding payment due to the intermittent heat and water. Without warning the water would turn off when one of us was in the shower. Instead of becoming irate, we laughed, but we felt nonpayment for utilities was warranted.

In the months before apartment living, we were forced to go to the post office and wait in line to make international phone calls home. It was always exasperating because we never knew how long we would have to wait, whether it would close for hours at lunch time, or worse yet, if the post office was closed indefinitely due to another strike.

Now was the first time we had the luxury of our own telephone. We had the added pleasure of going through an international operator, who was almost always a young Italian man. "*Buon giorno, signorina.* You just called Pittsburgh, Pennsylvania. Are you American? How long have you been living in Rome? Do you like Italian men?"

We took bets whenever we made an international call to see how long it would take before the operator invariably called back asking for a date . . . such was Italy in those days.

La Signora and Mario

The glove store was a tiny storefront hemmed in by larger boutiques on either side. If you didn't know it was there, it was easy to miss. The sales counter was long and narrow and the salesgirls crowded along its length, waiting for customers to enter the door. There were steps to the rear of the store leading to a cramped, disorganized storage room for gloves and miscellaneous items and supplies. I met Cecilia, a Jewish-English gal from London on my first day of work. She was a beautiful, vivacious blonde, and a natural comedienne. She reminded me of a young Angela Lansbury, the British actress. She gave me a quick biography of her background and told me she had a steady boyfriend Paolo who worked at a recording studio at Cinecitta. He got her occasional dubbing or acting jobs to supplement her glove store salary. Cecilia was a hoot and kept us constantly entertained and in good spirits. She was definitely a sassy lassie.

Mario's mother, *Signora*, was a buxom battle-ax who guarded the cash register as though she were a mother bear with a honey pot. The *Signora* was the only one authorized to open the register and make change, take American Express checks, or handle cash. Her whip-like tongue spitting out a string of orders in rapid succession brought up images of a Komodo dragon about to decimate her underlings. We came to immediate attention for fear of retribution. She was the maternal head of the family and she controlled her son and everyone else around her. The *Signora* was in charge.

Our sole responsibility was to convince the clientele to buy as many pairs of gloves as possible, although we never earned a commission on the quantity. Our commission was made on the bars of leather cleaning soap we sold. It never made any sense to me, and I never once made my weekly quota. Rather, I enjoyed speaking to the international crowd more than selling them anything. I even waited on Janet Leigh, an American actress. I was repeatedly reprimanded for spending too much time talking and laughing instead of selling. Retail was not my thing.

Mario was a real piece of work. Since he was afraid to confront his mother, he took his frustrations out on his lowly sales staff. He would march up and down the narrow store aisle with his arms crossed over his chest, urging us to make more sales, denigrating our selling abilities in the process, but always with a smile that resembled a sneer. He lined the salesgirls up on the stairs when he had a topic of importance to deliver. One memorable directive was demanding total allegiance to him. He threatened to run us over with his car if we ever reported him to authorities for working illegally without work permits.

He was like a character in an Alberto Sordi comedy which made it difficult to take him seriously. He was short and thin, almost sickly looking, with a sallow complexion. Mario dressed in expensive, fitted Italian suits and ties that were too loose for his scrawny neck. His broken English was like a sitcom script, particularly his, "Hi, Madame, ah . . . you fom Chicago, Miami?" or "Hi, Madame, ah . . . you fom New Jersey, Alabama?" always mixing up cities and states. It was difficult to keep a straight face even for customers.

It was great material for Cecilia. She was forever mocking Mario, calling him a *nob* when he turned his back to her, or a *dozy bugger,* and her comedic skits mimicking his broken English spoken with her British accent were worthy of an Oscar. With her curled hand on her hip, which was one of Mario's signature poses, she would launch into her lines. "Madame, you try smaller size. Better to stretch first. See? Oy, I put hole in glove! You fom Dallas, California? You give address and I visit."

Mario enjoyed chatting up all the tourists, keeping names, addresses, and phone numbers in a black notebook for future reference. He planned to take a trip around the world and visit all the unsuspecting souls who had innocently given him their names and addresses.

One day an elegantly dressed American woman came into the store. Molly waited on her.

"You speak English so well! You must have gone to school in the United States."

"Yes, I did," Molly said.

"Where did you go to school?"

"In Boston."

"Oh, my goodness, your English is *almost* perfect!" It was difficult to keep a straight face, but Molly played it to the hilt never revealing she was indeed an American.

Mario taught us how to size gloves properly. The customer had to place an elbow on the counter as we slowly and meticulously massaged the supple fingers of the leather glove until it was seated correctly on the customer's hand. Many times the customer claimed to have a size that only a child's hand would fit. It was like trying to squeeze into Cinderella's glass slipper and at times, it proved the undoing of the glove as the seams came apart. Mario would angrily glare at us as he hastily retreated to the rear of the store to retrieve a larger size. Needless to say, this *disastro* (disaster) was taken out of our pay.

I lasted only a few months. Since we were working illegally, Mario took every advantage he could in paying us a pittance of what a reasonable salary would have been. I quit when I could no longer tolerate the long hours and sub-standard earnings. My days were spent at home sipping *Sambuca,* eating pizza, playing cards, and routinely checking *The Rome Daily American* newspaper for jobs. It was the local English language newspaper that became my constant companion. I responded to many ads, but without fail I was told my Italian wasn't fluent enough, or I was offered a job in Turkey or Timbuktu and I wasn't willing to relocate.

The Rossellinis

I enrolled in more Italian classes and reluctantly accepted help from Gianni and his family. Gianni continually encouraged me. He was the poster child of optimism. His positive attitude kept me going and provided sustenance both physically and emotionally. At times I became discouraged wondering if my decision to stay in Italy had been wise. Was I taking advantage of Gianni and his family? Every day Gianni addressed me with his endearing *Bella di Gianni* (Gianni's beauty), accompanied by a smile and a big bear hug, which provided needed manna for my malnourished psyche. It didn't take much to make me happy in those days. My friends told me I followed Gianni around like a puppy. I suppose I did. He was so thoroughly good that I sometimes felt I didn't deserve him.

My temperament was volatile at times, and I was impetuous and demanding. It was like the sudden explosion of a pressure cooker. There was no controlling it, and I would suddenly jump out of the car at a traffic stop and refuse to get back in. He would slowly drive beside me imploring me in his sweetest, calmest voice to get back in the car. *"Amore mio, cosa ho fatto?"* (Love, what did I do?) He would cajole me and promise to be more understanding, but it really was never his fault. My inner voice told me to calm down, to think before speaking, to control my anger. My anger was deep-seated. It always surprised me since I never knew when it would erupt or where it had come from. Clearly, it was lurking in the shadows waiting to attack the nearest victim. Gianni just happened to be the recipient. Maybe I was afraid I didn't measure up, wasn't the person I wanted to be, and would never be as good as he was. He deserved better.

Besides the daily routine of helping Signora Giulia prepare lunch which was the main meal of the day, we would frequently visit Signora Giulia's father on Sundays in Cividella, a rural village outside Rome. He was a cherubic, jovial, white-haired man with rosy cheeks, and could easily have donned a red suit, a white fluffy beard, and posed as jolly Old Saint Nick on Christmas Day.

Going to his village was like going back in time to an era devoid of modern conveniences. The hillside was planted with twisted olive trees that must have been there for centuries. It was a serene vista and I sat under the lean-to appreciating the countryside, the fresh air, and listening to Gianni's cousin play the guitar. Having prepared the meal in advance, Signora Giulia settled into her father's rustic kitchen and had only to heat everything up for her customary, superlative Sunday dinner.

Other days I would anxiously await Gianni's return from work. I missed him terribly during the day. It was like missing an essential part that made me whole. His first order of business when he got home was to wrap me in his arms for a long, warm hug. I felt the calluses on his rough plumber's hands . . . they felt like old, cracked leather gloves. Sometimes they were covered with grease which he painstakingly removed with a special ointment and scrubbing cloth before taking a shower.

One day Signora Giulia reprimanded me, swatting me with a dish towel, when she caught me peeking through the keyhole of the bathroom door as Gianni was showering. *"Che stai facendo? Dai, dai."* (What are you doing? Come on.) His naked body was lithe and lean, and I enjoyed gazing at it endlessly as though I were admiring one of Michelangelo's sculptures. Instead of exhibiting anger, she seemed mildly amused. I was mortified! I could hear Gianni singing in the shower. She seemed to accept our devotion to each other without question. I often wondered if she thought this bizarre voyeurism typical of American women? Would she have been as forgiving if I had been Italian?

Signora Giulia was a remarkable woman with the stamina of an ox. She stood at her small gas stove for hours singing or cursing, depending if the sauce or the pasta came out exactly as she wanted it. As she cooked, I observed every step in her preparations, writing them down on scrap paper ripped from Signor Arturo's *Egeria* ordering pad. It was obvious she was flattered that I thought so highly of her cooking skills. "Pay attention. The dough has to be kneaded and then flattened with a rolling pin and then set out to dry." I took feverish notes.

"How long does the dough have to dry?" She could never answer with specifics.

"It depends on the weather, the humidity in the kitchen."

"How much flour do you use?"

"Just watch and take notes." She would invariably become impatient with my questions. Signora Giulia was less precise when it came to measurements or the amount of time each step took. When she made fresh pasta, she cut it by hand and stretched it out on the table top or the backs of wooden kitchen chairs to dry. After the meal ended, she routinely cleaned the kitchen thoroughly and mopped the floor, readying it for the next meal. She had to be organized in her tiny kitchen.

She appeared to have a solid relationship with Signor Arturo. He playfully pinched her behind or threw his arms around her, and she self-consciously shoved his hand away in embarrassment or tickled his mustache.

"*Arturo, per favore, basta. È imbarazzante.*" (Arturo, please stop. It's embarrassing.)

"Can't help myself. It's nice and round. Just one more little pinch." He smiled and playfully continued to try and hug her. It was clear they adored each other. It was heartening to see their affection for one another which was always on display. Signora Giulia would frequently pinch Gianni's cheek or they would affectionately tease each other. His parents were exemplary role models for demonstrating love and affection. My parents never openly displayed their feelings for each other or for us children, but I never doubted their love for us. As for each other, I was never sure.

Reaping the Benefits

As Christmas approached, we went to Piazza Navona and welcomed the *zampognari* (shepherds from the mountains of *Abruzzo*) who dressed in sheepskin vests, long, black capes, and wide brimmed hats, playing their emotive bagpipes and flutes.

Piazza Navona, my favorite Roman piazza with its magnificent fountains by Giacomo della Porta and Bernini, became a pedestrian mall with scores of booths selling Christmas ornaments, candies, trinkets, toys, and food. The aroma of roasted chestnuts permeated the crisp night air. The area was alive with music and decorated with thousands of twinkling lights, Christmas trees, and *presepi* (nativity scenes). Everyone was in a holiday spirit. My constant worries about future employment were temporarily put to rest.

"Let's go to our favorite restaurant for a *tartufo*. I know how much you like it." Gianni knew my weakness for the decadent chocolate ice cream dessert, the *tartufo* made famous at *Tre Scalini,* a landmark restaurant in Piazza Navona. We never left the piazza without treating ourselves. For chocolate lovers, it was like reaching an instant orgasm with your first taste, as it oozed deliciously down your throat. It was a divine indulgence . . . all tourists should skip the Vatican and head straight to *Tre Scalini.*

Another favorite spot was the quintessential *Tazza d'Oro* near the Pantheon which had been delighting patrons since 1944. Customers would wait patiently in line to get their cup of Joe every morning and stand at the counter enjoying their first *caffè* of the day. The addictive fragrance of freshly roasted coffee beans drifted through the open air entrance out into the ancient cobblestone square beckoning you to come in. Large barrels and heavy burlap sacks of coffee beans from all over the world lined the floor. Italian espresso and cappuccino became an addiction. Unlike the US where we have a cappuccino with frothy milk at any time of the day or night, the Italians only had cappuccinos in the morning and espressos later in the day. They could spot an American immediately if you were caught drinking a cappuccino after ten o'clock in the morning. It was a dead giveaway.

On Christmas Eve, we had a feast of seafood and fish with spaghetti and clam sauce, fried sardines, and a tray of fried zucchini and artichokes *alla romana,* but no meat, following the strict edicts of the Catholic Church. It was the only nod to religious custom. At home in Francesco Amici, we decorated a small Christmas tree to mark the occasion. *"Amore mio, vieni subito!"* (My Love, come here right away!) And then Gianni and I anointed it by closing the door to the room and making love under its aromatic branches.

"I get it. It's a religious experience instead of going to church." I smirked. The Christmas tree will always bring back fond memories, particularly picking needles out of my hair and feeling them prick our naked bodies as we rolled over them. With the door closed, the pleasantly refreshing evergreen scent filled the entire room.

I assumed Midnight Mass would follow—my own stereotypical assumption of all Italians that they religiously attended Sunday Mass. To my surprise, the Rossellini family had no use for the Pope or the church and never once went to Mass. In fact, I dragged Gianni kicking and screaming to Midnight Mass at the Basilica di Santa Maria Maggiore. He actually wanted to wait outside the church and seemed to have an aversion to stepping foot inside, like being dragged to the principal's office in elementary school. *"Vai, vai* (Go, go.) I'll stay outside." He could not be persuaded to enter the sacred edifice. Signor Arturo routinely blasted the Pope and the church, so it was no wonder that Gianni was infused with some of his same irreverent ideas. Conversely, Signor Arturo always had a kind word for Mussolini and attributed the good roads, the train system and educational reforms to him. He must have been a closet Fascist. Despite his political leanings, I remained extremely fond of him.

Christmas Day meant a festive lunch starting with *stracciatella* soup (egg drop) followed by pasta, roast lamb with potatoes, vegetables and other tasty traditional dishes. Dessert was usually a *macedonia di frutti* (fruit salad) laced with *Maraschino* liqueur, and an array of cookies, pastries, and *cannolis* filled with ricotta cream. The Italians were not into elaborate pastries like the French. Instead, they concentrated on their pastas and *gelato* which they did to divine perfection. French cuisine was renowned for its refined, artistic flourishes loaded with butter and complex sauces, but Italian cooking was still my preference for its robust, fresh, simple rustic flavors.

Christmas in Rome was a special holiday for me. Since I was Jewish I had never experienced Christmas from inside a Christian family. When I was in elementary school I would visit Christian friends just to see their Christmas trees and all the presents waiting to be opened. As a Jew, I thought I had missed something or even been cheated by singing all the Christmas carols in elementary school but never rewarded with the heap of presents under the tree with my name on them. My family celebrated Chanukah instead, but chocolate money wrapped in gold paper, even if this tradition lasted eight days, didn't measure up to the gratification of Christmas presents for a child.

In Rome I could unabashedly indulge myself with all the pageantry and payoff. Christmas with Gianni couldn't have been sweeter. It was a sense of belonging, of sharing the spirit of Christmas with someone I deeply loved. The true religious story of Christmas was lost on us. It was more secular in nature since Gianni and his family were non-practicing Catholics.

Gianni told me New Year's Eve or *capodanno* had a curious tradition. "The Fiat 500 can't stay on the street tonight. You'll find out why soon enough." As the clock struck midnight, Romans flung open their windows and balcony doors and hurled broken dishes, pots, pans, furniture, TVs, and broken appliances, even refrigerators to the street below. If you were not forewarned about this unusual tradition, it was highly likely you could find your car with a caved in roof or shattered windshield the following morning. I could not believe my eyes when I witnessed this astonishing scene for the first time. It was like something out of a doomsday movie. The Italians gave new meaning to the old adage of throwing out the old and bringing in the new. You would think the Pope would have tried to bring this literal interpretation to an end. The sidewalks and streets were littered with piles of debris for days after New Year's Eve.

10

Arrivederci Roma and Benvenuto a Roma

Molly returned to Boston in early spring. I lasted until late spring before my funds ran out, and I felt guilty accepting the continued generosity of the Rossellini family. Susan moved in with Giacomo's family. It was the final realization that our bond had been irrevocably broken. Giacomo had managed to pry her loose from our friendship by creating an impenetrable barrier around her. It was the demise of our relationship.

Not having Susan to talk to brought back my fierce desire to stand on my own and prove that I could do it without her. Otherwise it would mean submitting to my fears and accepting defeat. My continual struggle for independence kept me from moving into the Rossellini's and accepting their help. It was time for me to regroup and go back to the States to figure out how to support myself financially. Beneath the surface I was in a state of panic by the thought of leaving Gianni behind.

My parents were overjoyed to hear I was returning to Pittsburgh. "You've finally come to your senses. This time you'll come home to stay. Your room will be ready for you." My mother was ecstatic, bubbling over with enthusiasm.

"I'm not making any promises. We'll see how things go. The first order of business is finding a job. That's a definite." *Telling Gianni was another story.*

"Please, don't leave me. I can't live without you. We'll think of something. You'll find a good job. I'll help you. But please don't go." Gianni was distraught. How could I leave him? How could I make him so unhappy? We were inseparable and I couldn't conceive of life without him. He had left an indelible mark on my young life. The gnawing question was whether Gianni and I had a future together. It was a question that kept me up late into the night, but I didn't dare share my doubts with him. Gianni saw everything as black and white. It was simple . . . he loved me . . . end of story. Nothing else made sense. For me it was much more complicated.

Being at home in Pittsburgh was more difficult than I imagined. It was extreme culture shock. Everyone thought I looked like a foreigner with my short haircut and Italian clothes. Sometimes I would lapse into Italian, forgetting where I was. The American way of life didn't make sense to me anymore—I didn't fit in. Being without Gianni was depressing, and I spent most of my time in my room reading and thinking. I was miserable.

Not having money was a major issue, so I got a part-time job selling children's furniture. A full-time job was too permanent and I needed time to unscramble all the confusion I was feeling over my relationship with Gianni. Maybe eventually everything would come into focus. Major decisions required time and reflection. Every day I anxiously waited for the mail delivery to bring a letter from Gianni. With the words "*Ciao, amore mio,*" I was instantly transported to a warm, comforting place for a few minutes, but I ached to see him.

Molly and I kept in touch, and we both shared our unhappiness returning to the US and living with our respective families again. "Molly, I'm feeling so low without Gianni, really lonely. My parents are driving me crazy constantly asking about graduate school. I'm not ready for any of this. It's really getting to me. I'm totally depressed."

"Yeah, I know what you mean. I'm bored stiff living at home. I never thought I'd end up like this especially when living in Rome was so much fun, even without heat. Have you thought about going back?" *What a brilliant idea!* Molly verbalized what I had been thinking.

She came to Pittsburgh from Boston to visit me and during her visit we conspiratorially hunkered down to make plans for our triumphant return to Rome, like Roman emperors of yore. "Where will you get the money for your ticket?" I asked.

"You know me, I have many admirers. I waitress on weekends and guys have a weakness for me. They're the best tippers. Besides I have a full-time job as a secretary."

"You're something else. I'm selling children's furniture, and if I'm a bit short, I'll ask my mother to give me a loan from her secret rainy day cookie jar."

"How long do you think it will take to round up enough money?"

"Not sure. Maybe a few months. I want to get back to Gianni ASAP. We can meet in New York for the flight to Rome."

"Okay. The timing is your call. I already have enough money right now, so just let me know when you're ready to leave."

By July I had saved enough money for my ticket and a few months rent. I was elated. My stint as a salesgirl had paid off for a change. My parents were dismayed but said nothing. I had no idea how I was going to support myself long-term the second time around, but my separation from Gianni was over.

Gianni picked us up from the airport at Fiumicino on August 2, 1967. He squeezed me so tight I could hardly breathe. "*Amore mio*, I missed you so much." We headed to a *pensione* and dropped off Molly and our suitcases. Seeing Gianni again made me realize how much I loved him and had missed him. I belonged in Rome in his loving embrace. We were like two misshapen puzzle pieces that somehow managed to fit together to complete a whole. As soon as we arrived at his parents' apartment, and I was welcomed with hugs and kisses all around, Gianni and I made a speedy retreat to his sister's apartment one floor up since no one was home. His family didn't question our departure. We had precious little time alone to show how much we loved each other. The fact that Carla and Enzo could walk in at any moment didn't seem to deter us, and I'm sure even if they entered the bedroom we wouldn't have even noticed.

Via Valtrompia

Molly and I stayed at the *pensione* for four days until we found a furnished one bedroom apartment in an area called Monte Sacro on Via Valtrompia overlooking the Aniene River. It was a five-story, nondescript, institutional-looking, concrete building with an elevator and long balconies on every floor, like many of the newer residential apartment buildings outside the center of Rome.

"It's a lot newer than Via Francesco Amici. I like having a balcony. We can even sit out there, maybe put a little table outside and have a glass of wine." Molly put her hands on her hip as she discussed the possibilities. She was clearly considering it.

"The view of the river is nice too. We might even get a good breeze up there since it doesn't have air conditioning."

"Good point. The neighborhood is perfect. It has a butcher, pharmacy . . . and the market is one block away. We can walk everywhere," she said.

"Does that mean we'll take it?"

"The rent is ninety-seven dollars. Fits our budget. Sure let's do it." The floor plan resembled a railroad car with a long, narrow hallway, and all rooms at a right angle off the hallway. The apartment had a large bedroom, a bathroom, a small eat-in kitchen, a living room-dining room combination, and a good size utility closet. The windows were covered with slatted, wooden shades that rolled up and down to provide shade from the summer sun and some privacy, since there weren't any curtains. There didn't seem to be a problem with insects or mosquitoes even without screens. The furniture was cheap, modern, and bland; the walls were devoid of artwork and cried out for some creative touches. It would be fun adding some personality to it.

We celebrated our return and finding an apartment by going to a special summer performance of *Aida* dramatically staged in the ancient Roman ruins of Caracalla. The setting was spectacular at night, perfect for the Egyptian theme of the opera, even incorporating live camels and horses into the production. It certainly beat sitting at home alone in Pittsburgh.

Since we arrived in mid-summer, we took a few days to relax before pounding the pavement looking for jobs. Gianni had to work, so Molly and I used my questionable means of summer travel by hitchhiking south to the Amalfi Coast for a few days. We got an immediate ride from a man in a huge American convertible who took us as far as Positano, the perfect location to catch a ferry to Capri, the idyllic island paradise we had only read about.

After disembarking in Capri, Molly and I took the tram up to the main square to check out the stores and find a hotel room. To my unexpected delight, Molly made the acquaintance of a dapper- looking Italian in one of the boutique clothing stores who just happened to own a small hotel. Italian men had a definite weakness for Molly. She was capricious and flirtatious, tilting her head and batting her dark, sexy eyes to garner his full attention.

"So you own a hotel? How lovely!" Molly had a glint in her eye. She saw a perfect opportunity. He gave us a free room for as long as we wanted and promised to provide a room at a reduced rate, if I returned with Gianni in September. We met some interesting people there; an eighteen-year-old Brazilian millionaire who wined and dined us, a charming French couple from Lyon, and an American school teacher who said she would visit us in Rome. After three days of walking the narrow paths covered with arched thickets of purple bougainvillea, sunning on the rocks, and swimming in the turquoise water, I decided to take the train back to Rome. I missed Gianni. Molly stayed behind. I planned to bring Gianni back to Capri. It was a perfect romantic spot for lovers.

11

Lazy Days of Summer

When I returned to Rome, Cecilia my English gal pal, contacted me. "Hey, Luv. I told Paolo to bugger off. I saw him chatting up some girl, and I had it out with him. He's nothing but a randy wanker. I need a place to cool off. What do you say?"

"I'll talk to Gianni and see if we can borrow an extra bed somewhere. Molly's in Capri but I think she'll be okay with you crashing here for awhile."

"Thanks, Ducky."

Her relationship with Paolo was a tempestuous one, and when they fought, they had to return to their respective corners, needing downtime to collect themselves before resuming the bout. She and Paolo both had hot tempers, and occasionally I was afraid it would end in a fistfight, with Paolo on the losing end. A friend of Gianni's provided a single bed. We put it in the utility closet which was a cramped, dark space without windows, similar to a walk-in closet. It was claustrophobic and lacked fresh air, but Cecilia didn't seem to mind. Our rent was reduced even further.

The apartment never felt crowded during the summer. Molly spent her weekends in Capri, like legions of Italians heading to the beach for a reprieve from ninety degree temperatures. She left Cecilia and me behind to suffer through the heat unabated. We still had a sofa bed in the living room if we needed additional space for occasional visitors.

Our lives were carefree and open to change at a moment's notice. No one had yet established any hard and fast rules when it came to living with others and coping with their eccentricities.

Connie, the American school teacher we met in Capri, came to stay with us for a week. She was making her way around Italy for the summer and was headed for Florence after leaving Rome. Her trip brought back memories of my own traveling summer with Susan. When I left Italy to go back home, Susan and I lost touch. I missed her.

Jean-Michel, my former French boyfriend, wrote to me to say he would be in Rome for a few days. It was an unexpected visit since we rarely corresponded. He arrived with a tall, slim, French woman with a lovely, sculpted face and a perpetual frown. She towered over his jockey-like frame. She gave me the distinct impression she knew about our prior relationship and didn't like what she heard . . . I could tell from the way she glowered at me. *Wonder what he said about me?*

Gianni was curious to meet Jean-Michel, even though it was somewhat awkward. "Let's go dancing. Maybe we can go to the opera one evening. Do you think Jean-Michel would like opera?"

"I know he likes poetry and music so maybe he will." Gianni put everyone at ease with his irrepressible personality. One night we went to a disco, and the second night we went to see *La bohème*. Jean-Michel stared at me frequently throughout the performance. *Does he still have feelings for me?* I concluded he was a foppish Frenchman. *Why had he appealed to me in the first place?* Gianni was honest and loyal without hidden agendas, unlike Jean-Michel who was looking for a free ticket to the US.

"*Hai fatto mai l'amore?* (Did you ever make love?) He doesn't seem like your type." *Gianni got that right.*

"Nope, he's too scrawny and short. We were just friends. *I wasn't entirely truthful.* I think you're much more handsome and sexy," I said with a laugh, pinching his butt. Gianni had a deep, abiding love for me, which was something Jean-Michel had lacked. The French love poems he had written were an ode to himself as much as they had been to me.

After Jean-Michel and his gal pal left Rome, I started looking for gainful employment. I applied for a personnel job at F.A.O (Food and Agriculture Organization of the United Nations) paying nine thousand dollars a year, and I had a promising interview with a dentist who serviced the embassy clientele. He needed an English-speaking receptionist and dental assistant. Neither job panned out. Many of the businesses were closed for the month, so I was advised to wait until September when everyone was back from their holidays.

I put an ad in *The Rome Daily American* as an English instructor. Unfortunately, my college education had not prepared me for any specific job. My skill set was minimal. Molly, who was an experienced secretary, easily found temporary work with a secretarial service. My ad in the paper turned into a fiasco.

"Hello. Are you still looking for a job?" A man with a British accent called one day.

"Yes, still looking."

"This job would be interesting. It's working for a family . . . two adults, three children."

"Uh . . . as a tutor, nanny, cook . . . what?"

"Not exactly. They're nudists. Think you can handle running around naked?" Click. *What a jerk.* That was one of the more outlandish prank calls I received. My friends and I pulled similar moronic stunts in middle school, calling random phone numbers in the directory, and making up risqué names, like Hickey Creamer or Harvey Hard-on to shock the respondent, and then abruptly hanging up.

I needed a paying job desperately. My frustration and anxiety were building. If I didn't find a job soon, I might be forced to go home by

Christmas. Accepting defeat the second time around wasn't an option. The thought of a prolonged separation from Gianni was enough to keep me focused on every available means of procuring employment.

"What if I plopped myself down along the road at night near Villa Borghese sitting around a campfire?"

"You mean like the resident prostitutes on Via Pinciana?" Molly was amused.

"Yeah, exactly. I could attract clients and drum up a lot of business, don't you think? All I need is a mini dress, high heels, heavy makeup and drooping, fake lashes."

"You're kidding, right? They'd run after you for horning in on their territory."

"I could always offer to read them bedtime stories from my library of books to pass the time . . . okay, forget that idea."

Ferragosto was a national holiday celebrated in mid-August. There were countless Italian holidays which I always thought were just excuses not to work. Gianni and I decided to join the throngs of other Italians and spend three or four days on the Adriatic Coast visiting Rimini, Cattolica, and San Marino. Since we had limited funds, we thought we'd rough it by camping along the way to save on *pensiones.* Molly had agreed to join us, but she needed a lot of convincing since she wasn't keen on the idea of camping. Frankly neither was I, but some sacrifices had to be made, if we wanted to go. Not surprisingly, Molly soon lost her enthusiasm for camping and sleeping bags.

"Camping is for peons. It's dirty, smelly. You can't take showers. What if it rains?"

"Since when do a few rain drops stop you from going somewhere you've never been? You love traveling as much as I do. Come on, be reasonable." Sometimes Molly could be obstreperous.

"I know you want Molly to come with us. Okay, we'll stay in cheap *pensiones* if that's what it takes." Gianni capitulated.

"How did I ever deserve anyone so reasonable? As always, you're a sweetie. Molly will love the idea." He was quick to cave-in to her demands. I would have held out longer. We revised our plans to accommodate her, even though it meant stretching our finances.

The Republic of San Marino, one of the world's smallest countries, was a highlight of the trip. It's a medieval, walled town perched majestically on top of Mount Titano overlooking the Adriatic. We took a cable car up instead of driving the steep, precarious, winding road to the pinnacle.

"This place is really romantic, like Capri. I feel like a third wheel." Molly was tiring of her official status as our personal photographer. I wanted her to take as many pictures of us together as possible to commemorate our trip. Luckily, she was there to assist.

"Sorry, but I'm not sharing Gianni. He's all mine—no *ménage à trois,*" (a sex threesome) I joked. "Besides, you owe me a favor since we aren't pitching a tent." Gianni looked adorable in shorts and sandals. He put his arm around my waist in front of a wall covered with a tangle of vines and a profusion of purple bougainvillea. "Okay,

Molly. Let's frame it with the flowers in the background. Shoot!" She gave me a disparaging look before taking the picture.

I enjoyed browsing the souvenir shops and walking through the cobblestone walkways holding hands, like so many other couples in love. We enjoyed pasta and local wine at a tiny trattoria with a view from the terrace of other distant hilltop towns. There was a refreshing downdraft ricocheting off the ramparts. We were sorry to leave it for the hot and humid seashore a few miles away.

The Adriatic beaches had fine sand, unlike many of the beaches on the Mediterranean side, which were mostly rocky or had black volcanic sand.

"*Amore, vieni qua.* (Love, come here.) Lay down next to me. I want to take a nap and I could use a pillow. You're nice and soft." He ran his hand across my bare stomach. It sent shivers through my body and it had to be in the 80s. *Too bad we couldn't make love right here.* Gianni and I stretched out on the beach for a snooze, then frolicked in the water and relaxed at the seaside restaurants feasting on seafood, *gelato,* and each other. Molly took lots of pictures of us together. I was thoroughly content. The days seemed too short. Being in love made everything seem beautiful and wondrous, as though I were seeing everything through magical lenses. Cushy accommodations were of little importance.

Molly and I had time to talk. "At the end of August I'm going to Germany to see my sister. She's teaching at a military base there. Then I'm going back to Boston to see Jimmy." (Jimmy was Molly's high school sweetheart who was returning from Vietnam.)

"I'm really going to miss you. If it hadn't been for you, I probably wouldn't have returned to Rome so fast. You made it happen. I'll have to figure out what to do once you leave. I'm not going back home—no way, no how. I'm not leaving Gianni again."

"Do you think you'll marry him?"

"That's the sixty-four-thousand-dollar question."

Our romance continued to flourish, fed by our insatiable appetite for each other. At times it was so intense that it consumed me, and we became a single entity in body and spirit. Maybe our relationship was the closest I would ever get to nirvana. Our lives were intertwined in symbiotic satisfaction, locked together in a world that we alone populated. When we were apart, I was able to detach myself long enough to reenter daily life. Somehow I managed to cope keeping both worlds in perspective.

"I ran into Giacomo today near his parents' apartment building on via Luigi Pigorini," Gianni said. "Susan is living with him. They're going to Pittsburgh to get married. Giacomo is getting his visa before he leaves."

The squabbles I had with Susan and Giacomo when we lived together had taken their toll, and we were no longer in communication, although Gianni would occasionally see Giacomo. Susan claimed that Molly had been the catalyst in driving us apart and destroying our friendship. They never got along. I always found myself caught in the middle, never wanting to take sides, but I believed Giacomo was the real reason for our rift.

Either way, Susan and I drifted apart after having a long, enduring friendship. It made me sad to think our friendship was over. We tried to come to terms with our rift before she departed, but there was much left unsaid. Cecilia was leaving for England the middle of December. If all these departures came to pass, I would find myself in an untenable situation again, unless I found a job and another roommate.

Molly was the recipient of a 5000 *lire* note slipped into her hand, after a perfect stranger asked her for directions. She had incredible luck. We decided to treat ourselves to dinner at a well-known restaurant in Trastevere before she left for Germany. She used the rest of the money to buy presents for Jimmy and her parents, and then realized she didn't have enough money left over for a ticket home. Her parents said they couldn't afford to send her the money.

"How do you intend to get back to Boston?"

"I'm planning on borrowing the money for my ticket from the American Embassy or else flying on credit and paying it off at home."

"Can you actually do that?"

"Sure, *no problema*. I'm used to living on credit. It's the only way I can afford anything."

"You are definitely a marvel. It's amazing how you pull things off financially one way or another." Molly was very resourceful. I never ceased to be impressed. She even had a permanent secretarial job in Rome if she wanted it, but she decided she had to get home to see her true love. We made tentative plans to live together in Boston, if I ever decided to go home in the future, and if she didn't end up getting married.

12

Life Returns to Normal or Almost

My search for employment continued. Cecilia was suddenly out of her modeling job when she refused to work Sundays which would have meant working seven days a week. Obviously, the Italians had never heard of fair labor laws. Molly was luckier in keeping her job as a secretary until she left for Germany. She managed to wrangle three days in Venice with her employer picking up the tab, again demonstrating how she always managed to get what she wanted with her wily ways . . . such was *la dolce vita* (the sweet life). The spectacle of her shamelessly flirtatious means to an end would be missed. While she was gone, Cecilia had two girlfriends come in from London for a few days. They were a rather promiscuous lot and I feared for what dregs of society I would find lounging in the living room each morning. There was never a dull moment.

The Rome Daily American became my daily go-to newspaper while I was hunting for a job. It was also a means to reconnect to the world I had virtually left behind, although the newspaper sometimes bordered on a tabloid. It was chock-full of miscellaneous, quirky news items you would never find in *The New York Times*. Reading the newspaper was a diversion. It helped me focus on news outside my own insulated life of choice with Gianni.

The apartment on Via Valtrompia had some of the same problems as our previous apartment. You could never count on taking a shower. There were several times that Cecilia found herself in the shower when the water ran out, and she had just bleached her hair.

"Bollocks! What happened to the bloody water? I'm really brassed off!"

"Wait, I've got to give you a mirror." It always made me laugh to see her standing in the bathroom with purple hair and to hear some of her choice British expressions. It became routine to take advantage of shower time if we had water, regardless of whether we needed a shower or not. By French standards, that would have been blasphemous.

Having roommates, especially with one of them being British, was a good exercise in learning to get along with people who did things differently, had their own value system, and weren't always flexible. It was like an *insalata mista* (mixed salad) when you tossed in everyone's boyfriend. Negotiating was necessary and compromises had to be made. No one seemed to hold grudges for very long. We somehow made it work.

My mother wrote to inform me a college friend of mine had called "person-to-person." She said she told the operator I was "a-broad" and the operator laughed. She couldn't understand what was so funny and she requested an explanation. My mother had a wonderful Yiddish sense of humor, but she had trouble when it came to a double entendre.

She also included some recipes I had requested. Cecilia and Molly became my resident guinea pigs. They particularly enjoyed the apple cake and roasted chicken. Cecilia asked me to make chopped liver and noodle kugel for Rosh Hashanah. Even though I didn't have a chopper, I enjoyed figuring out imaginative ways of doing things without proper kitchen equipment. Cooking was a useful distraction when Gianni was at work.

Since Cecilia insisted we observe the Jewish holidays, I decided to make some of my mother's recipes, light the candles, and say the blessing using the prayer book my parents had sent me. I thought my Hebrew was poor even though I had taken ten years of instruction, until I heard Cecilia recite the prayers with her English accent. She sounded like an English gal from Liverpool impersonating an Israeli Jew from Tel Aviv.

We went to the Grand Synagogue for services on Yom Kippur, the holiest day of the Jewish New Year. It was educational to see how Italian Jews celebrated the High Holidays. Traditionally, Orthodox synagogues segregated the women from the men. The men sat on the first floor. We were ushered upstairs to the balcony or *loggia* where the women were seated. The women jabbered incessantly while the men did the serious business of praying below us. It seemed a contradiction when we were celebrating the Day of Atonement and being forced to listen to the ladies of the loggia. My family belonged to a Conservative synagogue where the men and women sat together, but no one had animated conversations while the service was in progress. At the Grand Synagogue it was so loud that you couldn't hear the rabbi speaking or the cantor singing.

"I'm convinced Jewish-Italian women must have the worst reputation for common courtesy. Remember the Signora at the glove store? She's a perfect example, don't you think, Cecilia?"

"Spot-on, the Signora was a corker. These women all remind me of New Yorkers who also have a horrid reputation for rudeness."

"Let's not forget Londoners," I added. After a short while we left in disgust. I'm not sure whether it had to do with the difference between Ashkenazi and Sephardic Jews or American and Italian Jews, but either way it was a totally unsatisfying experience. We would have to atone for our sins elsewhere.

Being Jewish in Rome was very different from being Jewish in Pittsburgh. In Rome there was a Jewish section called the "Ghetto" where the Grand Synagogue was located. The name disturbed me. It reminded me of the Warsaw Ghetto and the atrocities committed there by the Nazis. Roman Jews were unperturbed by the name. The connotation did not appear to elicit the same outrage and horror of Jews forced to wear Star of David armbands and live in a designated area surrounded by a ten-foot wall.

From my observations, they were not subjected to Anti-Semitism and seemed secure in their lives, unlike Jews elsewhere in the world. But the mere sound of the word, conjured up images of Jews being starved, beaten, and rounded up for the final solution awaiting them in extermination camps. Gianni and his family never once brought up my religion or questioned me about it. They were equally uninterested in discussing their own. Maybe this was typical behavior for most Romans. Jews were free to live peacefully and prosper like other Roman citizens.

Are Dogs Really Man's Best Friend?

Molly left for Germany and my time was spent trying to housebreak a puppy that Cecilia's boyfriend Paolo had given her. Cecilia had no clue how to housebreak a dog. His name was "Thor," short for Henry David Thoreau and he appeared to be a mutt, although Paolo insisted he was a purebred German Shepherd.

Thor was always underfoot. After the holidays, Cecilia and I decided to do some redecorating so we painted the kitchen including the furniture. Invariably, Thor would rush the paint cans, barking at them. The job took more time than we thought since he was getting in the way, and we had to shoo him out of the room. He even ended up with a painted nose like Bozo the Clown when he decided to stick it in a can of red paint.

The whole place looked decidedly brighter after we finished. We then bought a few plants for the balcony to add a bit of color. I wondered if we had been too hasty in freshening up the apartment since Thor began eating furniture legs, paper, shoes, and one very good bra. He was definitely an incorrigible nuisance.

"No, Thor, No! Bad dog, bad dog. You can't pee on my bed! See that closet door? That's Cecilia's room. Go pee there . . . Cecilia! Take care of your friggin' dog!" I had lost it!

Cecilia never seemed to be around when Thor needed to be walked or trained. Her absence was all too convenient. She probably arranged it that way to stick it to me since she knew I was the responsible type and loved dogs. So we now had another mouth to feed.

As weeks passed, Thor continued to wreak havoc in the apartment. He chewed up the bathroom rug, two more chair legs, and a section of the wall, adding to his ever lengthening list of *Items Destroyed by Thor*. Would he ever outgrow puppyhood?

"Let's take Thor to the country. He can run all over the place and pee wherever he wants," Gianni suggested.

"*Buon idea*," I said. "That's a perfect way to tire him out." Gianni and I took him for a ride to the outskirts of Rome where the rolling hills provided a perfect backdrop for a little exercise. Thor ran back and forth between the olive trees retrieving the ball, his tail whirling like a helicopter, propelling him up and down the hills. He was loving it. He was just a normal puppy who needed exercise, and when he was cooped up in the apartment all day, he found other ways to entertain himself and get into trouble.

We then went to a villa with acres of gardens and fields that included a pond stocked with a hundred ducks and tropical birds. Thor thoroughly enjoyed chasing them, but fortunately caught nary a one. Maybe he was a third-rate bird dog. I jokingly contemplated leaving him there. It wasn't his fault if he wasn't given training and was left alone most of the day. Dogs are hard to dislike, and I had grown up with two of them. Thor was slowly winning me over. He deserved better. Paolo should never have given him to Cecilia.

Thor continued his reign of terror. He began jumping into the toilet probably to cool off. He devoured my slippers, my Italian/English dictionary (maybe that's why he understood commands in both languages), a month's supply of birth control pills, and feasted on sections of a bookcase and several towels for good measure.

"Cecilia, when Thor finishes his destructive rampage, our landlady will be forced to rent the apartment unfurnished."

"I promise to replace everything he's eaten, Ducky. I'll buy you a new English/Italian dictionary to start."

"What about the more important stuff like furniture and my birth control pills?"

"Don't worry your pretty little head. I'll ask Paolo for a loan." Cecilia had planned to take Thor with her to England, but decided it was going to cost too much and he would have to be quarantined. It was clear to me that Thor and I were destined to be together in the not too distant future.

The following week we were invited to Gianni's friends' wedding. Italians really know how to throw a party . . . every two minutes someone made a toast, and by the time the espresso was served, all the guests were visibly bleary-eyed and drunk. The toasts became repetitive, even though they were delivered by different family members, but no one seemed to mind.

The meal was an event in itself, consisting of multiple courses: antipasto, mixed fish salad, two different kinds of pasta, two different chicken dishes, a veal dish, roast beef platter, and a green salad. Then for dessert came the wedding cake, *gelato*, champagne, fresh fruit, and finally espresso. We sat at a table eating and drinking wine for five hours.

"*Abbiamo mangiato come maiali.* (We ate like pigs.) I must have gained ten kilos in the time we've been here." I couldn't get out of my chair.

Gianni pulled me into a standing position. "But it was *fantastico*, right? There's nothing like an Italian wedding. It's all about the food." He was right about that. The marriage ceremony seemed incidental to the reception.

I wondered whether Gianni and I would ever have such a glorious wedding. *Would I wear a wedding gown, would we be married by a priest, a rabbi, both or neither?* Somehow I couldn't picture us in Pittsburgh having nearly as much fun. Besides, my father would disown me so who would pay for the wedding?

In my limited experience, weddings in the States tended to have food one step above cafeteria chow. Italians would be horrified. I fantasized while watching the bride and groom affectionately kiss and caress one another. *Would I look as demure and loving? Would I ever be ready to take the plunge?*

Cecilia the Charmer

It was always an adventure going out with Cecilia. One day we took a stroll along Via Veneto, a popular street for people watching and window shopping. Within minutes we were hotly pursued by a golden Cadillac driven by a fat, old man. It would have been understandable for a Roman, but we were shocked by the New York license plate.

"I rest my case about New Yorkers. They really are a cheeky lot. He must be besotted," she said. The lecher followed us everywhere, throwing us kisses.

"Maybe he thinks his behavior is acceptable since he's in Rome instead of New York. How did he get a Cadillac here?" I flipped him the bird to get rid of him while Cecilia strutted down the street with her dress hiked up in dramatic fashion just to whet his appetite.

"Get a load of his eyes. They're practically bulging out of his head," I told her. I was reminded of the headlights on the dirty Deux Chevaux in France. She always seemed to be on stage just waiting for a Hollywood director to discover her—a Hollywood and Vine moment. Cecilia was the ultimate drama queen.

She got a small part in a film and made fifty dollars for six hours of work which seemed like a fortune. Paolo said he would try to set up an audition for me to dub an Italian film in English. The following week Cecilia got another part in a film. Her future as an actress was on the upswing. At Paolo's suggestion she had professional pictures taken, and he distributed them throughout the movie industry anticipating she would soon land a substantive role.

The pictures made a difference. Soon afterward Cecilia got a part as a flight attendant in a movie starring Joseph Cotten, an American actor. Paolo managed to get Gianni and me jobs as extras for the day playing passengers on the plane. We were delighted at the opportunity to make some money.

The plane never left the tarmac, but Gianni was as excited as a kid running amok in a candy store since he had never been on an airplane before. I had been flying since I was three years old, so this insight into Gianni's sheltered life confirmed that he had done little traveling outside Italy. It made me wonder whether his life experiences had been too insular for someone who had always appreciated the adventure of traveling to parts unknown. Would he be willing to take risks like I had just for the thrill of it? We had led very different lives. Cecilia decided to extend her departure to January with the possibility of another part in a movie in the future.

The rainy season started in November. We had a huge thunderstorm one night and my favorite plant fell to the floor of the balcony The clay pot shattered into a million pieces. I tried to clean it up since I didn't want Thor tracking mud all over the apartment. The next morning I got a complaint from the *portiera* that the mud had dripped onto the balcony below us and the tenant was furious. She also lodged a complaint against Cecilia for cleaning her brush over the balcony and covering all her plants with blonde strands of hair.

"That hair is absolutely not mine! It must have blown here from somewhere else. That cheeky woman is a twit!"

"You're the only blonde in the building," I asserted.

"You can't pin that hair on me! I'm innocent. You won't get a confession out of me, Ducky. You'll have to draw and quarter me."

"Should we analyze the hair color and see if it matches? Let's get your brush."

"Uh no, stay away from my things. You're quite mistaken." Although she vehemently denied being the owner of the hair, she finally conceded she was indeed the guilty party. We both burst out laughing. We, in turn, complained about no heat. The *portiera* said she would turn it on when it got cold. She didn't consider forty-five degrees cold enough. She ignored our complaints. Even sleeping with three wool blankets didn't keep us warm.

The *portiera* and residents in the building looked at us askance from the very beginning of our occupancy. Young Italian women did not live alone in apartments, or have young men traipsing about at odd hours of the day and night. I was certain they thought all American and British women were whores. The only difference they saw between us and the ladies of the night was that we had a permanent roof over our heads, while the real prostitutes worked the streets. At least they were able to build fires to keep warm.

Paolo introduced me to his forty-year-old brother one day when I accompanied Cecilia to his brother's clothing boutique. I quickly acquired another admirer besides Gianni. He was infatuated with me even though he was married with two children. That didn't seem to deter him from flirting with me relentlessly. I was flattered by his attention. He told me I was as precious as a rare crystal, and said I was "*la fine del mondo*" (out of this world.) Honestly, I never encouraged him, but I rather enjoyed the admiration of an older man. He said he was going to start a novella about me. It brought back the flowery poems Jean-Michel had written. I was glad I inspired men to write. He probably thought if he lavished enough compliments on me I would finally capitulate and fall into bed with him, but my eyes were only for Gianni.

Hurrah! A Job at Long Last

My job search continued. In the middle of November I interviewed for a job as manager of a well-known American bookstore. The salary would have been sufficient to support me, but the owner went on a buying trip to the States, and I wouldn't know whether I had the job until he returned. Working in a bookstore would be ideal since I loved reading and would have plentiful reading material to keep me occupied. It sounded hopeful, but he never called me back.

It wasn't long after that disappointment, that the employment agency I signed up with called to tell me about a job opening in the telex department of W.E. Hutton International, a US stock brokerage firm. I jumped at the prospect. Because I didn't have a work permit, it was only a temporary job over the holidays, but there was always a chance it could develop into something more permanent, and I needed money desperately.

My training was on the telex machine. The telex was like a typewriter with a separate keyboard (teletypewriter) with a two-way, dial-up communication system. It provided a real-time means for international messaging similar to today's texting. The telex was the precursor of the computer and the technological revolution of electronic communication.

W.E. Hutton's headquarters were in New York with branch offices in London, Monte Carlo, Lugano, and Rome. The first time I used the telex I was spellbound typing, "Hi, what's happening in Monte Carlo?" and getting an instant reply on the very next line. I even carried on a flirtation with a coworker in London strictly over the wire. It seemed so strange, almost like magic to be instantly connected with people all over the world. It was exciting to be at the forefront of future developments in telecommunications.

This job changed my entire outlook. I looked forward to getting up each day and heading to the office. It made me feel productive and self-confident, and everyone spoke English, making it a stress free environment. As much as I loved the Italian language, by the end of the day after speaking it nonstop to Gianni, I would go to bed with a pounding headache.

There was one small caveat to my job . . . a Mr. Hesse who was a German stockbroker from Berlin. He was universally disliked. When the head honcho was away on business, Mr. Hesse would try to take charge dictating orders to everyone, but no one respected him enough to listen. After he made a snide remark about Jews, I tried to steer clear of him rather than be subjected to his offensive comments. Given his dogmatic personality and prejudicial remarks, it made me wonder what his parents must have been doing during World War II.

Winter Woes

In December we received a whopper of an electricity bill ... thirty dollars for two months. The last bill was ten dollars for four months.

"I'm convinced that old bag wants us to move out. She probably figures if she ups the utility bill, we'll hightail it out of here. Fat chance of that happening."

"That *portiera* is daft if she thinks that," Cecilia added. "We shouldn't pay the increase even if it means reading by candlelight. She isn't going to get away with her shenanigans."

"We should plan a counterattack. Maybe start a petition to get her ousted for harassing the tenants. I bet we could get everyone in the building to sign. They like her less than they like us, and that's saying something," I said.

On New Year's Eve, Gianni, Cecilia, Paolo, and I went to a nightclub called Maxim's for dinner and dancing. Instead of saving my Chanukah *gelt* (money) that my parents had sent, I bought a cocktail dress for the occasion. It was a gorgeous, shimmering, single shoulder Pierre Cardin copy for forty-four dollars and shoes to match for seven fifty. As we slow danced, Gianni whispered in my ear, "*Mi fa impazzire*" (You make me crazy) a compliment to how much he liked my sexy reproduction. He held me as close as possible and whispered again, "*Quando chiudo gli occhi vedo solo te.*" (When I close my eyes I only see you.) He made me feel I belonged to him alone, just the way I wanted it.

The nightclub had cheap decorations and sketchy clientele made only worse after we were served a cold, limp lasagne dinner. It lacked the New Year's Eve ambiance we were seeking, and it didn't put Cecilia and Paolo in a festive mood. Gianni made the best of the situation as he always did. "I'm happy just being with you. It's enough." He whispered sweet nothings in my ear and gave me little kisses. Cecilia was emotional the entire evening, either crying about her imminent departure from Rome and leaving Paolo behind, or complaining loudly about the nightclub's shortcomings, further dampening the atmosphere.

"What a bloody, beastly excuse for a club! I'd rather be at home bonking Paolo. What do you say, Luv, are you ready to leave?" She turned to me for affirmation. *She really likes alliteration.*

It was the perfect occasion for Gianni to use one of the many inimitable American expressions I had taught him. "Let's blow this joint!"

Driving home was as treacherous as always on New Year's Eve, trying to avoid any flying object thrown unexpectedly from a window to the street below. The streets and sidewalks were littered with all sorts of debris making driving and walking equally dangerous.

Home Alone

As I predicted, Cecilia left Thor with me when she flew back to London. I was actually glad she left him behind because he kept me company now that I was alone. I walked him along the banks of the Aniene River for miles. He enjoyed barking at the flock of sheep we encountered, grazing on the side of the river, sending them scattering in all directions. The shepherd would curse at me under his breath. When given the opportunity, Thor particularly savored eating their excrement like it was forbidden fruit.

I was never afraid living alone in Rome and would frequently take midnight strolls. It felt safe. There was very little violent crime then, and I was only warned to beware of pickpockets and ass- pinching men. With Thor by my side, I thought I had nothing to fear. Of course, if someone offered him a treat like sheep shit, all bets were off.

It wasn't long before Thor was in the limelight again. He enjoyed tormenting me. He ate a check my parents sent me. I caught him munching on it just before he ate the number one hundred. I had a friend who worked at American Express so I was hopeful he would cash it without any trouble if I pieced it together carefully.

Thor started behaving after Cecilia left, and I was beginning to enjoy my roommate-free existence. Gianni stayed with me on a regular basis.

Dinners were uncomplicated. Gianni told me to keep it simple. "Maybe a big green salad with some prosciutto and melon. We can pick up some cherries at the market for dessert."

"Sounds perfect." Fresh and wholesome. That was the Italian way.

At times I felt as though this must be what married life is like. Gianni would tell me his preferences before he left for work, and I would get up early to shop at the open marketplace a block from the apartment just like a normal wife. Since I didn't have to be at work until after noon, it gave me time to prepare a simple dinner in advance. Gianni appeared again after work, and we would either eat at home or go to his parents' apartment. It all seemed so natural, so satisfying knowing Gianni would be with me every day under the same roof.

There were days that were simply heavenly, and I was incomparably happy. All we ever needed was each other. I never wanted our times together to end. But I was brought back to reality when I had to pay the entire rent on my own. Gianni was already helping out his parents financially, and I knew he couldn't contribute to my rent. I couldn't sleep, and I became prone to anxiety attacks as the end of the month approached. I had no option but to find a paying roommate.

In January, we watched it snow from the balcony of the apartment. It only stayed on the roads for a few hours before it melted, but Italians had no idea how to drive in that kind of weather. They would either stop their cars in the middle of the road, jack them up and put chains on, or abandon them entirely creating massive gridlock. The temperature dipped to twenty-nine degrees, extreme for Rome.

We also had a few days of high winds over fifty-five miles per hour which caused extensive property and tree damage. The apartment building was across the street from the river, and there weren't any trees to buffer the wind, as it whooshed over the river. It howled eerily outside the building making the windows and wooden shades clatter. I deemed myself lucky after reading about heavy snow, zero temperatures and below in the US.

"Come here, *Bella*. Let's get into bed to stay warm and make love." It sounded like a rapturous night ahead. Gianni and I hunkered down in bed, weathering the storm. It was pure contentment.

13

My Prayers Are Answered

The stock market was on a steady decline, and when the North Koreans seized the *U.S.S Pueblo* on the high seas in January 1968, I doubted it would recover any time soon. Vietnam was still very much in the news. I found myself reading the newspaper more often, especially since I was advertising for a roommate in the *Rome Daily American* and wanted to check to make sure the ad was running in the classified section.

An American woman came to have a look. She had a scholarship to the Metropolitan Opera House to study Italian opera. She would have been an interesting choice. Maybe I could have gotten free tickets to the opera, but she said she didn't like the location even though it was a mere fifteen minutes to the center of Rome.

Toward the end of January, Mary Louise an Italian American from Chicago, answered my ad. She was a pretty brunette with dark, sparkling eyes and an engaging, cheerful, upbeat personality. She decided she liked the apartment well enough and said she would move in by mid-February. I told her I would give her a key when she gave me a deposit.

"By the way, I have a dog." Just as though on cue, Thor bounded into the room and catapulted himself toward her practically knocking her over. She jumped back in fright.

"Is *he* staying?" She motioned toward Thor who rolled over waiting to have his stomach rubbed. She ignored him.

"Yes, he lives here."

"Does he sleep in the bedroom?"

"He sleeps wherever he wants to."

"So that includes the bedroom?"

"Yep, I'm afraid so. He's a great companion and a super guard dog." *He's actually a total wuss if a stranger offers him a treat, but I decided to keep that little fact to myself.* She gave me a look of resignation and shrugged her shoulders. I wasn't sure she would follow through. *Thor was definitely an issue.*

Speaking of the dog, my hopes for Thor's improved behavior were short-lived, as he resumed his disobedient puppyhood antics.

"Thor, stop that! What are you eating? Oh, shit. You ate 2000 *lire* and my vaginal suppositories! Bad dog, bad dog! Go sit in the corner!" He slouched away with his tail between his legs, understanding I was clearly upset with him. "No treats today." *What if the suppositories poison him? Maybe he's a gay dog, confused about his sexuality? Should I take him to the vet or go to the bank?* I was able to piece the notes together with scotch-tape and decided on option two—I hurried off to the bank.

"I have a problem." I handed the torn *lire* notes to the bank teller. "My dog ate them." The teller laughed.

"Are you sure that's what happened to them?"

"It's the honest-to-God truth. I found the remains on the floor with my dog's paws on what was left of them. He definitely did it. No doubt about it. Can you please help?" The teller continued to smile and shook his head, before he handed me two new, crisp *lire*. *I don't think he believes me.* His reaction reminded me of the teacher asking the student, "Where's your homework?" and the student responds with, "The dog ate it." I suppose that popular retort crossed all cultures. I couldn't afford to have Thor eat the equivalent of even three precious dollars. Every *lire* counted.

In February The Vietnam War was in the headlines again. The "Tet Offensive," the Vietcong surprise attack on Saigon and other major cities, rattled the psyche of the American people. President Johnson found himself in a perilous position with events spiraling out of control. The stock market plummeted further in response to this tragic development. It left me feeling frightened as an American and sad at the loss of young lives in a war I did not support. After getting a full account after reading two newspapers, I was fearful for what might happen next. There were bound to be repercussions.

At work I got immediate newsfeed over the wire from New York, as the stock market continued to dive reacting to the international crisis. The Vietcong had dealt a tremendous blow to our confidence and resolve. Johnson was misguided to have suggested the Vietcong had been decimated. He must think Americans are naive or uninformed.

As much as I wanted to discuss these events with Gianni, Vietnam remained an unspoken topic. He was opposed to the war as most Italians were, but he didn't keep up to date with the latest headlines. It was an American war, not an Italian one—his interest was minimal. He definitely wasn't as tuned in to world events as I was. Living so far away from home made me feel unsettled and anxious when there was negative news about the war. I thought it best to stay current with what was going on.

Getting Acquainted

I really had been enjoying my independence, but Mary Louise moved in as promised. Finally, I had a roommate. She worked at the English School off Via Lucullo, coincidentally, the same street I worked on. She spoke fluent Italian and French, was very friendly, and most importantly, appreciated my sense of humor. She invited Gianni and me to join her and her boyfriend Francesco on a skiing trip to

Abruzzo after she moved in. She was pleasant and easy to talk to—definitely a good choice for a roommate. I lucked out for a change.

Thor was front and center again when he contracted worms. Paolo felt obligated to accompany me to the vet, since the dog was technically his and Cecilia's. The doctor confirmed that Thor was a *bastardo*, even though Paolo had assured us he was a purebred German Shepherd. I had always suspected the obvious truth since he never resembled one. Then he ate two Brillo pads and got violently ill, so I took him to the vet again. This time the vet determined he had an intestinal infection, and that the steel wool pads had nothing to do with it. He was given medication and put on a restricted diet of rice, water, and lemon for three days. Thor was becoming an expensive nuisance. Paolo planned to go to London the end of April to see Cecilia and propose to her. Thor was not accompanying him.

Mary Louise was terrified of him. He stole her fuzzy slippers and ate her favorite pen. She had a wild irrational fear that if she had direct eye contact with him, he would viciously attack her or wait until she was asleep and sneak up on her and pounce. She must have had a negative experience with a dog when she was a child. I assured her he was not a savage beast.

Feeling guilty for Thor's foibles, I decided to make chocolate chip cookies for her—comfort food always helped quell anxiety. "Gee, these cookies are *fantastico*! But don't ask me to forget what Thor did to my slippers and pen. They were my favorites. It won't work." My true intention was obviously transparent. She gave me a stern stare.

"Thor isn't a bad dog. He just needs some TLC and some training. Cecilia and Paolo never gave him either, poor thing. He's the smartest dog I've ever had. He understands English and Italian. He wouldn't bite a flea . . . okay maybe a flea . . . just give him a chance."

"No-siree-bob!" She was defiant.

Since the cookies were a resounding success and exactly what the doctor ordered, I was convinced they would eventually work their magic, and Mary Louise would come around and accept Thor as a basic, lovable dog. I was hoping my mother would send me a care package with some of my favorite items to share with Mary Louise to appease her, but she never did. I was still waiting for a kosher salami, rye bread, creamed herring with onions, kosher wieners, my Aunt Margaret's dill pickles, and a large tube of Colgate toothpaste.

The following week I felt emboldened to attempt my mother's strudel, substituting yogurt for sour cream which I couldn't find in Rome. "Mm-m-m . . . never had strudel before. I'll have to get the recipe for my grandmother. She's the baker in the family. Um . . . let's see, I taste raspberry, walnuts and the pastry is nice and crunchy." *Mary Louise liked it! Could cookies and strudel be the secret to winning her over?*

It was another success, and I was again flooded with compliments. This time I noted Mary Louise didn't mention Thor's latest rampage. She was beginning to lighten up. I even handed some strudel out to the neighbors and to our dreaded *portiera* as a peace offering. I figured, if they worked on her, the resident troll, they would certainly work on Mary Louise. Anyhow, some of my mother's baking finesse had passed on to me after all.

Now that I was basking in the glow of my baking successes, I decided to attempt a beef tenderloin with roasted potatoes. American beef was far superior to Italian beef. The tenderloin turned out to be a poor excuse for the real thing. The potatoes weren't much better and tasted like dried up spuds left over from the Irish famine. I thought I should stick to baking for the time being.

When I wasn't at work, I spent my time baking, shopping, and walking Thor. He went to the vet again for more injections. The vet mentioned there was a hepatitis epidemic in the dog world carried by river rats, and four dogs in the area had already died. Thor always played near the river, so I had to find another spot to walk him. He would miss the sheep.

"Thor is getting really big. What is he eating—pasta, steak, or did he eat one of those lambs he likes so much?" Gianni winked, wanting me to know he was kidding. He was surprised by Thor's apparent growth spurt.

"You know Thor eats everything—food, furniture, shoes, everything. He's an eating machine," I explained as Gianni laughed.

He seemed to grow larger every day. Maybe his puppy days were nearing an end. When I finally convinced Gianni to take me to the zoo, I was tempted to leave Thor there when I saw what appeared to be domestic cats in cages. If the Rome Zoo was so hard up for animals, maybe they would consider taking Thor off my hands. He might have proven to be their biggest attraction, especially if I provided a list of everything he had eaten and survived. I smiled at the thought. Thor was a pain sometimes, but I loved him and he was now mine.

Giacomo reported to Gianni that he and Susan were getting married in Pittsburgh in March. I thought about how happy they would be and wondered about the future of my own happiness and whether I too would marry one day. As was my custom, I diverted my attention to the newspapers and current events to avoid thinking about the future.

The US political news didn't disappoint; it continued to fascinate me. I wrote my father for his opinion on George Romney or "rejected Romney" as I coined him, bowing out of the 1968 Republican Presidential Campaign. He was born in Mexico and some voters thought it disqualified him for president. It might have contributed to his decision to withdraw.

It paved the way for "reluctant Rocky." Nelson Rockefeller was playing it cool and was waiting to gauge his chances before committing himself to running for president. I wondered whether he could win against Nixon, and of course Johnson. Most people agreed Rockefeller had been a good governor of New York. He shied away from commenting on the Vietnam War. It wasn't clear what he thought about it. From my perspective, I saw him as the only politician with a few pluses. Nixon, even though he had revamped his political approach and had made stabbing attempts at improving his personality and wit, still smelled like a rotten egg. He definitely was not a likable fellow.

The American political scene began to blossom further when Eugene McCarthy had a strong showing in the New Hampshire primary running on an anti-war platform. Johnson must have been shaking in his shoes. His forty-two percent of the Democratic vote was impressive. When would Rockefeller make up his mind, particularly since Nixon had captured so many Republican votes? I tried to keep myself fully informed about American politics.

The Vietnam War was still a looming issue. The student protest movement occupied major headlines in the US newspapers, as it became more ideologically radical. Not only were the protesters against the Vietnam War, they were against corporate America and governmental authority. They demanded social reforms for gays, women, and blacks. They were considered the New Left. The protests were becoming violent and deadly.

Mary Louise told me she was getting a new car. Most Italian cars had manual shift, and Mary Louise didn't know how to drive a stick shift.

"Think I'll master shifting gears?"

"I can just picture you lurching down Via Valtrompia to the wide-eyed stares and laughter of the Italian neighborhood. My brother Sid taught me how to drive his Triumph TR3 sports car when I was sixteen. Worse case scenario, I'll teach you how to shift if you need help."

We were becoming better acquainted with each other and getting along well, although I came to the conclusion that her sheltered Catholic upbringing had impacted her life deeply, particularly when it came to sex. I was certain she saw me as the wanton woman, and it sparked discussions of moral conflict in her relationship with Francesco who wanted to marry a virgin.

"Does it bother you that you aren't a virgin?" she meekly asked me one night.

"You gotta be kidding me. Well, okay . . . I haven't given it much thought. Let me think back to that historic day when I was still in diapers . . ." I couldn't resist teasing her.

"No, I'm really, really serious," she said.

"Does it bother you that you are?" I said.

"Well, um . . . I'm not sure . . . maybe yes and maybe no."

"What kind of an answer is that? It sounds kind of wishy-washy to me. You'll know when the time is right." End of discussion.

When I thought about these intimate chats which generally occurred late at night in the darkness of our room, I wondered whether my life in the liberating 1960s had been too liberating. I never considered myself to be promiscuous, never had one-night stands, but I had a few semi-long-term relationships before, during, and after college. How would Mary Louise fare with Francesco, if he were her first and last lover? It seemed incomprehensible to experience only one man's lovemaking virtuosity for the rest of my life. I would feel deprived and cheated, always wondering if I had missed out on something positively heavenly. What if I hadn't made love to Gianni . . . just think of all those lost moments of ecstasy? Mary Louise was definitely going to regret her decision, but then again isn't ignorance bliss?

14

Luck of The Irish

In March I lost my job. W.E. Hutton was under increased pressure to hire only employees with Italian work permits, or prove that Italian counterparts were unable to do the same job. They would have helped me obtain a permit, if I had agreed to stay on permanently, which I wasn't prepared to do. I called one of our biggest clients at W.E. Hutton, a top executive at Caltex, the petroleum products' arm of Chevron Italiana. It always helped to know the head honcho.

"Sorry to bother you, Mr. Costello. This is your fellow Pittsburgher from the telex department at W.E. Hutton. Hope you don't mind my calling. I'm out of a job. I wondered if you might let me know if there's any temporary work open at Caltex in the future?"

"Well, I'll see what I can do. So, you only want a temporary position—nothing permanent?"

"That's right. I like temporary jobs in case I have to go back home on short notice. But I could commit to at least six months." Accepting a permanent job was too much of a long-term commitment, a gamble, and I wanted to keep my options open. What if something happened on the international front, and I had to make a speedy getaway? There always seemed to be an excuse. *What am I really afraid of?*

"Fine, I'll check around. Leave me an address or number where I can reach you." Mr. Costello had always been kind to me and seemed genuinely interested in my welfare. We had lengthy conversations on the phone about work and current events. He told me he had twin girls around my age who were in graduate school in the States. Maybe that explained his fatherly concern. It never occurred to me that calling the top executive of a major company wasn't common practice for twenty-three-year-old, low-level telex operators. I was an independent thinker marching to my own drummer. I hadn't yet been tainted by rejection. It worked most of the time.

Being out of work, gave me free time to concentrate on my clothes. I noticed there was a dressmaker down the street from our apartment, and I stopped in to talk. She said she could make dresses starting at eleven dollars and coats for twenty-two excluding the material.

"I'm going to have some clothes made," I announced to Mary Louise. "You should talk to the dressmaker. Her shop is next door to the butcher's. The prices she quoted are too cheap to pass up. She has samples of her work and gorgeous fabrics to die for. I looked through her latest magazines for ideas."

"How do you manage to find all the bargains? You make every *lire* count. Wish I had your knack."

"It must be in my blood. My mother taught me well. I bought a light-gray, gabardine wool fabric for a dress, jacket, and matching beret. Very chic from the picture. The cost including the lining, zipper, buttons and her fee comes to forty dollars. Can't beat that."

"Gee, no kidding. Will you come with me to help pick something out? I need a few things to round out my wardrobe. My clothes look pretty frumpy compared to Italians."

"Sure, would love to. You know me and fashion . . ."

It turned out so well, I decided to have the dressmaker make a suit with a silk blouse for forty-five dollars. This was the life. Mary Louise decided to have two dresses made.

I cut my hair really short to speed up my fashion conversion to a stylish Italian woman. My haircut was round and smooth, cut close to the scalp with cropped bangs. It was the latest hair style I had seen in the fashion magazines.

"You look like a *cipolla* (onion)." Gianni couldn't contain himself when he saw me. I laughed as I looked at myself in the mirror. "Would I look better as a *carciofo*?" (artichoke) This time Gianni laughed. His teasing reminded me of Signor Arturo. Gianni definitely inherited his good nature.

He indulged my whims, particularly when it came to fashion. Changing my American image was paramount, and a haircut and Italian clothes would reinvent me as a *fashionista*. Having a few dresses made and buying platform shoes which were in vogue would aid the transformation now that I had some discretionary income. Italian women like the French always dressed fashionably, and I was determined to look just like them. Gianni couldn't have cared less if I walked around looking like a schlump. He loved me from the inside out.

Okay, I'm not Irish, but my ninth grade teacher used to call me Sandy McTavish. He thought I looked Irish with my dark hair and blue eyes. Mr. Costello called me from Caltex to arrange an interview with one of his managers. My interview went well, probably since Mr. Costello had set it up, and I was hired on a temporary basis to work in the telex department. Caltex was located in Ostia, a suburb of Rome, in a beautiful new air-conditioned building with its own cafeteria. My hours were 8 to 5 p.m, which were longer hours than I had at W.E. Hutton. Finally, I would earn considerably more, enabling me to expand my wardrobe and maybe even save some money. It sounded like an ideal opportunity. Spring had sprung.

On March 31, 1968, *The Rome Daily American* had a shocking headline splashed across the front page in large print. President Johnson decided not to run for reelection. It was an unexpected international bombshell. The Vietnam War had taken its toll, and

President Johnson was one of its casualties. Mary Louise and I spent our midnight chat discussing the whole matter.

"Gosh! What a shocker! I never saw that coming. At times like this I wish I were back home in the States. It makes me nervous, like a ship without a captain. Who do you think will run for president? I wonder how the Italian press will see it or the world for that matter?" Mary Louise was shaken.

"The Italian press will definitely have a negative take. But you know the government isn't pro-American, not with the Vietnam War still going on. They won't be able to kick Johnson around anymore, that's for sure. The next president, whoever it is, will have to end this war."

"It scares the bejesus out of me being on the street sometimes with all the demonstrations and strikes. Don't you feel isolated from the US being here? I don't like the way it makes me feel. It upsets my stomach. I feel queasy." Mary Louise needed some reassurance.

"Once the dust settles, we should have a better idea what's going on. Let's wait before we panic. Give it a few days. Don't worry. Everything will be fine."

My new job was working out well, and it kept my mind off the American political scene. The telex department consisted mainly of men, and they were extremely patient with me the first few days. They thought my Italian was excellent. Of course I didn't believe them, but it was nice of them to say so. My responsibilities consisted of transmitting wires nationally and internationally. I actually saw $27,000,000 pass over the wire in payment for an oil refinery in Rome.

This job was going to be exciting. It got even better when the personnel director offered me a whopping 170,000 *lire* a month (about $275). My jaw dropped in disbelief. I had to promise to stay at least until the end of May. For comparison, at W.E. Hutton I made 84,000 *lire* a month. It finally meant financial independence. Caltex was an international company, and I thought I could always use them as a reference in the States when I went back home. My return to the States was always in the back of my mind. It would come to the fore when I least expected it to, particularly when I was feeling homesick.

Turmoil at Home and Abroad

There was general unrest after Johnson's announcement not to seek reelection. More demonstrations and strikes were planned. The Rome University campus closed for two weeks in March after protests and frequent clashes between students and police. They raged against inadequate, antiquated school facilities; university policies; and insufficient faculty to student ratios. Two hundred students and police were injured.

The student protest movement was beginning to spread to other parts of Europe including Paris, Madrid, and London. What started as anti-Vietnam War protests seemed to burgeon into general dissatisfaction with the government and the entire educational system. The Italian government feared further protests and promised the students that reforms would be implemented quickly.

Gianni seemed disinterested in these events. Since he hadn't attended a university, he felt no connection or rapport with the demonstrators. "Why don't they stop demonstrating and go back to the university? I don't understand what they think they're doing. They should be glad to be getting an education."

He didn't seem able to relate to the principles behind their demands. My reaction to the student demonstrations in the States wasn't that dissimilar from his, and I had gone to college.

With my poor Italian language skills, I tried to explain how disgruntled the students were with their archaic educational system, but it was difficult to have substantive conversations on important topics such as these with my limited vocabulary. It would have made for a stimulating exchange of ideas, something I sorely missed. Even though I felt a disconnect from the political unrest of the time, I would have given it the attention it rightfully deserved if I had been wholly fluent in Italian.

On April 4, 1968, Martin Luther King, Jr., the eloquent, iconic voice of the Civil Rights Movement was silenced by an assassin's bullet in Memphis, Tennessee. Why would James Earl Ray shoot an innocent, non-violent leader in cold blood just because he disagreed with Dr. King's world view of tolerance and equality? I felt physically ill. It was the same feeling I had when John F. Kennedy was assassinated. It was a sickening, heartbreaking, grievous loss for the world. He was a great man with a vision.

There was rioting in black neighborhoods throughout the nation. At least a hundred cities in the US had violent demonstrations. A curfew was enforced. I sympathized with the protesters, but destroying property and setting their communities on fire was not the answer. Dr. King had proven that peaceful protests were an integral part of the civil rights struggle. Change would come over time, not overnight.

That same week, the American Embassy in Rome was surrounded by protesters. Things were getting ugly. Americans seemed to be universally hated. I was anxiously awaiting a letter from my mother to help me cope with the reaction of my fellow Americans. I was sure her letter would reassure me. She always knew what to say. When it finally arrived, Mary Louise placed it on my bed and to my dismay, Thor ate most of it before I got home from work. I was extremely upset with my German Shepherd imposter. Paolo promised to take Thor away to never-never land, but he never did.

At work I tried to keep the US political scene at bay while focusing on my daily responsibilities. Then after eating tainted clams in the Caltex cafeteria, I came down with a violent case of food poisoning. My supervisor Mr. Rossi, hustled me into a taxi and whisked me off to the doctor's office with frequent stops along the way so I could throw up. As we passed the revered Piazza Barberini, I was forced to leave some of my spaghetti *con vongole* (with clams) behind. I don't think I'll ever look at that piazza or clams in the same light.

It was terrible being so sick away from home. My coworkers were very sympathetic. I decided it was far more rewarding working in an office filled with men. Mary Louise cooked for me and generally nursed me back to health. She was very sweet and nurturing, and I began to realize we were forming a lasting, meaningful friendship.

"Shellfish is off the menu for awhile, dearie. How about some minestrone soup?" *I don't want to hurt her feelings, but I want my mother's chicken noodle soup.* Gianni came by every day to check on me and bring me some basic pasta with olive oil which Signora Giulia said would settle my stomach. Everyone had their own fail-safe home remedy, but my mother's was by far the best.

Over Easter I had a four-day holiday, but instead of days of sunshine, it rained continually. Gianni and I had to scrap our plans to go to Capri. Piazza di Spagna was filled with azalea flowerpots ready to burst into full bloom. Tourists returned to the city, but I didn't see many Americans. Could the American political unrest be keeping people at home? Rome was usually inundated with American tourists every spring. The traffic got worse, getting into restaurants was a pain; there were crowds everywhere and tourist signs multiplied like mushrooms on every corner. It took on an artificial facade most evident around the popular tourist attractions and shopping areas in central Rome, but this year was different.

Mr. Rossi was extremely nice and invited me and other coworkers to go fishing with him. He had two sailboats and was an enthusiastic sailor. He was always extending invitations to us for a carefree day of fishing or sailing. Sailing on the Mediterranean was a great, relaxing way to spend an afternoon at the end of a long work week, feeling the breeze and hearing the lapping of water over the bow of the boat. We would be lost in our thoughts, reenergized with fresh air and sunshine; there was no need for small talk, no need to discuss the world's state of affairs and its disintegration.

It was a friendly, stress free work environment, even though I spent most of the day speaking Italian. There was genuine camaraderie and we were always laughing and joking with each other. We became solid friends sharing many personal stories about our lives and loves. Mr. Rossi, who was married, was always giving me advice on the Italian male, most notably Gianni, which was very useful. The work itself wasn't as stimulating as I had originally hoped, but the salary and general atmosphere more than made up for it.

15

A Master Plan

I was getting homesick, but I would not consider leaving Gianni behind this time. In my youthful, addled, lovelorn brain, I felt our future together was in the States, not Italy.

"Come with me to the US. I think your life will be better there. There's more opportunity. You would be free to go back to school if you wanted."

"I don't know. I don't speak English. What if I couldn't find a job? I don't want to depend on you. You know I've never been out of Italy."

"But why not give it a chance? You're still in your twenties so you can do whatever you want. Look what I did on my own. I came to Italy and I couldn't speak Italian. It isn't that different."

After many conversations with him late into the night, I convinced him to give life in America a chance, that there was a better future waiting for him there. He just needed to take a risk and leave his beloved Rome and move to the US with me. At the time, it was the only way I would consider going back home—Gianni had to come with me.

My master plan was to leave for Pittsburgh on June 2, 1968, after I got my final paycheck. I would stay with my parents for two weeks, and then I would head for San Francisco. San Francisco was the chosen destination since it had a similar climate to Rome, was close to the ocean, and had a sizable Italian population—all attractive features to make Gianni feel more at home. Caltex also had its largest office in San Francisco so it was conceivable I might find a job there if Mr. Costello gave me a good recommendation. It seemed like a solid, workable plan, albeit rather ambitious. I had saved enough money for my airfare and rent for a few months.

"While I'm there hunting for an apartment and job, you can deal with US immigration here. Getting a visa should be a piece of cake. Giacomo didn't have any trouble."

"There's a big difference. Giacomo was raised in South Africa and works for an American airline. He speaks English." Gianni wasn't convinced it would be as easy as I thought. Instead of considering his valid point, I was optimistic it wouldn't be an issue.

My plan for Gianni seemed to end with his arrival. Not much thought was given to what would happen next, or what he would do there not speaking English. How would we manage to survive paying rent, food, and English classes for Gianni? Never once did it enter my mind. My youthful optimism assumed everything would fall into its natural place, without so much as an obstacle along the way. I didn't even consider there might be a problem. Mary Louise attempted to bring up the delicate subject during our late-night chats.

"So, let's go over your plan. Do you know what Gianni is going to do in San Francisco?"

"Not exactly, but I'm sure we'll figure something out."

"Well, what if he doesn't have any money to live on?"

"Oh, I'll find a job, and I'm sure I'll make enough to support both of us. Chevron has an office in San Francisco. If Mr. Costello puts in a good word, it should be a cinch."

"Really? How can you be so sure?"

I found a home for Thor with Gianni's help. Mary Louise tried to hide her glee at the prospect of not having Thor underfoot. I really hated to leave him and felt guilty about giving him away. The entire week he was a perfect angel, as though he sensed his days with me were numbered. He was going to the country where he had the space to run around at will, chasing all the birds and sheep he desired. I knew he would be happier there, convinced he was a bird dog. The apartment was eerily quiet when I got home. I could hardly bear it.

Before I left, Gianni and I treated ourselves to an excellent dinner at a restaurant called *Domus Aurea* overlooking the Colosseum. "What a beautiful view! It sure beats anything I've ever seen. The Colosseum is like the eighth wonder of the world. Just look at it." I was in awe.

"Do you think we can go see the Empire State Building? I've never seen a building that tall."

"Sure, we'll go on a tour of some of the US hot spots. You'll be blown away by the skyscrapers in New York City, and Times Square is kind of like Las Vegas! You'll be dazzled by all the neon lights." The food, service and warm evening breeze made the evening extra special. There was also dancing, all for six dollars and fifty cents a person. It was one of our last dinners out before my departure. We also finally made our long awaited return trip to Capri the following weekend with Mary Louise and Francesco. It was a fitting, romantic retreat where we could spend some quality time together.

"Mary Louise this could be the prime time for *you know what*." She blushed.

"Don't get your hopes up, dearie. We're just planning a nice weekend, nothing earth-shattering like *you know what*."

"Give it your utmost consideration. Capri couldn't be a better location for a little romance." I gave her a knowing smile.

We all got along famously. I wondered whether Mary Louise was still a virgin after the weekend. Somehow she seemed to have an extra glow and a spring in her step that had been missing before we left. Maybe I had planted the seed of doubt in her mind after our endless midnight chats. After she gave me a wink, I was flabbergasted to think she might actually have done "the nasty!"

In May, there was a major week-long mail strike. Strikes seemed to be a way of life in Italy. This time, even the telegraph messengers were on strike. It was a protest over the massive amount of electoral material that was being distributed all over Italy in advance of the Italian election day. Once the election was over, mail delivery resumed with an enormous backlog of mail. It would take months to straighten it out. I called my parents to let them know why my letters had stopped arriving. It was hard to imagine protesting union workers trying the same stunt in the States.

I left Rome on June 2 as scheduled and arrived home in Pittsburgh exhausted. My parents were overjoyed to see me once again. "So how about staying in Pittsburgh awhile to figure things out?" My mother was much more diplomatic than my father.

"I had plenty of time to think about it, and my mind is made up. I'm heading west. You know . . . *I left my heart in San Francisco. High on a hill, it calls to me . . .*" I couldn't resist singing a refrain from Tony Bennett's famous song, especially since my parents didn't know my love was joining me there. I conveniently left that little detail out.

My dad did not appreciate my cavalier response. "This is not a laughing matter. We want you to stay *here*." His voice was resolute, firm.

"There's a good chance I can get a job there since I have an inside track with the Managing Director of Chevron Italiana, Mr. Costello. Chevron has an office in San Francisco. If it doesn't work out, I can always go to graduate school." I calculated that mentioning graduate school might soften his stance.

My father eyed me suspiciously, but said nothing. My parents soon realized I could not be swayed from my decision. They probably concluded the farther away I was from Italy and Gianni, the better. In their way of thinking, at least I would still be in the United States. In hindsight, there were dark, looming clouds on the horizon, but I was oblivious to them. I was in love.

On June 6, my parents and I heard the devastating news that Robert F. Kennedy was assassinated by Sirhan Sirhan in Los Angeles after winning the California Democratic Primary. It brought back the overwhelming grief and sadness when his brother, John F. Kennedy, was assassinated by Lee Harvey Oswald on November 22, 1963.

"I just don't understand. This is horrible, just horrible." I was overcome with emotion. "He could have been president." I started crying.

"Why are there so many crazy people with guns?" My mother took my hand in hers to console me. "How could this have happened again in just a few months?" she added, referring to Martin Luther King, Jr's assassination in April by James Earl Ray. It was too much to bear. It was a sad day for America. This murder would tear the country further apart. We sat in silence watching the grim event unfold, captured live on television. As tears spilled out of my eyes, my father just stared at the television in disbelief. We were witnesses to a turbulent, violent time in our country's history. There was a premonition that more heartache would follow. Gianni wrote me to say how sorry he and his fellow Italians were over Bobby Kennedy's death. The world was in shock. This assassination would only add to the impression that Americans were murderous, gun-toting outlaws. Maybe we were.

Gianni also told me how sad he was since my departure. He watched me get on the airplane and wished that the window opened like on a train or bus, so he could give me one last hug goodbye.

"I watched the airplane as long as it was possible, until there was a small dot in the sky and then there was nothing. You were gone." Gianni was apprehensive about my departure and what awaited us in America, but he tried to remain optimistic that everything would work out in the end. He realized the sheer gravity of both of us leaving a secure, idyllic life behind in Rome. Maybe he thought the recent violence in the US was an omen that foreshadowed our future happiness. From all the Wild West cowboy movies we had watched, he must think everyone carries a gun. When we would meet again in California, life would never be the same.

After two weeks at home, I flew out to California. As previously planned, I went to a real estate agency in search of a suitable apartment and soon found one on Baker Street in Pacific Heights. It was an unfurnished, one bedroom apartment, and I had a lot of work ahead of me to make it habitable before Gianni arrived. It was a long July 4th weekend by then, and I was alone and unhappy. It was the first time I dreaded being alone. There was absolutely no one to talk to. It was sheer isolation when I needed companionship the most. Having Thor with me might have broken the deafening silence, and it would have given me a reason to go outside and walk him. It was an awful, demoralizing four days as I slowly sank into a major depression doubting my plan would ever be realized.

My thoughts turned to Gianni. *Is this the best choice for him? Can he assimilate into the American way of life, or will he regret leaving his beloved family and Italy behind?* I spent hours considering every possibility, and whether I was being unrealistic in asking Gianni to share my life in the US. I needed to talk to Mary Louise or Molly. There wasn't even a telephone. I was totally cut off from communication with friends and family. I sat on the floor propped up against the empty wall of the apartment and cried my eyes out. The feelings of desolation and panic overwhelmed me.

After the extended weekend, I ventured out of the apartment to find a telephone booth and called home. "We've been waiting to hear from you. Mary Louise called from Rome and said she wanted you to call her right away." My mother seemed concerned. "Your brother Sid called too. He's going through a rough time in his marriage. He also wants to speak to you. You're in great demand."

"Did Mary Louise say anything else?"

"No, just that it was important. She sounded serious."

I suddenly felt sick to my stomach. Something was wrong. Mary Louise's call was the most worrisome. I called her immediately.

"Would you believe it? The American Embassy turned Gianni down flat! They refused to issue a visa to a plumber. They said they didn't think he would ever go back to Italy once he got to the States. Gianni is really, really upset, and he wants to talk to you as soon as possible. I feel so bad for him I could cry."

When Mary Louise used her ubiquitous "really, really" you knew she was being serious. I was overwhelmed with emotion. There was no way I could stay in San Francisco without Gianni. My plan had gone horribly wrong. I called Gianni at 4 a.m. Rome time, not realizing the time difference. He was extremely relieved to hear my voice, but when I began to cry, he couldn't contain himself. His voice trembled.

"*Voglio morire. Mi sono distrutto, desolato.* (I want to die, I'm heartbroken, devastated.) I feel like the whole world has fallen on my back." His words made me sob uncontrollably. He could never bear to see or hear me cry. It made him wince, like it wounded him physically. This time it was worse than ever before, since it could not be rectified with a kiss or a hug. We were thousands of miles apart. It was out of our control; nothing would change the outcome. Before saying goodbye, he told me he loved me very much and *non piangere* (don't cry.) I sank to the floor of the phone booth shaken to the core. My tears welled up inside me, as I wailed like a baby.

I calmed down long enough to call Sid. He was distraught over his crumbling marriage and was despondent. I decided to take a side trip to Houston on my way back to Pittsburgh. He needed moral support and a sister's unconditional love after his separation from his wife. We could provide solace to each other. We were both going through difficult, trying times.

After my telephone calls, I ran back to the apartment and immediately packed up my belongings. I planned to make a plane reservation the following day, leaving the month's rent behind. There was no longer a reason to stay in San Francisco. I left my heart in Rome, not San Francisco.

Gianni and I spoke again the next day before I left for Houston, and he told me what happened at the American Embassy. "All they said was, 'I'm sorry.' When I got back in the car *mi sono messo a piangere.*" (I started to cry.)

His despair was palpable. He added, he must have been born *sfortunato* (unlucky.) He knew it could be difficult but never thought it would be impossible to get a visa, especially after providing three letters of guarantee and countless other documents. He did everything he thought he had to do to make it happen. "I saved 225,000 *lire* for the trip. I'll send you a check for a plane ticket back to Rome. We can live here."

Gianni said that after our phone call the previous day, he stood by the telephone for a long time thinking of all the money I had spent in flying to San Francisco and renting an apartment in anticipation of his arrival. He couldn't go back to sleep, so he left the apartment and started to walk, not thinking about where he was going. By the time he looked at his watch, it was 8 a.m. He had walked for four hours and had to take a bus home to get to work on time.

When I got to Houston, Sid listened to my story from beginning to end, as I cried again. The fact that Gianni had been rejected because of his occupation gave me pause. At the time, it never occurred to me that if we had gone to the embassy together and I told the officials we were going to be married, his entry into the US might have been granted. Better yet, if we had already been married, there wouldn't have been any question about admitting him to the US. In hindsight, maybe his visa denial was predestined. It was a fateful day. It defined the parameters of our future—it was a sign.

Sid tried to come up with possible solutions. "Have you ever discussed whether Gianni would consider going back to school? Maybe it's something to explore."

"No, we haven't discussed it, but maybe I should bring up the subject with him. I'm not sure how he'll react. He isn't very fond of classic education. He reads newspapers, but I've never seen him reading a book for pleasure."

Gnawing doubts seeped surreptitiously into my thoughts. *Why can't Gianni go back to school and continue his education? It could make it easier for him to find a better job. Is that the answer?* Mary Louise told me we should have thrashed all of this out before I left for San Francisco. She tried to warn me, asking me pertinent questions about what we would do if Gianni couldn't get a job and how he would support himself. But, I wasn't ready to listen to what she had to say. I was impulsive, determined. She sent me three salient points on the subject of Gianni returning to school:

> *1) Tuition costs*
> *2) Going to school means not working—no income*
> *3) He's twenty-six years old, set in his ways, and happy the way he is*

She promised to provide emotional support to Gianni while we figured out what to do next. At least he would be able to talk to her about how he was feeling. She was a dear friend to both of us and would understand and listen without interjecting her own personal bias.

Gianni sent me thirteen letters during my three weeks in Houston. Each letter I received sounded angrier than the one before as I continued to push him on going back to school. When I spoke to him on the phone, he was getting increasingly impatient with me.

"The educational system in Italy is different than in the US. It isn't simple to get admitted to a university. It's expensive, and I've been out of school for years. I don't want to study history or mathematics. In fact, I don't like school." As our discussion continued in his letters, his writing seemed to confirm this with his words written in bold capitals as though to emphasize the point.

"I'm willing to read and take classes in English. That I'm willing to do, but that's it." His letters became progressively more agitated, and he accused me of loving an education more than I loved him. "Why haven't you ever mentioned it before? Isn't it enough that I love you?" It finally reached a crescendo with "*Basta!*" (enough! stop!) The discussion was over. "If you want to return to Italy, I still love you and will wait for you, but a university education is not going to happen."

Since analyzing relationships was one of my preeminent pastimes, I finally understood that education had a great deal to do with ours. Like my father, I enjoyed reading, being informed about current events, and having meaningful conversations. It had been an essential ingredient in all my prior relationships . . . choosing cerebral men who were knowledgeable and learned. I enjoyed intellectual sparring and weaving, much like a boxer beating his opponent to the first punch. This element was missing from our relationship. Instead, we had passion.

Sid and I spent three weeks listening to each other's tales of woe trying to come to terms with our lives. His divorce was inevitable. My future was uncertain.

As soon as I was back in Pittsburgh, I decided to return to Rome. I wrote to Mr. Costello and told him what had happened and asked if he could help me get my old job back, and whether there was anything he could do for Gianni. He wrote back promptly:

> *I will certainly do what I can to help. We can probably work something out for him. Please encourage him to go to school. This is important! Why am I being so helpful? I feel young people in love who are serious and want nothing more from life except the right to work hard and be together certainly deserve a helpful hand. Besides, you seem like such a nice, sweet person who deserves a real chance at happiness.*

Mr. Costello never ceased to amaze me with his kindness. He never disappointed. Why couldn't my father have been as understanding? Gianni sent me an express letter on August 8 with a check to pay for my airline ticket back to Rome. I was leaving the first week of September. In my agitated state of mind, I didn't hesitate in my decision. If I had stopped long enough to really confront the situation and accept it, I might have concluded it was a clash of two different worlds that posed serious, irrefutable obstacles. Our future together was cloudy at best, but I was young and not prone to reflection about my own life or ready to admit the inevitable truth.

My mother accepted my decision with a sigh of resignation. My father stopped talking to me. I never explained what happened in San Francisco. It was too painful. My emotional bond with Gianni was like a magnet that defied the earth's magnetic field. He was my life, my first true love, and I was unable to pull myself away from his powerful hold.

In late August, 1968, the Democratic National Convention was held in Chicago. My parents and I watched it on television. It turned into a deadly encounter between thousands of student anti-war demonstrators and Mayor Daley's henchmen, police, and the National Guard. They used tear gas and billy clubs to beat back the protesters who were trying to march to the convention center. By the end of the convention, over a hundred police officers and protesters had been injured. Hubert Humphrey was eventually nominated as the Democratic candidate amidst a backdrop of chaos and violence.

My father gave me his assessment. "This anti-war stuff is out of control. The police did the right thing. Those thugs should be punished."

"Dad, you know a lot of people are opposed to the Vietnam War. Those students are around my age, and I agree with them."

"You kids are full of ridiculous, idealistic views of the world. If you break the law, you should pay the price." He wouldn't look at me.

"I don't think they should be beaten to a pulp for demonstrating. Isn't free speech important? It didn't have to get bloody. Let's drop it. It isn't worth talking about if you won't listen to me."

"So you could be one of those kids, is that what you're saying?" My father's voice started to rise in anger. My mother, sensing we were about to get into a heated argument, grabbed my arm and led me into the kitchen. She couldn't handle another upsetting disagreement. The announcement that I was returning to Rome had already set the stage for battles to come.

Even though I agreed with many principles of the protest movement, I wasn't willing to put myself in the line of fire as so many college students had done. There didn't seem to be a need for me to take an activist stance that required a physical defense of my positions. Getting beaten up and arrested wasn't the answer to the conflict in Vietnam. Social discourse, intellectual discussions, and other non-violent means were more in keeping with my nature. In my mind, the most virulent element of the political unrest could be left behind when I returned to Italy. Besides, I was drowning in my own self-inflicted drama.

16

A Joyous Return

I arrived at Fiumicino Airport on September 7, exhausted and emotionally drained. When I saw Gianni's smiling face when I exited customs, all I could do was cry. As soon as he had me in his arms, I felt my legs buckle under me. Gianni held me upright as he kissed my face and neck uttering, "*Amore, ti amo, ti amo.*" (I love you, I love you.) He repeated it over and over again, as I tried to regain my balance. I felt like I was in an altered state. The passion I felt for him defied description—intense, all-consuming. There was no turning back. We clung to each other, like ill-fated lovers. How could things have gone so wrong? Why hadn't I listened to Mary Louise? Gianni was just as emotional as I was. We stood together embracing, as though we were conjoined twins unable to be separated or it would mean certain death. *Where is our relationship headed? How can I ever live without him?*

While I was gone, Mary Louise's two Italian grandmothers had come to stay with her, and they weren't leaving until October. Gianni's sister Carla said I could stay at her place until I figured out where to live. When Gianni and I were together, we talked over our circumstances. "I wish we could live together, but I know we can't," I said.

"You're right. I'd like to get an apartment together too, but I have to pay my parents every month. I don't have enough money to do both." The sad truth was that Italian working-class men lived at home paying their parents room and board until they married. I knew if Gianni earned enough to help his parents financially plus pay rent for our own place, he would have done it. He wasn't bound by Italian custom, or he wouldn't have fallen in love with an American.

I went to see Mary Louise. "I have a favor to ask. I'm staying at Carla's temporarily, and I know things are complicated with your grandmothers being here, but do you think I could move into the closet?"

"Of course you can. My grandmothers are sleeping in the bedroom and I'm sleeping on the studio couch. Cecilia's old room (the closet) is open for business."

"What a relief. I hate imposing on Carla and Enzo. I'd rather impose on you," I laughed. "You know how much I've missed you and our late-night chats. We need to get caught up. It was a nightmare being in San Francisco without Gianni, and it was a bitch in Pittsburgh. My dad was impossible."

"I know how hard this has been on you and Gianni. I wish I could have helped," she said.

"But you *did* help. You were there for both of us, talking us through it. Gianni told me he wouldn't have survived without you. You're a real friend. I never thought he wouldn't get a visa." Mary Louise could have injected a reality check, but she remained silent for now. It wasn't a discussion I was ready to have.

I was thankful for Mary Louise's friendship and her gracious hospitality. It would be crowded until her grandmothers left, but it felt so good to be in Rome. The closet reminded me of a prison cell without a window, but I didn't even mind the claustrophobic confines. Being reunited with Gianni was all I wanted or needed. Cecilia returned from London about the same time I did and tried relentlessly to persuade us to let her move back into the apartment. Mary Louise vetoed the idea and said we really didn't have enough room now that we were sharing the apartment with her grandmothers. Besides, I was now occupying her space. Cecilia was crushed. We continued to see each other a few times a week for dinner. It was the least I could do to appease her.

"I found a new job while you were gone," Gianni said. "Now I'm working for an agency that supplies drivers for the producers and directors at Cinecitta. I really like it." The demoralizing experience of being refused a visa due to his profession must have inspired him to change his line of work. Cinecitta was a major Italian movie studio.

"That's great! Tell me about it."

"The hours are long and I'm tired when I get home, but it pays well. I met John Huston, Carter DeHaven III, and Stanley Kramer."

I was impressed. They were among the celebrated Hollywood titans making movies in Italy during the 1960s. I now understood why he never called Mr. Costello at Chevron.

Gianni worked late hours, and we didn't see as much of each other those first few months, but we were satisfied to be back together in Rome. As long as we could speak to one another and know that we would be apart for only a matter of days or weeks, we were able to handle our separation without too much angst. The discussions we had about furthering his education were put to rest. They were *verboten*.

Life Returns to Normal

I went to see Mr. Costello to say hello. "Well, well, well. If it isn't the rolling stone at long last. Sorry things didn't go as planned in San Francisco. I appreciated your letter, but you didn't really go into detail. Gianni never called me."

"You're right . . . things never go the way you plan them . . . um, it's a long story, so I won't bore you with the details. Actually, Gianni got another job that might pan out, so that's why he didn't call."

"All right, but my offer still stands. As for you, if you want your old job back, it's yours for the taking. We haven't hired a replacement yet. You're hard to replace." Mr. Costello smiled.

"Fantastic! I'd love my old job. Thank-you so, so much. I can't tell you how much I appreciate everything you've done for me. Won't Mr. Rossi be surprised?"

"He told me he missed you and your corny jokes." At last things were returning to normal.

My job responsibilities at Caltex had grown since my return. Mr. Rossi needed my help in another department, so for part of the day I was relegated to the secretarial pool where I was doing complicated translations, only made more challenging with the clattering of sixteen typewriters in the background. It made it hard to concentrate with the cacophony of noise. The rest of the day was spent in the telex department sending and receiving messages from around the world. I tackled my new responsibilities with gusto. It was an opportunity to prove my worth. A few months after my return Mr. Costello transferred to the New York office. He had been my kingpin at Caltex. My job might be in jeopardy and evaporate with his departure. There was reason for concern.

My job kept me busy during the day fortunately, since Gianni was not as available now that he was working for Cinecitta. He began traveling, sometimes for two weeks at a time. When Gianni's out-of-town stints lasted more than a week, I received letters from him.

One letter in particular remains vivid in my memory. After dropping off Mr. DeHaven, he was driving back to his hotel along the ocean when he got caught in a fierce thunderstorm with powerful wind gusts, whipping up the waves along the beach. "*Il tempo era bruttissimo* (the weather was terrible). It started to rain like a river and I could see the waves getting bigger and bigger. It was like a tempest." Even though he was driving slowly, he was terrified the car would be swept into the sea, as lightning lit up the sky and the waves crashed onto the road flooding it. Suddenly, a huge lightning bolt struck five to ten meters from his car ". . . *tutte le scintille in aria*" (the sparks exploding in the air). He pulled off the road and got out of the car, shaken by the lightning strike only a few feet from the car.

After standing in the rain for some time, too nervous to drive, a car miraculously appeared and stopped to pick him up. He was thoroughly drenched and unnerved by what had happened. He couldn't wait to get back to Rome. He ended his letter with "*Voglio baciarti. Mi manchi tanto amore.*" (I want to kiss you. I miss you very much, Love)

After that letter, I always worried about him when he was driving in unfamiliar places. It scared me to think he could easily be in an accident, given the long hours he spent on the road. Gianni was an excellent driver, but I certainly couldn't say that for the majority of Italian drivers he would encounter on the road. It only fed into my tendency to worry and overthink everything.

While he was gone, I occupied my free time baking. It was therapeutic. I attempted challah, my mother's best recipe, and I made three loaves decorating them with caraway seeds instead of poppy seeds which I couldn't find in any market. Although they didn't taste like my mother's scrumptious, sweet, delectable challah, they weren't bad for my first attempt. Gianni's family devoured two loaves. Baking bread took practice and patience.

For Yom Kippur Cecilia and I went to the Grand Synagogue again, like the previous year, hoping our past experience had been an aberration. "Nothing seems to have changed. The loggia is just as noisy as last year. I still can't hear the cantor sing or the rabbi speak with the nonstop talking. Those women can't seem to keep their mouths shut. What a waste of time!" I shook my head in disappointment.

"Blimey! Those birds are a bunch of cheeky twats. Why can't they take their chittering outside?" Cecilia was just as annoyed.

"Italian Jews are definitely a breed apart," I concurred. "It's like a triple whammy being Italian, Jewish and female—a lethal mix. You would think someone would get the hook and drag them downstairs and toss them in the street."

"Yeah, like rubbish!"

We left once we determined it would not get any better. Outside the synagogue, we saw balloon and souvenir vendors selling their wares. It was an odd carnival-like atmosphere considering it was Rosh Hashanah. Italian Jews were decidedly strange compared to their American or British counterparts. The Jewish New Year Italian style seemed to be only about a celebration, instead of a time to reflect upon the past year's transgressions. The women of the loggia should atone for their sins by asking God for forgiveness. It would be our last attempt at observing the High Holidays at the Grand Synagogue.

The Cinquecento

The bus to work took one hour and twenty minutes each way. Since Gianni was now driving a much larger Fiat to accommodate his exclusive clientele, he gave me his little gray *Cinquecento*.

"Take the car, but be careful if it rains. It's very temperamental. You might have to stop and dry off the spark plugs if they get wet."

"Can you show me how to do it? I don't know much about cars— cylinders or spark plugs."

"Do you know where the engine is?" he asked with a grin.

In response I started to walk to the front of the car. He laughed since the engine is in the rear like a Volkswagen Beetle. The *Cinquecento* was like a lawn mower, loud and slow, but it cut my traveling time in half. I grew to love it dearly and took very good care of it. It was a cinch to park on the street, since it could fit into incredibly small spaces. I even learned to creatively park it perpendicular to the curb or even on the sidewalk, like other Romans who parked their cars at haphazard angles that defied description. It was like a toy car. Parking spaces were a scarce commodity in the crowded, narrow, ancient streets.

One day when I was taking a shortcut back from work I turned down a one-way street, and as I rounded a curve in the road, I slammed into a car backing up the narrow one-way street. I got out of the car and broke down crying, as I examined the buckled front end of the car.

"Look what you've done! You ruined my car! What the hell are you doing going in the wrong direction on a one-way street?" I yelled.

"I'm sorry, Signorina. Please don't cry. You're right. It's my fault. I don't know what I was thinking." Rather than get into an altercation with the driver, who was clearly at fault, I decided not to call the police since I didn't have an international driver's license. Most of the damage was done to my beloved *Cinquecento*. The other driver apologized profusely for causing the accident when he saw how distraught I was over the damage. He was also grateful I didn't want to involve the police, but he didn't offer to pay for the damage, and I was too upset to ask him. We both decided to leave the scene before we caused a hopeless traffic jam. Cars were already lining up behind me impatiently blowing their horns. Soon I was on my way again as the car limped home to Gianni.

When I entered Gianni's apartment, I broke down crying again, as I tried to explain that I had been in an *incidente* (accident). His first reaction was alarm, worried that I had been injured, and he grabbed me exclaiming, "*Amore Mio!* Were you injured?" He hugged me tight as I continued to cry. Once I assured him I had not been hurt, his demeanor immediately turned to relief. He never once asked about the *Cinquecento*. I was soon smiling through my tears, as he gently teased me playfully about the *piccolo incidente* (small accident).

I eventually managed to save enough money to get all the dents taken out of Gianni's *Cinquecento* and have it painted. It came to a grand total of fifty dollars. It was the least I could do to repay Gianni for his generosity. It looked brand new, and Gianni insisted I keep it. I felt so fortunate to be the recipient of Gianni's love and generous spirit. Now that he was working exclusively for Carter DeHaven III, he enjoyed a steady income with perks, like traveling in style. The downside was he always had to be available like an ER surgeon, getting interrupted abruptly at dinnertime, or during our private time together. Gianni's job put him in close proximity with many American celebrities. It made me hopeful that being surrounded by English-speaking people might encourage him to go to school at least to learn English.

Occupying Time Italian Style

Since Gianni was out of town frequently, I loaded up on books starting with the *Last of the Just* by André Schwarz-Bart and the *Magician of Lublin* by Isaac Bashevis Singer. I bought five books and hoped they would fill my hours alone in the evenings. Reading was a passion I shared with my father. It would also give me time to get my absentee ballot in order, since the November election was coming up. It was my civic duty to vote. Gianni couldn't quite understand my fervor when it came to politics, but it was a subject I enjoyed talking about, particularly with my father.

For mindless entertainment when Gianni was around on weekends, we enjoyed going to the movies to see the infamous spaghetti westerns like *The Good, the Bad and the Ugly* with Clint Eastwood who was popular in Italy. They were always dubbed in Italian, and I thought it was funny to hear Italian coming out of Clint Eastwood's macho mouth. For some reason, Italians preferred dubbing to subtitles. It explained why Cecilia had gotten so many dubbing jobs at Cinecitta.

Other favorites were the Italian comedies: *Il Medico della Mutua* with Alberto Sordi and *Il Commissario Pepe* with Ugo Tognazzi. Both actors were accomplished comedians. You didn't have to speak Italian to understand the nuances of their body language or facial expressions. There was plenty of slapstick in Italian comedies. Westerns and comedies were far easier for me to understand than dramas where the dialogue played a more important role. We spent many entertaining weekend afternoons at the cinema. It actually helped improve my conversational Italian, although at times I came out with something more descriptive of the Wild West than present day Italian colloquialisms. Gianni would tell me I was *simpatico* (charming), as he laughed at my newly learned expressions.

We also enjoyed dinners out with friends at little hidden family *trattorias* where Gianni would take charge of the ordering. "Excuse me, can you make something special for my girlfriend? She likes a good pasta." Invariably the chef would prepare a surprise dish off the menu. We always ate very well. "Compliments to the Chef. *Grazie mille*." (Thank-you very much). He never failed to thank the waiters and staff.

Food was like a primordial Italian activity of supreme importance and enjoyment, not unlike the French. It always amazed me that no one ever refused his requests. Only wealthy, loyal patrons in the US could expect the same treatment and only at the most expensive restaurants. The food was delicious everywhere. I was a glutton for pasta. It was no wonder I gained several kilos living in Rome.

On certain Sundays the Rossellini family had *pranzo* (lunch) at an outdoor restaurant along Via Appia Antica, a road lined with large flat cobblestones from ancient Roman times. If I squinted into the distance, I could almost visualize Romans in their horse-drawn chariots rattling over the stones, as they triumphantly made their way into Rome. Much of its length was flanked by Mediterranean umbrella pines and private villas. The quaint outdoor restaurants along the ancient road were festooned with grape vine trellises or flowering vines draped with twinkling lights. They had a rustic country feel far removed from the usual hustle and bustle of central Rome. We spent many lazy Sunday afternoons there.

We also listened to a lot of Italian pop music. The lyrics were full of love and longing, the melodies unforgettable. I still remember the words from *Il Mondo,* a romantic love song sung by Jimmy Fontana. I first heard it on the radio. It became the number one song for weeks on the Italian hit parade. Gianni used to sing it to me until I finally broke down and bought the record.

Life was good. We settled into a normal routine, like any other couple enjoying our time together and making it through the days when we were separated. It was a life I treasured without stressing over the future and what was beyond the horizon. For now, I was content with how everything had fallen into its respective place. Our uncertain future was pushed away deep into the recesses of my brain, dormant for the time being, like Mount Vesuvius.

"Hey, Luv. Want to come to my modeling job? It'll give you something to do instead of pining away for Gianni. It's dull as dishwater around here." Cecilia intended to rescue me from a life of loneliness.

"Are you working late again?"

"Looks that way. I'll be buggered (tired) by midnight, but I like the money. Paolo's brother will be there. He'll be gutted (sad) if you don't show up. You know he still fancies you."

"Well, I wouldn't want to muck things up," I said with a chuckle. "Can we get something to eat first? I'm famished."

"Brilliant! I'm chuffed to bits (pleased) that you're coming."

It was a good way to whittle away the time when Gianni was away. Sometimes, Cecilia would work until midnight, modeling clothes for out-of-town clients. She modeled clothes effortlessly with elegance and grace. She had obviously been attentive at her modeling classes, in contrast to her less than stellar academic learning. She knew all the right moves, as she strutted around the showroom striking poses. She made it look easy. It was an opportunity for me to become well acquainted with the latest fashions. One of the perks of the job was getting to keep some of the clothes she modeled. I in turn borrowed Cecilia's clothes since we wore the same size. It was a win-win situation for everyone, and it kept me busy when Gianni was gone.

During the modeling show, Paolo's brother stood behind me with his hands on my shoulders, whispering sweet nothings in my ear. It was a pleasant distraction and amusing to me that he hadn't given up hope of landing me in bed—hope springs eternal. It made me wonder if he ever completed his novella.

Mr. Rossi offered to give me another dog. I was afraid to even bring up the subject with Mary Louise given her primal fear of Thor. She would occasionally recall one of Thor's naughtier moments, like destroying a favorite pair of shoes or emptying the trash can in the kitchen and leaving remnants scattered the full-length of the apartment from the bedroom to the living room. She would have been totally stressed out if I brought another dog into the picture, even though I was tempted.

Gianni and I drove to the country one day to visit Thor. He hadn't forgotten us and greeted us with kisses and yelps, jumping three feet in the air, as though we had just returned from a long trip. When we got into the car to leave, he squeezed into the back seat panting excitedly thinking he was going home with us. It made me sad to leave him behind again. I felt as if I were abandoning him for a second time.

Occupying Time American Style

"Hey, Luv. Let's get an apartment together. I really need a place to live and living with you would be dandy. Staying with Paolo is beginning to get on my nerves. I don't have any privacy." Cecilia was hoping to work her magic on me.

"I'm really sorry, but I won't leave Mary Louise. She's counting on me to stay on once her grandmothers leave."

"Then talk to her again. Ask her to give me back my closet room. I'll do whatever she wants. I'll even take out the dustbin."

"That's a shocker. You really think she'd believe you? You never once helped with the trash. It was too smelly, or you were too busy, or you made a speedy exit, claiming you had to be somewhere."

"I promise. Cross my heart or whatever you Americans do. We can watch the telly together like old times."

"All right, I'll give it one more try, but she already turned you down once. If I can talk her into it, you owe me. Don't forget it." After much cajoling and negotiating, Mary Louise agreed to give Cecilia her closet back once her grandmothers left. We both had our reservations about this decision.

In October, Mary Louise and I painted the utility closet and hung a few pictures to make it more inviting. We also disassembled a wardrobe in the closet to give Cecilia more room and reassembled it in the bedroom where we needed more storage.

"Why didn't we do that before now? The closet actually looks like a room. *Che idioti.*" (What idiots.) I turned to Mary Louise in amazement.

"We'll have to thank Cecilia for getting us to be creative. She won't believe it's the same closet," she said.

"As always, too bad she wasn't around to help. We'll have to see if she holds up her end of the bargain and takes the trash out," I added.

"I wouldn't hold my breath." Mary Louise examined our finished work. She was pleased with the results—a vast improvement.

Our apartment continued to go through a metamorphosis. We painted a few more pieces of furniture and bought two oriental scatter rugs and new lamps. My mother sent my black and white bedspread from home along with matching curtains that we converted into skirts for two night tables. The ambiance of my Pittsburgh bedroom was reborn in Rome. We were more than satisfied with our decorating skills. Ever mindful of losing my job at a moment's notice, these activities helped keep my anxiety in check. Besides, Gianni was out of town again so I had plenty of time to kill.

The Rome Daily American became part of my daily routine. I read in astonishment that Jackie Kennedy married Aristotle Onassis on October 20, 1968, to be known forevermore as "Jackie O." It was five years since John F. Kennedy's death. What a newsworthy bit of celebrity gossip. He was twenty-three years older than she was, and not the least bit attractive, but he was a Greek multimillionaire shipping magnate. He gave her a whopping forty carat diamond ring to commemorate the occasion. Sadly, she had chosen money over love. It was hard for me to imagine marrying someone solely for money and notoriety, but lots of women did. Gianni and I were a shining example having fallen in love first.

As Halloween approached, Mary Louise and I searched everywhere in Rome for a pumpkin and ultimately found one in a small, open marketplace in Trastevere. We carved it into a happy Jack-o'-lantern, inserted a candle, and placed it on the balcony once the sun had set.

"Maybe we should ask the *portiera* if it's okay."

"Are you kidding?" (I said that a lot to Mary Louise. She was such a goody two-shoes.) "I think it might cause the most excitement around here in a long time. Some unknowing Italian will probably report a fire on the fifth floor."

"Do you really think so? That would be terrible. What will people think?" She was aghast.

"When are you going to stop worrying about what people think? Go with the flow." I loved pulling her chain. We both decided it made us feel more at home celebrating one of our own holidays after celebrating enumerable Italian ones. I was American to the core, but sometimes the Italian experience made me wonder if one day I would succumb to Rome's seductive charm and become a member of the large American expat community.

It Pays to Have Connections

Mr. Costello called from New York to inform me that Chevron New York was planning to cut back on employees in the Rome office, and it was doubtful I would have a job much longer. It was nice of him to let me know in advance. He arranged an interview for me with Mr. Martinelli, formerly of Pittsburgh, who had lived a few blocks from my parents. He needed a secretary who spoke three languages and took shorthand in all three, so the interview proved futile, but we had a long chat about Pittsburgh and reminisced about the Pirates and Steelers. He was a big sports fan and missed going to the games. He was an excellent contact and Mr. Costello urged me to call Mrs. Martinelli who always welcomed fellow Pittsburghers.

My salary remained 170,000 *lire,* so rent money was not an issue, as long as I kept my job. With Cecilia sharing the rent, I was only paying thirty dollars a month. I began to get uneasy about the future of my employment and decided to try and save more money, just in case I got sacked.

Getting and keeping a job was a constant problem that created undo stress in my life. Much of it was my own doing, since I insisted on only temporary jobs. If I had accepted a full-time job from W.E. Hutton when they offered it, I wouldn't be in this predicament now. My fear had always been the permanency of a full-time job would create problems in itself and remove any flexibility in the direction of my life. Besides, boredom might have set in. It also would have forced me to make a decision about Gianni, and I was not yet prepared to do so.

The 1968 election was over and Richard Nixon was elected our thirty-seventh president, even though he hadn't gotten my vote. Shortly afterward, I read in an Italian newspaper that an assassination plot to kill Nixon was uncovered in New York. An Arab immigrant from Yemen planned to carry it out. I had to wait until I got *The Daily American* to verify the facts. Although I wasn't happy Nixon had become president, I certainly did not want him to meet an untimely death like John F. Kennedy. Just the thought of it made me tremble.

Soon after Nixon's election, Mr. Costello returned to Rome for a meeting and came down to my department to see me. "Have you been following the political news out of Washington? You always have an interesting take on it. Glad Nixon won. He's good for business."

"My dad is a Republican too, plus a businessman like you. He must be jumping for joy."

"But what about you? Did you vote absentee?"

"Yep, I sent my ballot in just in time to be counted." We were interrupted before he could ask, "Whom did you vote for?" I was saved from telling him I didn't vote for his guy.

Before leaving, he gave me the name of the manager at Goodyear and told me to call him. He said he spoke to the administrator at Caltex. My job was secure for another month. He advised me to continue trying to reach Mrs. Martinelli. We had been playing telephone tag, but I told him I was determined to reach her. You could never tell what this connection could mean in the future.

Mr. Costello was instrumental in helping me with my job search. He treated me almost like a daughter in his attempt to keep me employed. My interview at Goodyear as a market researcher went well, but I was told I wouldn't get a response for a few weeks. In the meantime, I seemed to be in great demand at Caltex. I was put in charge of running the General Service office in addition to my other duties. It was too bad the decision on my status was in the hands of the New York office.

When I got home from work to tell Gianni I still had a job for at least one more month, he had some unsettling news. "My mother is really sick. She has high blood pressure and circulation problems. The doctor wants to put her on medication. When her arm and shoulder became numb, I thought it was her heart, but the doctor took an electrocardiogram and said it wasn't a heart attack."

"I promise the medication will work and get things under control. My mother has heart problems and the pills do work." I reassured Gianni. It brought back worrisome memories of my own mother's heart problems. She suffered from angina. I could always tell from the alarm in her face that she was experiencing another bout of unexpected chest pain. It would throw me into a state of panic wondering if she would weather the attack without calling an ambulance. After popping a nitroglycerin tablet under her tongue, she quickly recovered.

Gianni's concern was understandable. Signora Giulia was put on a strict diet to address her excessive weight which probably contributed to her health problems. Then a few days later, Signor Arturo had a bit of bad luck. He fell and broke a bone in his foot and was hobbling around in a cast.

"Gianni, tell me what I can do to help. I'm free to go to the market or whatever else your parents need."

"*Grazie, amore.* Let's hope they're better in a few days. I'll do my father's deliveries. I don't want them to worry about anything."

"Give me a list of what I should buy at the market. I know your mother likes her fruit ripe and only buys one brand of prosciutto. Maybe you should check with the doctor first about her diet."

They were like family and they meant the world to Gianni. I wanted him to know he could depend on me when things got tough. He had always supported me during trying times with my father. Gianni found time in his busy, unpredictable work schedule to make Signor Arturo's water deliveries. I did the shopping. At least we were both there to lend a hand.

Winter was coming, and I couldn't resist having a coat made that I saw in *Vogue Italia*. It was a fine, red wool with a Napoleon collar and black, shiny buttons. The whole project with lining and buttons would cost forty-three dollars. After suffering through last winter, I thought it was worth it to be better prepared this year. I should have been saving my money instead of frivolously spending it—the scourge of youth. Job prospects were looking bleak. At the time, it was more important to be fashionable.

I justified my decision by telling myself the blue and white checked coat I had originally worn to Europe was beginning to show its wear, and it wasn't nearly warm enough. The dressmaker said the coat would be ready by the end of November. Gianni never questioned these decisions. He seemed to accept my proclivity to spending money on fashionable clothes without question, even though it might not have been the sensible thing to do.

"You always look beautiful. I don't care what clothes you wear or don't wear. Naked is even better," he turned to me with a wide grin. I playfully slapped his arm for his last comment. He bestowed frequent compliments on me and made me feel beautiful. Italian men knew instinctively how to treat women. It was in their genes—it came naturally.

The dressmaker finished my coat just in time for colder weather. It looked just like the picture in the magazine. I was really enjoying having my clothes custom-made on limited funds. It would have been impossible to do the same thing in Pittsburgh. Living in Italy definitely had some perks.

November weather brought dull, gloomy days with cold rain. "I read about a famous monastery in Farfa that I'd like to visit. The weather is awful but we can stay inside. There's a lot of art to see there."

"Actually, I've never been there. You make me laugh because Farfa is only a few kilometers from Rome, and you know more about it than I do, and I'm the Roman."

"I'm glad to be your tour guide for a change." Its historical significance intrigued me, and Gianni was happy to take me for a change of scenery, although he had no interest in its present or past architectural glory.

The monastery was originally built in the VI century. Over the centuries, it went through periods of deterioration, even burning to the ground, but rose from the ashes with major reconstructions in the VIII and IX centuries. It wasn't until the Middle Ages that it flourished and prospered as a Benedictine enclave, becoming renowned for its cultural and political importance throughout Italy. The coffer wooden ceiling from 1494, ancient frescoes depicting Bible scenes, and *The Last Judgment* were well worth the visit.

My interest in art, architecture, and archeology only intensified while traveling in Europe and living in Italy. They held no fascination for Gianni. Perhaps, being surrounded by antiquities and precious art objects all his life made him indifferent to their wonders. I was sorry we did not share common interests. Maybe over time, Gianni would learn to appreciate them if I dragged him to enough museums and archaeological sites.

As raindrops dripped off our noses, we kissed in the courtyard of the abbey in the shadow of the XIII century bell tower. Then we meandered through the labyrinth of narrow streets in the village before returning to Rome. Everything was gray and brown; the surrounding fields were sodden. But for me, the day had been a success since I was doing what I enjoyed most—exploring antiquities and fine art with the man I loved most in the world. Northern Italy was again experiencing major flooding. We were looking forward to a longer holiday ski trip with Mary Louise and Francesco during Christmas week and New Years.

"Let's have Thanksgiving American style. It might be fun showing Gianni and Francesco how we celebrate one of our own holidays. It'll brighten up a pretty dreary month."

"That's a great idea!" Mary Louise sounded excited. "But where do we find a turkey? I don't think Italians eat turkey. I've never seen one at the butcher's."

"Neither have I, but I'll start searching. Then we can decide on stuffing, but that should be easy to make from scratch. We definitely won't find Pepperidge Farm stuffing mix anywhere. Not sure we'll find cranberry sauce either. We'll use our noggins improvising."

"I can make my grandmother's special creamed onions. They're yummy." Mary Louise was anxious to pitch in. I was hoping Gianni would be pleased to know what we were planning.

The tom turkey which embellished most American tables at Thanksgiving proved elusive in Rome and was nowhere to be found. What we did find was a scrawny, unappetizing specimen, a far cry from its wholesomely plump US brethren. We concluded it had to be the female counterpart, or maybe it wasn't even a turkey. We couldn't be sure, and the butcher didn't evoke confidence in his fumbling identification. He probably figured we wouldn't know the difference. He was right.

The meal wasn't our best effort. The turkey or whatever it was, was tasteless, but Gianni and Francesco appreciated all the work we put into the feast. "*Hai fatto bene.*" (You did a good job.) Gianni said the stuffing and creamed onions were *interessante*—a euphemism for not great. He always encouraged me and never criticized, not wanting me to feel guilty about presenting him with a mediocre meal when food was so important to him. My feeble attempt to introduce Gianni to a small part of Americana had been a flop. It had more to do with my struggle to come to terms with whether he could ever settle for the American way of life.

17

Can This Be Happening?

At the end of the month I was given notice that my job at Caltex would terminate before January. Mrs. Martinelli, the referral from Mr. Costello, arranged an interview for me with a forty-year- old American criminal prosecutor from Philadelphia who had an office in Rome. His name was Albert Ferrantino. He was swarthy-looking but attractive, with slicked-back, oiled hair and dark, penetrating, deep set eyes, an older version of Rudolph Valentino, a silent film star from the 1920s. A cigarette seemed perpetually glued to his lips. He had an intense, driven quality which was downright intimidating.

He stared at me for an inordinate amount of time, sizing me up. It felt like he was undressing me with his eyes. It was unnerving. There was something menacing about him.

"So how long have you lived in Rome?"

"Almost three years."

"What do you do for entertainment? You look like someone who enjoys a good time."

"Um . . . I really enjoy eating out." His inappropriate comment rattled me. "The restaurants are a lot better than the Italian ones in Pittsburgh. So I definitely like going out to dinner, although I've put on a few pounds." I deflected his comment with my seemingly inane response and tried to ignore his. Red flags were being thrown in every direction.

"Don't worry about your weight. I bet you look sexy in a bikini."
Is he making a pass at me?

We talked casually for about an hour, unlike a formal interview, and I was taken aback when he suddenly asked me out for dinner. *He must have taken my response about dinners seriously.* That should have been a warning sign of things to come. Acknowledging there were a disproportionate number of fellow Pennsylvanians in Rome, I told him I was busy and declined his invitation. It seemed odd to me that I was there to interview for a job, and he had the *chutzpah* to ask me out.

Later that week, Albert called to offer me a temporary job as his receptionist. He was one of the few lawyers in Rome who provided legal advice to Americans abroad. I was still working eight hours a day at Caltex, but I accepted his offer since my time at Caltex was about to end. It would make for a very long working day. Instead of considering the possible consequences of working for a man with a hidden agenda, I stupidly decided to give him the benefit of the doubt.

Our ski trip over Christmas to St. Moritz was firming up. We were going with a group of twelve others besides Mary Louise and Francesco. We wrangled a very good deal with a travel agency catering to organized groups. I was excited since I had never gone skiing and neither had Gianni. Needing necessary ski paraphernalia and wanting to look snazzy, I bought ski boots and a fiery red jacket with matching pants without a second thought. I might not be able to ski, but at least I would look like an Olympian skier. Saving money definitely wasn't a priority in those days.

A holiday break was something we could definitely use, and Gianni and I looked forward to the upcoming trip. We were all suffering from exhaustion. Gianni spent long days at work, I got home after 9 p.m, Mary Louise arrived an hour later, and Cecilia got home after 11 p.m. We rarely saw one another.

A Christmas with Consequences

Mary Louise got officially engaged to Francesco on her birthday in mid-December and Cecilia's birthday was a few days after that. We had a lot to celebrate including the fact that all three of us were now twenty-four years old. Mary Louise was leaving for home in April to plan her wedding. She was hopeful that Francesco would be able to get a student visa since he was studying to be an engineer. Once they got married he would automatically get American citizenship. It seemed a simple process unlike Gianni's disappointing rejection.

"Why is it so easy for him to get a visa?" Gianni said rhetorically in a quiet voice.

"I don't know, especially when it was impossible for you." He clearly hadn't expected me to answer. Gianni's demeanor immediately changed. It was a touchy subject. It must have brought back emotions best left in the past. His face registered overwhelming disappointment as he turned around abruptly and walked out of the room. *Why had I opened my big mouth?*

It happened without warning while shopping for Christmas gifts in a department store. When I reached into my purse to retrieve my wallet, I discovered it was missing. I frantically retraced my steps thinking it had somehow dropped along the way. But, I soon realized it was gone forever, never to be found, along with two hundred dollars for my ski trip. The store detective just rolled his eyes as if to say, "What do you want me to do about it?"

Gianni consoled me with, "*Non ti preoccupare,*" (Don't worry) a familiar refrain. Pickpockets were rampant in Rome, particularly in crowded stores at Christmas time. I should have known better. Gianni had repeatedly warned me. It shattered my hopes for a Merry Christmas.

"I'm so so sorry you can't come skiing with us. It won't be the same without you and Gianni." Mary Louise gave me a comforting hug.

"I was really an idiot going into a store with all that money. What was I thinking? I feel like a complete dunce."

"It could have happened to any one of us. I've done dumb stuff too. Don't beat yourself up over it." She was a one-person cheering team.

"I know, but I was looking forward to getting away. I'm so tired. My body craves rest and relaxation. Skiing would have been fun, and I could have recouped sitting in front of a fireplace, spacing out with a glass of Sambuca."

"Well, we'll miss you." She gave me a last hug, picked up her suitcase, and left for St. Moritz. It was upsetting to see her leave. I could have kicked myself in frustration. When I got to Gianni's, he kept giving me little squeezes and rubbing my back, trying to make me feel better. He didn't seem to mind the cancellation. It was surprising since I knew he had been anxious to go skiing.

I was thrown into a life-altering dilemma a few days later on Christmas Eve. We were sitting in Gianni's living room. The stolen funds were still on my mind, and I wondered how everything would have been different, if I hadn't stuffed that money into an already bulging wallet. Gianni approached me with a smile and reached into his pocket. For a moment I thought he had found my wallet.

"Here's a little gift for you. I love you. *Buon Natale*." (Merry Christmas).

Instead, he withdrew an engagement ring, took my finger, and slipped it on in front of his beaming, delighted family. It was a beautiful oval emerald surrounded by tiny diamonds. I was speechless—there was a prolonged, awkward silence. It was at that moment I realized time was not on my side. A decision had to be made soon about our future. The inevitability of the proposal should not have surprised me.

It was a natural conclusion to a relationship that had lasted nearly three years. Gianni waited, but I didn't utter a word. I was stunned.

"It fits perfectly. What do you think?" He must have assumed it was a foregone conclusion so a response was unnecessary. I couldn't look him in the face. Instead, I focused on the floor and the irregular patterns in the terrazzo tiles. They looked like random splotches of paint thrown from an artist's palette. *How do I keep it together? My face can't convey fright or he'll be destroyed, crushed, humiliated in front of his parents. He was so sure of my response that we even have an audience for the announcement.* I tried to elicit a facsimile of a smile, but my facial muscles remained rigid almost frozen. I was sure the color had drained from my face. My heart began to race and I broke out in a sweat. I felt faint.

His family did not appear to notice my unusual response. They hugged and kissed me, never realizing I was in shock. It felt like I was having an out of body experience. Whatever was happening wasn't really happening to me, but to someone else across the room. I was not a participant, but an observer to my own life. It was not what you would expect from someone who just got engaged. It should have been one of the most joyous moments in my life. This was not a normal reaction. The twinges of doubt could no longer be contained. They exploded like the sudden release of a jack-in-the-box. I had my first panic attack.

After a few deep breaths and controlled breathing, I finally regained my composure. I responded in a subdued voice, "Yes, it's beautiful. *Perfetto.*" (Perfect.) I gave Gianni a kiss and hugged him hoping I sounded convincing. Mary Louise would be surprised to learn that her erstwhile roommate was engaged, *or am I?* The weightiness of the ring on my finger seemed a mere mirage . . . a dramatic scene in a theatrical production with a tragic finale. There was no way I could tell my parents. The thought of my father's reaction was horrifying. He would surely disown me. *How do I handle this dilemma without destroying Gianni? Oh my God!*

The hours at Caltex had been reduced, and I was spending more time at the law office. The long hours alone when Albert was meeting a client for lunch gave me too much time to dwell on the implications of the engagement ring. It made my finger throb, almost to the point of being painful, yet I couldn't remove it. If I looked at it, the essence of its meaning made my heart pound uncontrollably. It was not a good sign.

To quell my ever increasing fear, I left the office to get the newspaper at the corner kiosk for my daily infusion of world news. It was always much worse than my personal crises. Israeli commandos had attacked the Beirut Airport and destroyed thirteen Middle East Airline passenger planes. It was in retaliation for an Arab attack on Israelis at the Athens Airport. Middle East peace would remain challenging, *so will my life*. These terrible events briefly took my mind off the ring and other deliberations. Then suddenly everything came crashing down, like an avalanche accidentally burying me. Sheer panic erupted. I couldn't breathe. *What do I do about my relationship with Gianni? How can I accept an engagement ring when I have doubts about our future? Why did I allow this to happen? What have I done?*

My head was reeling with the magnitude of what had happened and what it would mean for our relationship. At work, I tried to act normally, pretending to have things under control. I told Mr. Rossi about our engagement and about the robbery resulting in our cancelled trip. It was good to focus on work and have activity around me.

"Why don't you and Gianni come skiing with me. I'd like to meet him. I'm going to Scanno. There's plenty of snow this year, and I haven't gone skiing for awhile."

"We really aren't skiers. We'll embarrass you. We'd cramp your style."

"No you won't. You can always sit by the fire and get drunk. We can celebrate your engagement and the New Year." *I feel conflicted about the reason for the invitation. Just saying the word "engagement" makes my blood pressure rise. Maybe a change of scenery can clear my head.* Scanno didn't have the same caché as the Alps, but it was only 150 kilometers from Rome to the Abruzzi Apennines. My fashionable ski clothes would finally be put to good use. My troubling thoughts were pushed to the back burner for now.

We drove to the Apennines on January 1, 1969. The mountains blanketed with snow glistened like brilliant crystals in the sunlight. I put on my ski goggles to shield my eyes from the blinding glare.

"*Che bello!* I've never seen so much snow." Gianni was ebullient. "Let's have a snowball fight." He picked up a handful of snow to make a snowball. He threw it at me and there was a loud splat as it disintegrated on impact, sending icy crystals up into my face. I threw one back as we both laughed.

I hadn't seen significant snow since being in Switzerland with my parents. Its vast whiteness concealing all the barren ugliness of winter was serene and calming . . . a perfect remedy for my agitated state.

Gianni had never gone skiing, but he confidently pushed himself off on his skis like he had done it countless times before. We took the ski lift to the top of the mountain. After Gianni expertly descended the slope, he waved to me to come down. I stood frozen to the same spot for at least twenty minutes before gaining enough confidence to ski to the bottom.

My body seemed to have a life of its own, with legs going one way and torso the other, like a disembodied marionette. I fell at least ten times on my way down. Fortunately the snow was fresh and powdery, or I would have had bruises from head to toe. Wearing flashy red ski clothes had not prevented me from being an uncoordinated amateur. I was on full display as I caught the bemused attention of passing skiers. It was mortifying.

We had a grand time off the slopes, sitting in front of a huge, stone fireplace sipping aperitifs and snacking on pizza—just as I had imagined. The air smelled of aromatic burning wood used to stoke the pizza ovens. It reminded me of winters at home when we stayed in a rustic ski lodge with open-beamed ceilings and overstuffed furniture covered with worn but comfortable cushions. On our first night many of the guests removed the pillows to sit on the floor near the fireplace. Before long, we were all talking and joking like old friends.

One of the guests struck up a conversation after detecting an accent. "Where are you from? Do you celebrate *capodanno* (New Years) in the same way?"

"I'm American. It really isn't that different. We hoot and holler and drink champagne instead of *Spumante*. At midnight we all kiss and have fireworks just like Italians. *Cin-cin!*" (Cheers!) I held my glass of *Spumante* up high and took a sip.

Italians have an uncanny ability to be friendly and fun-loving, even when thrown together with total strangers. For them the glass is half full; for me it's always half empty. Gianni thoroughly enjoyed himself.

"*Buona notte, Bella. Sono stanco.*" (Good night, Beautiful. I'm tired.) He collapsed into bed after a full day of skiing and carousing. He was asleep the moment his head hit the pillow. I draped my right arm gently over his torso. My ring finger had ceased throbbing. Maybe it was feeling content being the symbol of Gianni's affirming love. It was strange that he never once asked me about the ring or whether we should set a date. He must have sensed that all was not right. I was terrified he might ask, and I had no idea what I would say to him. As he slept peacefully, I ran my hand over his chest, resisting hugging him tight for fear I would wake him. I closed my eyes and fell into a restless sleep.

18

A Regrettable Decision

Caltex unexpectedly asked me to stay at my job for an additional two weeks, and Albert wanted me to start working full-time. I found myself in a quandary. If I passed up Albert's offer, he threatened to hire someone else even though the salary was far below what I was earning at Caltex. It wasn't worth it to give Caltex extra time only to be out of a job in two weeks. If I explained the circumstances, maybe a compromise could be reached. Otherwise, I would have to quit my job at Caltex and reluctantly take Albert's offer.

"When I told you I needed you right away, I meant it. Do you want this job or not?" Albert wasn't happy. His voice was loud and threatening as he scowled at me.

"I know you're angry, but Caltex was counting on me too. I feel an obligation to help them out. My supervisor went on vacation for two weeks, and they want me to cover for him."

"You know what? I don't give a fuck about Caltex. I need you here now! You can't jerk me around." He was beginning to frighten me. *He definitely has anger management issues.*

"Please, Albert. Try to understand . . . I didn't know this would happen."

"You really piss me off! You seem to make a habit of it."

"Albert, I'm sorry. Be reasonable. I need the job. Can we talk about it?"

After endless negotiating with Caltex and Albert, I agreed to work afternoons at Caltex until the end of the month when Mr. Rossi returned from his vacation, and at Albert's office in the mornings. No one was entirely satisfied with this arrangement. Albert wanted to pay me through his office in Pennsylvania to bypass the paperwork involved in getting me a work permit. The temporary part-time schedule complicated the process. As I had already learned, obtaining a proper work permit for international employees put additional constraints on employers, and Albert wanted to circumvent them.

Albert's office had living quarters in the rear of the apartment behind the office. The bathroom that was used for clients was also for personal use, and Albert left it in deplorable condition. Without fail, I found myself cleaning the bathroom on a daily basis with a mop and bucket more like a maid than a receptionist. My mother facetiously asked me if I had gone to college to be a maid. I had never shared my housekeeper job at Penn State with her. However, my mother's point was well-taken. It made me question whether I really wanted to work for him.

I continued to look for a better paying job than Albert's. Working for Albert worried me, and I didn't trust him. He clearly was not a proponent of proper office protocol. He was too friendly, too personal, and treated me like a girlfriend instead of an employee. Why couldn't he keep a professional distance? If I could find another job, I would feel more secure, not always on guard waiting for something unforeseen to happen.

I had an interview with the HIAS Service (Hebrew Immigrant Aid Society) as a social worker. When I told the interviewer I had a bachelor's degree in social work from Penn State, he seemed immediately intrigued. HIAS provided assistance to the flood of Jews leaving Poland. They wanted someone who had counseling and interviewing skills. I mentioned my volunteer job at a VA mental hospital working with a psychiatrist who ran group therapy sessions. He was the guy who chased me around his office. My second volunteer job was more pertinent. I told them about spring break in Harlem my freshman year and working for a community outreach organization.

"What did you do in Harlem? Sounds like quite an experience."

"It was. We stayed with local families and interviewed residents: drug addicts, prostitutes, ex-cons, and other people on the fringes of society." He leaned over his desk taking notes. *He's interested.*

It was dangerous work, but my recollection was mainly about my girlfriend Emma, the cockroaches, and being pelted with vegetables while walking down the street—at least they weren't throwing knives.

At the end of the interview he said he was sorry, but I didn't get the job. He had been duly impressed, but I couldn't speak Polish or Yiddish, prerequisites for the job. My mother would have been a perfect candidate. She spoke both languages fluently. Maybe I did have some skills I hadn't put to good use yet. It would have saved me from my current predicament with Albert, and I would have been doing something meaningful.

I called home to wish my parents a Happy New Year and tell my mother about the job I almost got. My father said two words to me before handing the phone to my mother, "Hello" and "Goodbye."

"Your father is still upset with you. I've tried to reason with him, but he won't listen. You know what he's like."

"Do you think he'll ever forgive me?"

"If and when you decide to come home, I think he'll get over it. He can be very stubborn . . . just like you."

"Like father, like daughter I guess." There was no point in belaboring the subject. He was going to make me suffer. Whether he would forgive me was moot. The subject of the engagement ring remained unspoken or there would have been hell to pay. It would have only poured gasoline on an already incendiary situation.

Albert continued his onslaught making sexual references to female anatomy during our conversations, particularly favoring my breasts, and telling crude and vulgar jokes. He attempted to stroke my face or pat my butt, and I rebuffed each of his advances. His behavior was the forerunner to what would later become known as sexual harassment. A siren should have been going off in my head. I didn't know how to react. If I complained, he could fire me and I needed the job. It was incongruous with his strong Catholic upbringing, which he openly discussed with me. Albert clearly had unresolved issues and was morally conflicted. I was sure he knowingly and regularly committed mortal sins. *He really needs confession.*

"Can you fill me in about Catholicism? Like original sin, mortal sins, confession?" I knew Mary Louise would be knowledgeable on the subject, since she had gone to parochial school and remained a devout Catholic.

"Why the sudden interest in Catholicism?" She furrowed her brow and looked at me quizzically.

"Albert is Catholic and he talks about it a lot. Goes to church, and whatever else Catholics do . . . uh, you know, like the wafer and wine bit at communion." She shook her head and gave me a disapproving look.

"Sorry, didn't mean to offend you."

"You haven't. Go on."

"I'd like to understand some of its basic teachings for future reference. At least I'd sound informed. Right now I feel just plain ignorant. I can't add anything to the conversation when Albert brings it up."

"How much time do you have?" she asked.

"As much time as you need." She started with original sin and Adam and Eve. It would be a long night. I didn't tell her about Albert's objectionable overtures. It would make it too real, and I wasn't ready to accept the inevitable conclusion.

When Albert wasn't making advances, we had interesting, provocative, philosophical discussions about his past trials, criminal law, the death penalty, and other intensely stimulating subjects. He clearly had a brilliant mind. If I ever committed a murder, I would definitely want him to represent me. I doubted he ever lost a case. *The problem is he would likely be my first victim.*

He stopped at my desk one morning. "Listen, I want you to be well-dressed for my clientele. My tailor said he can make some suits for you. You'd look more professional. I want to set up some fittings."

"Do you really think that's necessary?" *The whole idea doesn't sit well with me even though I relish the idea of some new clothes.*

"Yes, I do. Custom-made suits would be more in keeping with a prestigious law office which this happens to be. Remember, we're dealing with a lot of wealthy people, darlin'." He made several appointments for me with his tailor. I was beginning to feel like a kept woman and Gianni wasn't pleased.

"Albert is an idiot, an asshole. Why are you still working for him?"

At the same time Albert began to denigrate Gianni. "What do you see in that guy? You deserve someone cultured, refined." Albert couldn't resist making snide remarks about Gianni whenever he had the opportunity. Did he see him as a threat?

"Are you saying *you're* cultured and refined? Should I repeat some of your dirty jokes?"

"You're quick with the retorts," he laughed.

"Remember, I'm engaged." I flashed my ring finger at him. He looked at it in derision.

My brother Sid wrote and said he was coming to see me in March. His nasty divorce was pending and he needed to get away for some R&R. I was delighted he was planning to visit his baby sister. I loved him dearly and wanted him to meet Gianni and his family. I also thought he might hit it off with Cecilia or at the very least, she would be a distraction. He would be amused by some of her favorite English expressions like, "Hi Ducky!" and "That's really dodgy," or "I can't find my knickers" (English slang for panties).

204 | S a n d r a   P e l a n n e

Celebration and Consternation

A surprise formal invitation to a cocktail party arrived in the mail from Mr. and Mrs. Martinelli. They were friends of Mr. Costello and he might have suggested inviting me. It would give me the opportunity to make connections so I was more than happy to attend. It was being held at their villa. They were one of the leading families in Rome and the impending social event was written up in the celebrity gossip column of the *The Rome Daily American*. Since the invitation did not specify bringing a guest, it didn't seem appropriate to bring Gianni with me.

"*Non preoccuparti.* Those people have sticks up their asses. We have nothing in common." I reluctantly left him at home.

I had to pinch myself when I drove up the long driveway to the Martinelli's luxurious villa in a cocktail dress, evening coat, evening bag, and earrings . . . all borrowed from Cecilia, and parked my Fiat 500 between a red Ferrari and a silver Rolls Royce. The party was a lavish affair. There was a live quartet playing classical music in a corner of the grand ballroom. The women wore long, elegant gowns *haute couture* no doubt with dazzling diamond and gold jewelry; the men wore formal attire. Even the waiters were wearing tuxedos. They carefully glided through the crowded room of guests carrying silver trays of delicately prepared *hors d'oeuvres, petits fours* and endless glasses of champagne. Vases of exquisite flower arrangements with pink and white orchids and lilies were placed strategically throughout the villa. An eclectic mix of contemporary and Renaissance paintings adorned the walls. The setting was stunning.

It was incredible to find myself—a young, naive, nobody—hobnobbing with rich and famous Romans, distinguished Americans, and European diplomats, sipping champagne and nibbling on smoked salmon and caviar. I surveyed the room admiring several ornate Venetian crystal chandeliers, before sashaying into the congested room trying to appear confident. I was hoping I wouldn't stick out like someone fully clothed walking into a nudist camp. I concluded I was the youngest one there and the only single woman. It was utterly amazing and slightly intimidating.

"Hello, young lady. Are you a friend of the Martinellis' daughter, Ana?" an aristocratic older woman in a lace and beaded gown stopped in front of me. I was caught off guard.

"No, I'm Mr. Martinelli's friend," I blurted out. She looked at me in surprise with widened eyes.

"I mean Mr. Costello's friend who is friends with Mr. Martinelli." She looked confused. "Sorry. I work for Caltex. Mr. Costello is my boss. He's the Managing Director." She seemed satisfied at last as she trotted off with her champagne flute in hand.

The Martinellis had done me a huge favor, but why had I been invited? Even Albert, who knew the Martinellis personally, hadn't received an invitation. It was thoroughly exhilarating being in that spectacular setting, flitting around and chatting with the movers and shakers of Rome's elite. It never would have occurred to me in my wildest dream to be invited to such an event. Not wanting to pass up a prime opportunity, I took names and phone numbers of many of the guests, much as my prior sleazy glove store owner Mario had done. It was networking at its finest. If I contacted one of them at a later date for a possible job and they had conveniently forgotten me, I would reference the Martinelli's gala party of the year which I had the privilege to attend.

Gianni ended up in the hospital for ten days with an eye infection. The doctors wouldn't release him until they determined the source of the infection. He had to take a medical leave from his job because his impaired vision prevented him from driving. His American producers were very sympathetic and told him not to worry. I spent a portion of every day visiting him in the hospital.

"*Come stai, amore?* (How are you?) I'm sorry I'm not in bed with you. You look really unhappy." It brought a weary, half smile to his lips. It was distressing for me to see him looking so helpless in a hospital bed. "Do you want a back rub?"

"I'm really fed up being in bed. I want to go home. My eyes are the problem. It isn't my body. Last time I checked, (he looked under the sheet) everything was working." I smiled. All I wanted to do was silently slip under the covers and reassure him with a big hug that everything would be fine.

I had time on my hands while he was in the hospital. I started reading some new books that were highly recommended by Albert, *The Crime of Punishment* by Karl Menninger and *The Ginger Man* by J. P. Donleavy. It seemed an odd pairing going from a thoughtful review of the American justice system to the steamy escapades of Sebastian Dangerfield. In retrospect, it was a conflict clearly visible in Albert's split personality. He would have been an intriguing patient for Sigmund Freud, the father of modern psychoanalysis. I'm certain he would have uncovered repressed sexual fantasies and deep-seated issues in Albert's childhood.

My last day at Caltex was January 31, 1969. I would start working at Albert's full-time. Although it meant putting up with his antics for more hours per day, it was only a fifteen minute bus ride. It gave me an extra hour and a half of sleep, and I was feeling sleep deprived. Albert kept me entertained with recollections of past murder trials he had prosecuted, impressing me with his courtroom prowess. From his stories I assumed he must have been a formidable opponent in the courtroom. His stern countenance and determination to win, using whatever theatrics were deemed admissible in court, would have been enough to frighten me into confessing my guilt.

His office was cluttered and disorderly with messy files piled high on his desk and covering every inch of the floor; his bookkeeping and notes were indecipherable.

"Look, I should have warned you. I can be slovenly when it comes to my work. Believe it or not, I know where everything is."

"But aren't you paying me to put things in some order?"

"It actually might make it harder for me to find things, but I'll overlook your fastidiousness if I can gaze longingly at your ass when you bend over."

"You will never be boring. We won't go into what other words I can use to describe you." I gave him a dismissive look. *Why don't I tell him to stop talking to me like that?*

"Do what you have to do." He kept his humor about it as I attempted to reorganize his files. The office was devoid of much interaction with others except for an occasional client. I missed the security and friendship of Mr. Rossi; it was too quiet and sometimes I felt apprehensive and afraid being alone with Albert. These fears were never shared with Gianni. He would have insisted I quit. Maybe I was overreacting. I was dreading Mary Louise's departure in April and tried not to think about it. She had become a dear friend. Would I ever see her again once she moved back to Chicago?

Another general strike was planned for February 5. The newspaper reported that an estimated 10,000,000 workers would protest. It truly was a wonder how the Italian economy survived these strikes. There was a funny article in the paper about a postcard taking sixty-two years to get to its destination only thirty-four miles away. After living in Italy and withstanding all these strikes, it didn't surprise me in the least. During the last strike, the empty land across the street from our apartment building became a dumping ground while garbage workers were on strike. People threw trash out the windows like they did in the Middle Ages. Another bubonic plague was just around the corner.

Sid wrote to say he would be in Rome in March. Hopefully, all the strikes would be over by then. He had his international license, passport, and his vaccination certificate. I was planning to arrange as many dates for him as possible to keep him occupied and entertained.

There was an Italian ambassador's daughter and the daughter of the president of one of the largest companies in Italy to consider, both friends of Albert's. And of course there was Cecilia practically sleeping in the same room with him. It was going to be great seeing him.

"Sid will be here the middle of March. I'm so excited to see him. I know you'll like him. He's very funny. He's really depressed and needs a break since his divorce. We have to keep him occupied."

"We'll have a good time, *non ti preoccupare* (don't worry). Maybe he'll find a girl at Trevi Fountain." Gianni knew that would make me smile.

"Just like you? He should be so lucky."

The middle of March was a perfect time to visit. The Spanish Steps would be filled with flowers from top to bottom for Easter. The wild plum trees and mimosas were already in bloom. I hoped he wouldn't mind bringing me a care package of pantyhose, bras, bobby pins, and Empirin for the persistent headaches I had since I started working for Albert.

Nixon came to visit Pope Paul VI and caused quite a commotion. I was on my way to work on a bus during a protest when it was surrounded by a sea of humanity pushing, shoving, and waving placards. It was a veritable mob scene. The students vowed to take down St. Peter's Square brick by brick. Italians made protests a way of life.

"You look upset. Did something happen?" Albert confronted me as I entered the office.

"I had a scary experience on the bus. Protesters blocked the road and stopped the bus. They're upset over Nixon's visit. I planned on going to St. Peter's Square to see him arrive by helicopter . . . I need a minute to calm down." I took a deep breath and placed my purse on a chair.

"You aren't still planning on going are you? I wouldn't advise it."

"No, I decided it was safer to watch his visit on TV."

"Good girl. Sound decision."

I tried to keep a physical distance between us for fear Albert would try to put his arm around me to console me. My reservations working for him were becoming more concerning.

I went to visit my friends at Caltex hoping they might hire me back. They mentioned a slight possibility that I might be able to assume my old duties. I confessed that I was much happier there with them and I missed their camaraderie. Unlike Albert, Mr. Rossi had always been a total gentleman and had never said anything inappropriate or off-color to me even in jest.

My Big Brother Sid

Sid arrived on schedule. We set him up in the living room on the sofa bed. I was thrilled to have his company, and Gianni and I showed him the sights of Rome, Villa d'Este in Tivoli, and the Appian Way. He seemed to enjoy every minute and grew genuinely fond of Gianni, noting his positive view on life. Sid suffered from the same affliction I did—C.H.E.S, the cup-half-empty-syndrome.

"Gianni really is optimistic. It's refreshing, seeing as I'm generally on the depressed side. I should spend more time with him. Maybe it'll rub off on me . . . I can definitely see why you're in love with him. He's a good guy," Sid said.

"Isn't it fascinating that you can't speak Italian and he can't speak English, but you still manage to communicate on some level. I haven't heard you laugh so much in a long time," I said.

"Like I said, he's easy to be around. I can figure out what he's saying just by his tone of voice, his facial expressions, and his body language. He uses his hands like I do. I think I'll take some Italian classes when I get back home. Maybe go to a few operas with Dad. It's a great sounding language. It rolls off your tongue like *che cazzo* (what the fuck) or *non me ne frega*." (I don't give a damn) Obviously, Gianni was teaching him some choice Italian phrases.

Gianni drew people into his world seamlessly. He had a magic touch. His honest, affectionate nature put people instantly at ease. Sid's spirits were clearly uplifted being with him. After his crushing separation from his wife, Gianni's positive vibes filled him with good humor. Gianni thought Sid was very *simpatico* (charming).

We managed to have an abbreviated Passover seder with Sid sitting at the head of the table. I tried my best at making chopped liver, *charoset* with apples and nuts, and matzo ball soup for the holiday. The Jewish holidays were important in our family and I wanted Sid to feel at home. It was essential for him to have the best time possible so he could briefly forget his divorce.

"Man, these matzo balls are so hard I can bounce them off the floor." He grabbed one from a bowl in the kitchen. "Here, catch!" He tossed one to Gianni who caught it with one hand. Sid told him he could be Roberto Clemente, a World Series right fielder who played for the Pittsburgh Pirates. It took awhile to try and translate. Italians don't play baseball. We spent the whole night laughing. It was good therapy for all of us.

Since Cecilia was sleeping in the closet adjacent to the living room, I was not surprised when I walked in one morning and found her "knickers" (panties) on the floor. I quickly picked them up and deposited them on her bed since I didn't want to embarrass Sid. It became an inside joke every time Cecilia would ask, "Where are my knickers?" we would both burst out laughing. Their unavoidable coupling was a good thing for everyone but Paolo, but we weren't about to tell him about Cecilia's indiscretions of which there were many. She had mentioned Sid's good looks on his arrival, so I knew it was only a matter of time before finding the errant panties.

While Sid was visiting, I quit my job. It was inevitable and poor judgment on my part to think I could keep Albert under control. He was beginning to have a detrimental effect on my emotional state.

"You have an appointment with my doctor. You need to figure out what's wrong with you. I insist you go so don't try to get out of it. I'll pay him. That's one less thing to worry about." Albert stood his ground waiting for my response.

"You're right. I don't want to go. What's the point? He might find some incurable disease that I'm better off not knowing about. Maybe he'll tell me to relax and go to the beach for a few days. You'd have to give me time off."

"If that's what the doctor orders, fine . . . we'll talk about it. But I insist—you're going." Albert gave me no choice. He was definitive. His voice was powerful and firm. It reverberated off the walls in the small office with the same iron determination he must have given in his impassioned closing arguments in court. He never realized that he was the cause of my ailments.

With constant headaches and persistent weight loss, the doctor prescribed tranquilizers and vitamin injections. Anxiety attacks were becoming commonplace before leaving for work, and I was having trouble breathing. I realized D-Day was coming when Albert's advances became too frequent to ignore and took on a more sinister nature. It worried me that I might not be able to fend him off.

As predicted, one day he literally picked me up and threw me down on his couch in the rear of his apartment, pinning me down with his body.

"Albert! Get off me! You've really lost it! Get off! You're scaring me!"

"Calm down, quit fighting. You know I've wanted you for a long time." He kept trying to kiss me as I struggled to get out from under him. I kneed him in the crotch and he flipped onto his side reaching for his groin. I took advantage of my opportunity to escape. I ran out of the office in a panic, leaving my coat and purse behind. *Was he going to rape me?* Even if I needed a job in desperation, I promised myself I would never set foot in his office again. Despite his brilliance as a prosecutor, he was a volatile, unpredictable man with a demonic side.

Extremely upset, I ran as far as Via Veneto to find a telephone and called Gianni. He came to get me immediately. Sid was with him. "Are you serious? He actually jumped you?" Sid was furious. "That son of a bitch! Wait until I get my hands on him." Sid stormed up to Albert's office to have *words* with him.

It was sheer luck that my big brother was there to protect me. That wasn't always the case. When I was nine years old and Sid was sixteen and David was fourteen, two boys I was playing with shoved me into the bushes just to show me who was boss. When I ran home crying and asked Sid and David to defend me, they told me to fight my own battles. I was so mad at them I went back and beat both boys up, bloodying them single-handedly. But now was different. He defended his little sister. Gianni couldn't contain his fury at Albert, and I had to physically restrain him from following Sid.

"*Che testa di cazzo!* (dickhead) *Figlio di mignotta!* (Son of a bitch) *Li mortacci tua!*" (insults to dead relatives). There was a string of insults and other equally rich expletives. Gianni paced angrily up and down the sidewalk pounding his fists together, his hair disheveled, spewing out curses like venomous spitballs to no one in particular. Gianni would defend his lover to the death—my Roman gladiator. If he had confronted Albert, there would have been a nasty fight. Sid returned with my purse and coat. Albert denied doing anything improper and said I had misinterpreted his actions. There was no way to misinterpret his blatant attack. It was too bad we had to end our relationship on such a sour note. I should have prosecuted the prosecutor.

Months after this incident I received a letter from Albert as though nothing had happened. He enclosed a newspaper article about himself, commenting that it was good publicity. I didn't read it. He ended his letter with:

> *P.S. You should see the present secretary. She's a descendent of German aristocracy. . .*
> *6 feet tall, blonde hair, all legs and tits! Guess why she got the job? That's wrong you evil minded virgin.*

Years later I had the shock of my life. I learned that Albert had entered a seminary to become a Roman Catholic priest. Confession hadn't been enough to absolve his guilt. It took me days to digest this unbelievable news. My assumption that Albert was struggling with his inner demons had been correct. He was seeking redemption from the Catholic Church for committing countless mortal sins, but whether he was able to forgive himself would remain unknown.

After two weeks in Rome, Sid rented a car and we drove to Florence, Venice and then to the French Riviera. Gianni had to work so I left him in Rome and told him I would take the train back. Getting a room in a hotel was a bit awkward at first since we didn't know whether to check in as brother and sister or husband and wife. We concluded that brother and sister would sound kind of kinky since we stayed in the same room, so we checked in as a married couple but asked for separate beds. That seemed to work out just fine since Europeans don't always share the same bed. I was taking the train back to Rome, and Sid was planning to continue on to Paris and London before flying back home.

We had a notable stay in the posh Hotel West End in Nice. During the night, I woke up to the sound of running water. Sid was peacefully snoring on the other side of the room. Someone must be taking a bath or shower, but it seemed to go on much too long. I switched on the light.

"Sid, wake up! Something's wrong. Can you hear that? Doesn't it sound like running water?"

"It's nothing. You probably dreamed about the ocean. It's your imagination. I don't hear a thing. You worry about everything . . . go back to sleep."

He turned over groggily, muttering something unintelligible with his back to me. Just at that moment part of the ceiling fell on my bed with a thud. Water cascaded down the chandelier and gushed out of a gaping hole in the ceiling. I leaped out of bed to avoid getting crushed by dropping plaster. At the sound of the collapsing ceiling Sid fell out of bed hitting the floor like a ton of bricks. It was a dramatic way to be awakened at 2 a.m.

Sid and I cowered in the corner of the room laughing hysterically. It was unavoidable—I peed my pants even with my legs crossed. We called the front desk to report the emergency. As predicted, a hotel guest upstairs had forgotten to turn off the faucet in the bathtub. We hurriedly packed our suitcases and were led to another room by hotel staff as a stream of apologies in English and expletives in French, followed us down the hall. Sid had a great sense of humor, and I knew he would recount this incident to our parents in his own unparalleled, comedic style. It was an unforgettable night, one for the books.

During our road trip together we had time to talk. I needed to share my thoughts about my relationship with Gianni, trying to clarify and understand my increasing doubts, and how things had come to a head with the engagement ring.

"I'm so conflicted about Gianni. I love him more than anything in the world, but I'm so worried I'll make him unhappy."

"Why do you think that?"

"You know what I'm like . . . always getting my own way, argumentative, impatient, expecting men to do whatever I want when I want."

"Well, I know you wrapped a few boyfriends around your finger."

"When I worked at that VA psychiatric hospital at Penn State, the psychiatrist I worked for told me I would drive men crazy. I had the evil eye. That crazed old man used to chase me around his examining room. Maybe he was right, but he was *already* crazy."

"Really? That's a good one," he laughed. "It's healthy to talk about it. It might help you make the right decision. Marrying Gianni is a huge leap of faith. Who's to say he would make it in the States. He's a simple kind of guy."

"Yeah, you're right. He could get eaten alive if he isn't ready for it."

"Sit down with a piece of paper and make a list of pros and cons to marrying him. See what you come up with."

"All right, I'll try to do that, but a list may not be enough to convince me. The decision has to be made on a deeper level, not based on a list."

"You're always so damn serious. Lighten up. I'm on vacation."

"Can't help myself. If I decide to call things off, it will be like a death knell. I can hear the bell tolling . . ."

"Uh, so melodramatic . . ." Sid was teasing me, but it was an intimate talk about my life. I was inching toward the conclusion that my future with Gianni was questionable. I knew if I married him and we lived in the States, he would do whatever I wanted. Maybe he would even go back to school and learn English or further his education to learn a new skill, even though he wouldn't want to.

"You know Gianni is a selfless, genuine, uncomplicated man with a heart of gold. He doesn't hold grudges, doesn't have hidden agendas, isn't neurotic like I am. He's transparent. All he has is love, not just for me but for life and everyone around him."

"That's clear. He's a great guy. I won't dispute that."

"I'm demanding, controlling, complicated. Gianni's love brings out the best in me, but I know it won't last. Nothing good ever does. I would make him miserable."

"You're right," Sid said. He looked at me askance. "We do have a tendency to see things in a negative light, the cup is always half empty." His divorce, soon to be final, was still fresh in his mind, and he understood the grief of losing the love of one's life. "Look, I'll be there for you from beginning to end. It meant a lot to me when you came to Houston."

"I know it did. But you also helped me after San Francisco. I was a mess."

"Yeah, and so was I. My wife slept with my best friend . . . that big, fat shit. And she admitted it didn't happen just once. They were only thinking of a good lay. Never thought of what it was doing to our two sons. Then once I moved out, she threatened to keep me from seeing them. It still feels like crap."

"It was so hard on you. Just so awful with the two kids caught in the middle."

"You know her mother and dad told her to get me for all I'm worth. What a couple of *schmucks.*"

"It will take awhile before you stop getting upset over it. At least you can always talk to me. I'm not sure how everything would have gone down if you hadn't been here for me. I need you just as much, bro."

"You should talk to Mary Louise, to someone who can be objective, someone with a different perspective, a woman's perspective."

"Yeah, Mary Louise has good insights. The time just never presents itself. Maybe I'm avoiding it." The option of living in Italy permanently had never been given serious consideration. Before I met

Gianni and fell hopelessly in love, I always planned to return to the US, go to graduate school, and get a job. That probably explained why I never wanted a permanent job . . . I could keep my options open and flexible if I decided to leave on short notice. It meant not making long standing commitments.

Seeing my brother made me realize how homesick I was for my family. I also missed all the conveniences and efficiency of the American way of life, and the opportunity to succeed if you worked hard at it. Italians were used to being taken care of by their socialist government. It created an environment that repressed the work ethic and made it even more unlikely that an entrepreneurial spirit could flourish.

I couldn't picture myself putting up with all the bureaucratic nonsense as an expatriate and not having total command of the Italian language. It would have put constraints on my future career options. Living in a foreign country made me realize I would always be viewed as a foreigner no matter how long I lived there. Americans were particularly disliked, the Vietnam War fueled the fire, and I often worried about a possible assault on my basic democratic freedoms.

Soon after Sid's departure I received a postcard from Paris with the greeting, "Hi wife: Can't help but laugh when I think of the West End Hotel. Tell Cecilia I'm having trouble sleeping at night without someone to *talk to*." (Sid's subtle reference to "screwing" Cecilia, and how we had registered in hotels as a married couple.) It briefly brought a smile to my lips. I missed him terribly.

19

The Point of No Return

Mary Louise and I finally did get a chance to talk about the black cloud hanging over my head ready to release the ten plagues. She offered her thoughts on the subject. "I know your plan was to have Gianni follow you home like Susan's Giacomo and my Francesco. It's true I feel our future is in the States, not Italy."

"That's what I thought."

"The difference is that Francesco is planning to be an engineer, and I guess the US government sees that as a plus and will give him a student visa. It's a profession that's in demand." She continued, "Gianni is a tradesman, a plumber. Not to denigrate what he does, but the US government was looking at it from a different angle. They want people with professional careers who can help grow the economy."

"I guess you have a point. I never thought of it that way before."

Mary Louise had touched upon the essence of the problem. When Gianni's visa did not materialize, my doubts began to germinate . . . uncertainty and ambivalence crept into my muddled brain and confused me. Then he gave me an engagement ring I was ill-prepared for.

"If I married him and convinced him to live in the States, I know I would try to make him fit into my American middle class life starting with his occupation. In the end I would destroy our happiness." Mary Louise placed her arm on my shoulder to comfort me. "He's perfect the way he is. He doesn't carry any extra baggage like I do." Tears began their route down the side of my nose wetting my lips. I could taste their saltiness. "Sure, we have our fights like all couples do, but they're nothing. After a few *porca madonnas* (nasty insult to the Virgin Mary) or *non mi rompere gli coglioni* (don't break my balls), they're over and forgotten. It's what I love most about him."

Transporting him to my world in the US was misguided almost bordering on cruelty, like forcing a carefree dolphin swimming in the blue Mediterranean to spend his remaining life in the confines of a shark tank. It was a no-win situation. Either way, it wouldn't work. We were doomed. Maybe it was providential that he had been unable to obtain a visa. The writing was already on the wall, but I couldn't see it through the fog of love. Rome was the center of his world and he seemed content with how he fit into the scheme of things. It was predictable and secure.

"I can't bear the thought of making him unhappy and manipulating his life. It would destroy him. How would he handle the pressure of the fast-paced American life? And for what . . . just to please me?"

"That's true," she said "and *you* in turn would become anxious and depressed. Don't forget that. Gianni would be at a distinct disadvantage. He's already told you he doesn't want to go back to school. You have to listen to him and accept it."

My vision was blurry with tears cascading down my face. "My love for him is so intense. I've never felt like this about anyone else. He's part of me. I'm just the wrong choice. This is all my fault. How could I be so cruel to leave him now?" It was going to be a difficult struggle to make him understand and difficult for me to accept, but I knew it was the only rational decision to make. It would sear a deep wound into both of us, branding our souls for life.

Mary Louise listened as my feelings poured out in anguished gasps, my tears burning my reddened eyes. She knew telling Gianni our future together could never work out would be one of the most challenging moments of my life. I had to decide how and when to tell him and to have the courage to actually carry it out. It was a sacrifice that had to be made for Gianni's future happiness and for mine.

Soon after my emotional conversation with Mary Louise, Mr. Rossi called from Caltex to offer me my old job back. I started in mid-April. Now at least I would be able to concentrate temporarily on something other than my decision to leave, turning my attention to things mundane, like spring fashions. It gave me a few months to let the weight of my decision sink in. Thankfully, Mary Louise postponed her departure until the beginning of June. She would be there to help me through this. I hesitantly wrote Molly to tell her I would be joining her in Boston, and that I would need her emotional support after saying goodbye to Gianni for the last time.

Gianni and I went to Venice with Carter DeHaven for a few days. Mr. DeHaven knew I would entertain Gianni if I came along as his guest, and he admitted he enjoyed having me around as a fellow American. It was nice of him to invite me and I was happy to oblige. It was yet another opportunity to avoid the inevitable conversation with Gianni.

"Let's go to Piazza St. Marco and feed the pigeons," I said. "And then what about a gondola ride?" Gianni had never been to Venice before. The gondola ride was Gianni's Venetian highlight and we took several rides while we were there. He joked around with the gondoliers who took us on excursions up and down the Grand Canal and under the Rialto Bridge to view the Venetian palaces and hotels dating from the thirteenth to eighteenth centuries. They were romantic bittersweet rides since I knew we would never again do it together.

We then walked the labyrinth of narrow passageways which provided glimpses into ancient Venice. At several points along the way we got lost or followed a path to dead-end at a canal, and Gianni had to ask a Venetian for directions back to the piazza. At night it was particularly difficult finding our way around. There were no lights along the passageways, and it seemed at times like we were descending into a mysterious underworld lured by Hades and Persephone. We held hands gingerly proceeding forward until a dim light from a window would appear, giving us assurance that we were headed in the right direction.

It was intriguing, watching visitors cart their suitcases everywhere. Water taxis, unlike cars, could only deposit passengers at designated stops, forcing them to find their own way to a final destination. All commerce was conducted by boat. Packages and other materials were unloaded and delivered via wagons or other rolling devices using ingenious methods to navigate hundreds of bridges and steps. It was part of the daily routine for Venetians, but extraordinary to observe as outsiders.

We visited the Doge Palace, the Bridge of Sighs, and the island of Murano to watch glass being blown into intricate creations by resident artists. We were the usual curious tourists, hitting all the top tourist attractions. It was wonderful doing some traveling with Gianni to new places. Even though we both agreed we preferred Rome, Venice was an amazing city to visit and explore.

We did a lot of drinking and eating with Mr. DeHaven and his friends. The food in Venice wasn't nearly as good as Rome, but we did have delicious *bigoli in salsa* (thick spaghetti made with anchovies and onions) and *fegato alla veneziana* (thinly sliced liver with onions), the only way to eat liver besides my mother's chopped liver. We browsed the stores and marketplaces, but found the merchandise was much more expensive than Rome. All I bought was a pair of sandals to commemorate our trip to Venice together, although Gianni had no idea it would be our last.

The finality of that thought would bring on waves of sadness, but I wasn't ready to face our inevitable discussion. Gianni was happy and I wanted him to stay that way as long as possible. My decision would land a crushing body blow to end his happiness for the foreseeable future.

"How would you like to come out to Cinecitta with Gianni to watch John Huston direct a film? You said you'd like to see some live action." Since I had once expressed an interest, Mr. DeHaven's invitation was a welcome surprise.

"Sure, would love to. Who's in the movie? Any actors I might know?"

"The movie is *The Kremlin Letter* starring Patrick O'Neill, David Boone, and Bibi Andersson, the blonde who is always in Ingmar Bergman's movies, the Swedish director."

"Yeah, I've seen all of Ingmar Bergman's movies. They were inspirational. I usually left the movie theater scratching my head trying to figure out all the symbolism and imagery. We had Bergman movie groups to try and analyze them. I spent a lot of time at the movies instead of in class when I was in college."

Mr. DeHaven smiled. "You're not alone."

It was amazing to actually see John Huston direct a movie in person. It was a bedroom scene, and Gianni and I were allowed in after the actors' main love scene had been filmed. The presence of strangers might have impacted their spontaneity. The actors were still lounging in bed smoking while John Huston directed the remaining scene in the quiet, darkened studio. The only light was focused on the two partially clad actors in bed. It made me feel like a voyeur looking through a peep hole at a couple's intimate liaison. Mr. Huston coached the actors in a calm, reassuring voice before the scene began. The scene proceeded smoothly without interruption. Seeing a famous director like John Huston in action was a special treat.

There was only one other equally exciting Hollywood encounter I had in California the summer before I started college. A Universal Studio tour was on my "must do" list. During the tour, the bus stopped suddenly and I looked out the window to see Cary Grant climb out of a white Rolls Royce convertible. I was so excited I almost fainted. He was my idol and the most attractive man I had ever seen. It had been a stroke of luck being in the right place at the right time—again.

Strikes & Strife

On May 18, 1969, I rushed over to Gianni's to watch the launch of Apollo 10 and to see history in the making. Unlike the US, Italy did not have color television yet, but it was breathtaking nonetheless to see US astronauts in space and to imagine the limitless exploration of a world yet to be discovered. It was a historic moment that Gianni and I shared. Our remaining days together were tinged with sorrow, but Gianni never knew that an ending to our romance was now in sight.

General strikes were happening so frequently that it was sometimes a month before I received a letter from home, or my mother received one from me. And then once the deliveries resumed, letters would arrive in huge mounds all out of chronological order so it would take another month to get back up to speed and put events in their proper order. It was still a mystery how commerce continued with these delays. Mary Louise was in a panic since she was planning to leave for Chicago and still had to ship out two trunks and several boxes, but the strike prevented it. Strikes disrupted making plans and completing essential duties. It was a destructive element in Italian life, but we were all hostages to them without recourse.

Finally, the strike ended and Mary Louise left Rome as planned with her luggage and excess baggage in tow. It was a sad day to see her leave. I would miss her terribly. My confidante was gone and we would never have another late-night chat. As a result of the strike ending, I got a barrage of mail along with a telegram from Molly.

FOUND CHARMING APARTMENT. RENT 230 DOLLARS. BEST POSSIBLE SITUATION. WIRE ADVICE IMMEDIATELY. MOLLY

The reality of my decision was starting to sink in and I knew the days were numbered before I would be forced to tell Gianni of my impending departure. I cringed at the thought of telling him. It was an unforgivable cowardly act to delay the agonizing moment of truth.

A few days later I got a letter from Molly with more specific information. She said our new address was 466 Commonwealth Avenue in Boston. She didn't describe the apartment except to say it had a garbage disposal and a dishwasher, obviously the two most important features for her. It was devoid of furniture and the two hundred thirty dollar rent sounded exorbitant to me. Anticipating my reaction, she enclosed an article about Boston rents going through the roof with rent hikes of twelve percent and more. I wasn't up for complaining at this point, trying to keep a panic attack under control. Maybe the higher price was justified since it was a convenient location with the MBTA stop right outside the door. She asked for an additional fifty dollars for a phone installation and for buying kitchen utensils and other necessities.

To add to the stress level, Cecilia and I began having issues over the rent. At first she refused to pay the June rent as well as the electricity bill. Since she decided to leave for England before the lease was up, she thought she could shirk all financial responsibilities and stick me with the remainder of the tab.

"Why do I have to pay the rent? Paolo cut my funds off so I'm a bit short this month, Ducky. I'll send it from London after I get a loan from my parents."

"I know what that means, Cecilia. You have a habit of conveniently forgetting to repay your debts. Once you leave here I doubt I'll ever hear from you again."

"Not true, that's totally not true," she asserted.

"Didn't Mary Louise and I give you a place to stay when you needed it? It wasn't easy rearranging the apartment to make room for you, but we did. And this is how you repay us?"

"I'm short on money. You aren't being fair."

"I don't have any more money than you do. But I'm responsible . . . you might even say reliable . . . but *you* on the other hand . . . I wouldn't expect you to pay the rent by yourself. You're just taking advantage of me." My temper was rising.

We finally came to terms but not without a battle, and we were again living in semi-tranquil cohabitation. Then at the end of the month she surprised me by deciding to leave the day before the July rent was due. Cecilia turned out to be a royal British *stronza* (shit). She reneged, even though she had agreed to pay her portion of the rent and electricity bill.

We had a heated argument the day she left. Our paths will probably never cross again. After all we had been through together, it was a hard pill to swallow. I was sure Sid would be as equally disappointed in her as I was. When I wrote Mary Louise to tell her about Cecilia's irresponsible behavior, she responded immediately.

> *Boy, the more I think about Cecilia the angrier I get to think of how we went out of our way to make her move in. I hope you've learned a lesson, dearie!*
> *You insisted so much not to hurt her and got a big kick in the pants for it.*
> *The next time learn to say "No!"*
> *I'm not trying to say to forget about friendship, but under certain circumstances one cannot sacrifice one's own happiness or comfort for the sake of others.*
> *CHARITY DOES BEGIN AT HOME! I guess I should step down from the pulpit and stop preaching, huh?*

Sid wrote to say he knew I was returning home (my parents had told him), and he wanted to stay in touch. He asked whether I had spoken to Gianni. His divorce was final. He started dating again. "I took Miss Ugly of 1969 out last Friday night, and all I can say is that she looked like the lost twin of Marsha the Mongol." Sid never failed to amuse me. Every letter I received from him made me realize how much I could use his support now. It had been so comforting having him in Rome. He helped me come to terms with my decision to leave. He was a good listener and never judged me for the independent path I had chosen. Both my brothers had gone to college, married young, and had successful careers. They had taken the path most parents would be proud of. I had not. Had I been a huge disappointment?

In July the weather started getting hot and humid. Gianni and I drove to the Marmore Waterfall about two and a half hours from Rome near Terni, Umbria. It wasn't Niagara Falls, but it was scenic and the mountain air was refreshing. The falls were constructed by the ancient Romans who were masters of engineering feats, as the aqueducts and the Colosseum demonstrated. The mist created by the waterfalls was as soothing as a massage on such a hot day. It beat fighting the snarled Sunday traffic at the beach.

"It's a beautiful place, tranquil, a good place to relax."

"You're right," I said. "Let's take it easy until we have to go back to Rome. It's so nice just getting away from the city with all the noise and traffic." We strolled around the area for the afternoon and sat by the water enjoying the natural beauty surrounding us. It was a perfect time to breathe in the fresh air and feel the cleansing mist, wash over me. Water has a restorative property that rejuvenates the spirit and at that moment it was a welcome relief to my turbulent, muddled brain.

In the evening after we got back to Rome, we went to Via Veneto for coffee and people watching. We sat at an outdoor café with other patrons, staring at the array of characters parading down the street. It was like a scene from a Federico Fellini movie with openly gay couples, primping prostitutes, pimps, and one cross- dresser all gussied up carrying a white purse and wearing a blue skirt with a matching shawl. The nude look was overtaking the fashion world in Rome after Brigitte Bardot was photographed wearing a transparent top. Seeing it on Bardot was one thing, but to see it on some of the oddballs, strutting down the street was quite another. It was a totally bizarre fashion statement, but on full display on Via Veneto.

Gianni and I were just happy to be together. We walked back to the car holding hands, the night dark and steamy, our bodies pressed together as Gianni pulled me close for a kiss. Each one of these intimate moments was etched in my mind, cataloged forever.

We had a survey team from Chevron, New York, visiting for two weeks to evaluate our department's efficiency and work output. They concluded that my work was exemplary. They wanted to put me in charge of the entire telex department. I declined the offer. My deposit on the Boston apartment had already been paid. If the offer had come six months earlier, I wondered whether I would have given it serious consideration. It was still not what I had envisioned for my future. The business world did not hold any fascination for me. It seemed mundane, routine, and I was sure I would tire of it over time. My life could have gone in a completely different direction if I had accepted that job. Fate played a heavy role in my life.

My parents sent me a generous birthday check, and my father, now that I had decided to come home, was communicating with me again. He offered to send me an airline ticket back to Pittsburgh which I declined. What I wanted most of all was my parents' understanding, not their money. After three and a half years of making my own decisions, I was going home on my own terms.

I sat down and wrote my mother a letter sharing my deep, personal reflections. It was cathartic collecting my thoughts and putting pen to paper. It always cleared my head and put things in perspective. She was instructed to keep it confidential, not to divulge the contents to my father. My mother was sympathetic to my emotional plight, and I wanted her to understand what I was going through. Women have the ability to empathize, men not so much, and my father, not at all.

Dear Ma,

My life has reaped nothing but mediocrity and unhappiness. Once I leave here I will be a lost soul floating in space with nothing tying me down, no roots, no foundation. My job at Caltex hasn't given me the satisfaction I had hoped for. It's just a job nothing more. I want to make a difference in the world, to achieve something meaningful and fulfilling.

My love for Gianni is deep, profound. The thought of leaving him makes me sorrowful, grief stricken. The pain is real. I will miss him, yearn for him. But we can never be together, never marry, never have children, never grow old together. His love for me is the only constant in my life; it makes me feel secure, grounded, and I am about to leave him behind afloat in a morass of regret. I may never recover. I feel like my life has already been lived.

My depression was real, my heart ached—I never mailed the letter.

The Long Goodbye

My twenty-fifth birthday was tinged with sadness since I knew it would be my last with Gianni. The year before had been spent in miserable solitude waiting for him to arrive in San Francisco. The girls at work bought me flowers and gifts. Gianni gave me a beautiful gold chain, a bouquet of roses, and had a big dinner party for me with a birthday cake. His parents were like family, and I was about to kill any hope for beautiful little Italian American grandchildren by abandoning their beloved son. I doubted they would ever forgive me.

On July 20, 1969, the employees in the Caltex cafeteria watched Apollo 11 and Neil Armstrong land on the moon and proclaim as he put his left foot down on the surface of the moon, "That's one small step for man, one giant leap for mankind." It was an exhilarating moment but the step I was about to make would cast a shadow over Neil Armstrong's giant leap. It was a step into a chasm of uncertainty with a prolonged, festering open wound to follow.

Gianni and I were invited to Porto Ercole as guests of Carter DeHaven. It was an affluent coastal resort town two hours north of Rome. We stayed at Il Pellicano, an exclusive hotel with a cluster of beautiful, individual villas nestled into the side of a cliff overlooking the Tyrrhenian Sea. There was a spectacular view of the water from the large veranda. We sat in relaxing lounge chairs watching cruise ships and private yachts silently glide by our vantage point peacefully sailing up and down the coastline to unknown ports, or dropping anchor in a remote cove to swim in the aquamarine water. I pictured myself on the deck of one of those fine boats with Gianni by my side. We would sail away together traveling the world. No one could find us to interfere with our happiness. Lovers forever. It was a pleasant thought and briefly put me at ease. With the constant sea breeze came the scent of wild rosemary and sage growing on the nearby hillside. There were orange and lemon trees and tropical flowers as far as the eye could see. It was a perfectly heavenly escape. Thank- you Mr. DeHaven.

We were supposed to return Sunday night so I could get to work on Monday, but the train workers went on strike and there was no way to get back to Rome. It was the first time I rejoiced at one of the multitudes of strikes in honor of Italy's illustrious train workers. It was a day of jubilation, a day to give thanks. The delay gave us additional time to savor the moment. While Mr. DeHaven was having meetings, we spent our time making love, picking flowers and lounging on the veranda. It was a joyous, romantic getaway.

The day of reckoning was drawing near. First I had to inform my landlady that I was going to use my deposit for the last month's rent, and then I had to speak to Gianni; there was no turning back. I was going to make my airline reservation.

Final Preparations

Gianni and I planned to go to Taormina, Sicily, for a week in August. It would be the opportune time to disclose my impending departure. El Al had a flight to New York on September 5, and I made a reservation with a connecting flight to Pittsburgh.

My belongings were organized and ready to be shipped out. It reminded me of my dress rehearsal before I left on the *Queen Elizabeth*. All I brought with me on that life-altering voyage was a garment bag and a pigskin tote. This time I was carrying a gift for Molly, Mary Louise's bronze bust wedding present, four paintings, a radio, a camera bag, a purse, and two new suitcases. It was exhausting just thinking about it. I hid everything in the closet so Gianni wouldn't see what I was planning.

Gianni and I had an unforgettable week in Taormina walking on the beach, dining alfresco and making love.

"*Amore mio, che successo?* (My Love, what's the matter?) There's something wrong." As our last day in Sicily approached, it was hard for me not to appear preoccupied. I was distracted, lost in my own tragic world. It was time to open Pandora's box. The ominous, looming cloud rolled in and obscured the sun. The delicate, vibrant colored flowers suddenly disappeared into a blurred sea of gray, and then everything went black. The dreaded moment had arrived.

The possibilities of misunderstanding or misconstruing my words kept my explanation to a minimum. It was difficult to fully explain in Italian, that the reason I was leaving was to preserve his future happiness. How do you make someone you love understand that? My candid discussion with my brother and Mary Louise could not be replicated. It would have required an interpreter. It would provoke anger, resentment, or worse, he might blame himself.

Instead, I opted for a simplistic explanation. "There's something I have to tell you. I know you're going to be upset, but I've made a decision. I'm going to Boston to live with Molly. I want to go to graduate school. I'm sorry, please forgive me. I do love you more than anything, but this is something I have to do." It was concrete, succinct and entirely inadequate. It was heartless, cruel. It was a lie. He was stunned by my words.

"*Non capisco, amore.* (I don't understand). What are you talking about? Tell me the real reason. I want the truth. Why, why? Why can't we get married? You can't leave me. You can't do this." He sat down hard on the bed almost losing his balance. He looked at me in bewilderment like I was speaking in tongues, not comprehending the words. There was no consoling him. My explanation was a hammer blow to the heart. The words were empty, hollow. We spent the night clinging to each other, drowning in our sorrow, expressing our undying love, and crying until there were no more tears to cry.

It was the saddest night of my life, but I knew it was the right decision. My days of innocence abroad were over. I was about to say goodbye to the man I loved most in the world. My life was shattered into a thousand little pieces. The puzzle pieces which had once miraculously fit together had now been irrevocably torn apart. My love for him would never cease. In hindsight, it was a cowardly way to end a beautiful, poignant love affair that had changed me forever. The contrite explanation I gave him lacked maturity and sensitivity. It would always leave unanswered questions in his mind. He would always wonder why I had *really* left. My explanation was shallow, dishonest.

Coming home from Sicily must have been my penance. The train was overcrowded and I had to stand for four hours, and then eight and a half additional hours scrunched up on a wooden bench without room to even move my foot sideways. The Roman gods were angry and were punishing me mightily for causing such unhappiness. I was miserable, distraught.

My breathing problems returned. I hadn't had a full-blown anxiety attack since I worked for Albert. The depth of my despair made me ill. I couldn't eat or sleep, convinced that Gianni would suffer the most after I left. He would be reminded of me everywhere he went and have lingering memories haunt him. We had shared over three years of happiness and had wonderful memories, but it would be an agonizing journey over time before we could simply cherish them for what they had meant to us. We had loved each other so fervently, so passionately.

It would be easier for me to go to a new city where I would not associate him with everything I did, although he would always be in my thoughts. My actions would inflict a deep sense of loss for both of us.

"You don't have to give me back the ring. I gave it to you because I love you and want to marry you. I don't want it." He thought my keeping the engagement ring would preserve our love from ever dying. "You'll come back. I know you will." His unshakable belief in my return only made my guilt more acute, my despair deeper.

Signora Giulia and Signor Arturo took the news badly. They would either look at me sadly and shake their heads or avoid looking directly into my eyes altogether. They wanted me to be their daughter-in-law, and this news was devastating. They must have asked Gianni for a reasonable explanation, trying to understand my motives, but he would not have been able to provide one. Our once happy, entertaining family meals gave way to silent, strained gatherings, similar to a Catholic wake I had once witnessed. Since I had vacated my apartment in preparation for my departure, I was staying with the Rossellinis, probably not the best planning on my part. Gianni was sleeping at his sister's. It made for many awkward dinners.

The only conversation was to ask politely for platters to be passed around. Carla, who was like an older sister to me, was the only one to venture a question after the dinner was over. "How's Molly? I haven't heard anything from her in a long time. Gianni said you want to live with her in Boston. Is that true?" I assured her it was true but never offered any more details. It was like actors in a tragic play and we were all playing our parts until the last act.

Molly, who was a particular favorite of hers and Signor Arturo, had sent postcards periodically to stay in touch. Signor Arturo always said she reminded him of Signora Giulia when she was young and *una bombola* (a doll.) She could never bring herself to ask me the more probing question—why was I *really* leaving? A heavy weight was again sitting on my chest weighing me down. It was physically painful to take deep breaths, and my breathing became labored, as though I was on the verge of a heart attack. Every time I looked at Gianni and saw how sad he looked, it would bring fresh tears to my eyes. There is nothing good in "goodbye."

20

Returning to The US

"*Quando ritornerai?*" Gianni wrote me to ask when I was coming back. I wrote him and told him he deserved to find everlasting love and happiness with a wonderful Italian woman who would treasure him as I had, and "*No amore mio, non tornerò mai.*" (No my love, I'm never coming back.)

The feelings of profound loss overwhelmed me at unexpected times. I could be driving to work, going for a walk, or eating a simple meal, and all of a sudden sink into the deepest depression. It would plague me like an ugly mythological Kraken appearing from the depths of Hell to terrorize me. Sleeping soundly became a thing of the past. For years afterward I had recurring dreams of Gianni and longed for just one more night to have him hold me in his arms. Overall, they were happy dreams except for the occasional ones when he would ask, "*Perché, perché?*" (Why, why?)

My three and a half years in Europe were a time for adventure, a time to foster new friendships, to fall in love as only a freshly minted idealistic twenty-two-year-old could, and to mature. College had provided factual and conceptual knowledge. After graduation there were no deadlines, no curfews, no papers to write, no parental guidance, no reason to question my youthful belief in my invincibility. My mind was open, unafraid, and unencumbered with conventional wisdom. I was naive, malleable like silly putty. I viewed things from different perspectives, different cultures, different languages, and made decisions independently and collaboratively.

The unexpected and exhilarating happenings in those years made life energizing. Nothing was predictable or mundane. Each day brought new and exciting challenges which had to be solved one way or another. Marriage was for all the twenty-somethings who never envisioned doing anything other than what the previous twenty-somethings had done. It was conventional expectations which shackled my independent nature. It wasn't what I had foreseen for my future. I wanted to be thrilled, to love and be loved, to live an adventurous life to its fullest degree, eking out every last drop of an adrenaline high.

My early twenties were not an age for mature, insightful reflections, or analysis of one's actions. Decisions were made without fully anticipating the reaction or consequences. Looking back on those years I now realize my relationship with Gianni was my "coming of age." It was a transitional milestone that moved me from a carefree, adventurous life into a world of full-fledged adulthood with all its convoluted complexities. The emotion I felt at the time was raw and painful, and I would learn and grow from having experienced Gianni's deep, enduring love. It would provide a solid foundation to build upon in the future when I was ready to fall in love again and accept all its promise and joy.

The 1960s were years of turbulence and change both socially and economically. Women began thinking of more than becoming housewives or mothers and putting their aspirations on hold. My years abroad gave me resilience and strength that helped mold me into the woman I was to become. They nourished and sustained a great love that would be remembered for a lifetime. They were both visceral and thought-provoking, much broader and encompassing than any four-year-college education could ever have provided. I was on the cusp, finally crossing the threshold into adulthood, bruised and battered, yet ready to confront the future with all its promise.

Life Goes On

The transition to living my life in Boston after my traumatic departure from Rome was not an easy task. Molly was initially generally supportive since she understood what I had been through, but after a few months she became exasperated with my prolonged depression. It was difficult for her to have a roommate who was constantly collapsing in tears and recounting a painful loss of my one true love.

"It's tough being around you sometimes. You're starting to drag me down with you. We need to start traveling again. We both love it and my job definitely has its perks. We can get a free room anywhere in the world at one of Sheraton's hotels." (She worked at Sheraton Hotels & Resorts, an international hotel chain.)

"You're right. My traveling days came to an end when I left Rome. I've had too much time to think. I've dug a hole so deep I can't seem to climb out. Where do you want to go?"

Our first trip was to Aruba. We met a few guys at a bar and hung out with them for the week. I wasn't the best company, but I tried to be pleasant. I ended up with a Dutch guy who was boringly ordinary . . . definitely not my type, but he made the time go by quickly. I was slowly returning to an even keel emotionally, although Gianni was never far from my thoughts.

For Christmas Molly and I went to Nassau on our second trip where I met a British hotel clerk who was charming and good- looking. He was my first blonde. We immediately clicked. Since he was a hotel employee, I was able to sneak into his room without much fuss. I fell for his British accent. Steve and I had a relationship that lasted a few months—nothing too serious. I flew back to Nassau on several weekends to stay with him and go to the beach on Paradise Island. Time was passing and the pain I felt leaving Gianni for the last time was receding into just happy memories.

During the winter of 1969, I got a job as an administrative assistant at a mental health center in Cambridge, Massachusetts, near Harvard Square. At times I was asked to lend a hand with the group of children attending programs at the center. The children were kindergarten age or younger and suffered from emotional trauma and developmental delays. I enjoyed working with them and watched Stan, the child psychiatrist, interact with them. He was a brilliant doctor and had written many articles about children and child psychiatry. He was affable and caring, and he encouraged me to consider getting a masters in education. Stan said I could go to school and still work at the center part-time. Lesley College had a graduate program in education and was only a few blocks from the center. It was walkable. Everything was beginning to fall into place, but I wasn't ready to make a commitment to graduate school.

After a year of working at the center, I met Robert who was three years younger than I was. He was a chemist and worked for a large scientific firm in Cambridge. He wasn't my usual type—he had a broad-shouldered, well-built body; a baby face with blue eyes, and long, blonde hair almost to his shoulders. I guess I could describe him as a hippie. He was intelligent and well-read with a fondness for hard rock and drugs, introducing me to a variety of both. Living in Europe I had managed to miss the drug scene and I was curious. I approached drugs with trepidation and felt Robert would ease me into it because he was knowledgeable and understood the effects and interactions of each drug. The one glaring point of contention was his lack of worldliness—he had never traveled. Even so, we began a long-term relationship. I insisted he cut his hair, and I enrolled in the graduate program at Lesley College.

I was spending more time at Robert's than on Commonwealth Avenue, and when our one-year lease ended, Molly decided to get her own place in Boston. I moved to Brookline which was an easier commute to my job in Cambridge. I found a spacious, two bedroom apartment in an early 1900s building with an eat-in kitchen and separate dining room. It even had a working fireplace, a small exterior porch, and a one-car detached garage behind the building. It was on a quiet tree-lined street, conveniently located near Coolidge Corner.

What I needed was a roommate to help with the rent. I placed an ad in *The Phoenix*, a local newspaper known for its classifieds, and before long I had a new roommate, Karen. She had a job at a college in Boston and turned out to be a perfect choice. She was mature, honest, and respected my privacy as I did hers.

My relationship with Robert continued to evolve, and he fell deeply in love with me. I was fond of him and he was a sensational lover, particularly when we were high on grass (marijuana), but I began to feel stifled and trapped like a bird whose wings had been clipped. It was a relationship destined to crash and burn. As the third year approached, I was looking for an exit strategy.

In late fall of 1973 Robert decided to visit a friend in Ohio. "I'm going to visit Jim. I want his advice about something and need to see him face-to-face."

"Anything you care to discuss with me?"

"I will when I get back." Robert gave me a mischievous smile and a wink. I immediately became alarmed. I was all too familiar with his seductive tone of voice. His whole demeanor spelled trouble—he was going to propose.

21

Soulmates

I became preoccupied with thoughts of Robert and increasingly worried about what I was going to do when he returned. Getting out of the apartment and concentrating on something else could ease my fears. I went to World Tire, a bare-bones commercial tire store in Cambridge known for selling quality radials. I had just ordered my first car, an orange Toyota station wagon and wanted to buy radials since it didn't come equipped with them. New England winters demanded radials.

As I stepped into the entrance, a handsome man about my age approached me. He was roughly six feet tall, slim, with a sharply angled face and prominent nose. He looked very European . . . *maybe French?* He was just my type. His straight light brown hair fell over his bushy eyebrows. I'm a glutton for bushy eyebrows. Dressed in a dark brown turtleneck sweater, tweed jacket with suede elbows and corduroy slacks, his appearance spelled sophistication and sexiness—very *de rigueur* (fashionable), and my first thought was *what is a man like this doing in a tire store?*

"Can I help you? Are you looking for any particular brand of tires?"

I was flabbergasted. "I actually need an education on radials since I know absolutely nothing about them, and I want to buy them for a car I don't even own."

"Well, that's an interesting story. Why don't you come into my office and I'll spend time getting you educated. I'm Claude Pelanne." I felt he was about to educate me on something other than radial tires.

We spent the next hour and a half behind a closed door, talking about everything *but* radial tires. We shared our life experiences. He was born in New York City but had grown up in France with his French parents and three brothers. *Bingo! I pegged him perfectly.* He was totally bilingual. In 1963 he returned to the States with his family to go to college at Tufts University in Medford, Massachusetts. His family moved to New Canaan, Connecticut. He enjoyed acting and became a regular performer at Tufts' "Cup and Saucer" and in the French theater department, acting in plays by Molière and Becket.

In 1967 he graduated with a BA in French and political science and entered a PhD program in French, but soon decided he didn't really want to be a French professor. When he dropped out of school, he was drafted into the army and sent to Vietnam for a tour of duty from 1968-1969. His experiences in Vietnam were traumatic, and when he returned he needed to process what he had witnessed and decompress. His older brother Marc lived in Nassau and worked as a pilot for Out Island Airways. He decided to go to the Bahamas for a month for some R&R and island hop with his brother.

We talked about food, books, travel, art, politics, and all the things we shared in common. I finally met a soulmate. During our time in the closed office, his boss Lee, who was his best friend, kept sticking his head in to see what was taking so long. "Haven't you sold her tires yet?" I'm sure he was wondering what was going on. As the conversation drew to an end, Claude managed to sell me used tires off Lee's car. He told me I was a real chiseler but then asked me out to dinner. It was fortuitous, at least from my point of view, that Robert was in Ohio, so I accepted.

Claude made dinner for me. It was a delicious *poulet Basquaise* (chicken with peppers and tomatoes). He could cook! How marvelous! I immediately called Karen to tell her I wouldn't be home and would see her the next day. It was love at first sight. Claude and I spent the night making love on a double mattress on the floor of his Bohemian-style studio.

When Robert returned on Sunday night, the die was cast. I was going to break his heart. It was a gut-wrenching conversation with a bewildered Robert, looking like he had been struck by a Mack truck. He just fell apart. I felt guilty that I put him through this overwhelmingly, distressful experience, but after meeting Claude there was no other option.

"I hope I can make you understand. It was fate—kismet I suppose. I didn't mean for it to happen. I didn't plan to meet anyone else. It just happened."

"But I love you and I thought you loved me. When I left on Friday, we were happy . . . we were together—ready for the next step. How could this happen so suddenly without warning? Can't we work it out? I don't even want to think of breaking up. I can't . . . don't ask me to." The whole night was just awful.

The next few weeks I continued talking to Robert, trying to be supportive and sympathetic. I felt tremendous compassion for him and what he was going through. It was a reminder at how deeply I could hurt another human being. *Hadn't I done the same thing to Gianni?* Robert was in a very dark place. I was afraid he might do something terrible like overdose on one of his many drug concoctions. Molly told me I was making it worse by continually staying in touch with him and that I should make a clean break. I listened to her. He ended up in therapy, took a leave from his job, and went to Key West to recover.

Molly and I had already prepaid a Christmas vacation to Rio de Janeiro when I met Claude. I now had no interest in going. It meant leaving him behind in Boston. I agreed to go but Molly was thoroughly annoyed. I was not my usual excited self, as I always was before traveling to parts unknown. The seventeen-hour flight to Rio was grim. I spent the better part of it sitting on the toilet in the tiny lavatory.

"Molly, I think I have cancer!" I was hysterical. "I'm bleeding and it burns . . . and I keep feeling like I have to pee."

"What you have is a case of too much sex."

"What?"

"You have a bladder infection. I know because I've had one."

"Are you sure? What do I do about it?"

"As soon as we land in Rio, we'll call the US Consulate to get the name of an English-speaking gynecologist."

I was tremendously relieved to know that Dr. Molly had diagnosed my ailment. It wasn't what we had envisioned for our vacation, but I needed medication right away if I was going to make it through the trip. I ruined Molly's vacation and she accused me of being a Debbie Downer. Rio was a fascinating city with beautiful Brazilian women in these infinitesimal bikinis. I decided I'd go back some day when I could better appreciate Ipanema Beach and Rio's other attractions.

Travels with Claude

Claude and I planned a trip to the Yucatan, Mexico, in February 1974. Our itinerary took us to New Orleans where we stayed for a few days with an old school friend of Claude's. From there we flew to Merida with a connecting flight to Isla Mujeres, an island located off the Yucatan peninsula. We chose this remote destination since neither of us had ever been there, and it sounded like a romantic spot to provide sustenance to our blossoming romance.

We had a wonderful time together, and I got to see a facet of Claude's theatrical side. He kept me in stitches, performing little comedic skits using strange voices and making faces. His rubber-like face contorted into uncanny grimaces. He was a natural comedian. I was overjoyed to have chosen a humorous man with an abundance of personality, wit, and intelligence, who could cook and do laundry.

There was one unforgettable incident that turned into our first "tiff." We had to wake up at dawn to catch a ferry to the mainland in time for a bus leaving for Chichen Itza, one of the major ancient Mayan ruins in Mexico. While dressing for breakfast the day before departure, I spotted an enormous bug climbing on the wall and reached for the closest object to hurl at it . . . our sole alarm clock. It smashed the bug and shattered into tiny pieces.

"Look what you've done! It was a harmless bug not a man-eating tiger!" he yelled.

"But I needed to act quickly and I wasn't about to touch that icky thing with my bare hands. The clock did the trick."

"So now, how are we going to get up in time for the ferry, huh? Ever think of that?"

"We can ask the desk clerk to wake us."

"You think we can rely on someone to wake us at 4:30 a.m.? I doubt it. This is a sleepy Mexican island and everything moves in slow motion." He was very angry with my spontaneous reaction to annihilating a solitary insect the size of a small truck. I felt like an assassin. The night receptionist pulled through for me after I pleaded with him and flirted just a wee bit. We received an early morning call in time to make the ferry. Our first argument was over, but I learned early on that Claude was not a patient man.

When we weren't traveling somewhere, I was busy studying. In May 1974, I received my masters degree in education. I also got a Massachusetts state certification to teach children with special needs. The Cambridge School Department hired me as a learning disabilities specialist and placed me at the Agassiz Elementary School. Stan was sorry to see me leave the mental health center, but he was glad he had been instrumental in my choice of a future career.

As July approached, Claude was busy arranging a trip to West Africa with a stop in Paris. He had been invited by Monsieur Charron, a friend of his parents who worked for the United Nations Development Program and was stationed in Dahomey (now Benin), West Africa. Claude saw it as an opportunity for possible employment at the United Nations. I was not about to let him go alone.

"I've always wanted to go to Africa and I'm off for the summer. What an exciting trip!"

"But Monsieur Charron doesn't know you, and I can't just bring you along like a suitcase."

"Why not? Why can't you ask him? Tell him it's extremely important for me to go with you."

"What's so important? You'll still be here when I get back. I'll only be gone six weeks."

"Six weeks! Are you serious? That's a long time. You can't go without me."

"Is that so? Who died and made you boss? You're a royal pain in the ass!"

I was furious and locked myself in the bathroom and wouldn't come out. It was our second fight. Eventually Claude came around to my point of view particularly when I mentioned how lonely he would be traveling to remote places without his trusted companion. He left two weeks before me to minimize the imposition on Monsieur Charron and his wife since we were staying at their house. We were given separate rooms with beds enveloped in cocoon-like mosquito netting. As soon as the lights in the house went off, I sneaked into his room via the adjoining bathroom. It became a nightly stealth operation. The mosquitoes were our only witnesses.

We traveled throughout West Africa and made stops in The Ivory Coast, Senegal, Dahomey, and Ghana. As I had learned living in Italy, traveling was an education. The Ghanaians were like the Italians of Africa in friendliness and hospitality. We met John, a teacher who was so thrilled we were visiting Ghana that he traveled with us on local mammy buses all over the country to introduce us to Ghanaian culture. It was the first time we were in the minority—two white Americans surrounded by black Africans. It was a lesson in humility.

There was a particularly telling incident one day. We were all crammed on a mammy bus when we noticed two light-skinned black women dressed in African garb sitting in the rear. They were obviously American and stood out like sore thumbs.

As the day progressed I became violently ill with stomach cramps and needed a bathroom desperately. It was the onset of dysentery. John asked the bus driver to make an emergency stop at the nearest gas station. The Ghanaians on the bus were very sympathetic except for the two women in the rear. They made rude and hostile comments about the bus having to make an emergency stop for us. They failed to realize that John and his fellow Ghanaians viewed them as foreigners just as they viewed us—we were Americans. It was not germane claiming Africa as their ancestral home simply because of their skin color and wearing African clothes. When the bus stopped, I was hoisted out the window. It was the quickest exit to the bathroom . . . the passengers cheered me on.

We stopped in Paris on our way back from Africa to visit Claude's array of family—aunts, uncles, and cousins. We remained there while I recuperated from dysentery. Claude was very solicitous and took exceptional care of me. He admitted, "I'm so happy you insisted on coming with me. I never would have had as much fun alone."

When Claude found out the United Nations was not hiring white American males, he enrolled in a masters program at Boston University School of Communications in broadcasting and film. When Karen moved out to get married, Claude moved in. After his graduation he got a job as a producer and then executive producer at a Boston TV affiliate of ABC.

Marriage & Beyond

We were married on May 24, 1975, in Pittsburgh at my parents' condo. I wore a slinky, shimmering, floor-length, blue tank dress embossed with butterflies with a matching jacket and scarf. The small ceremony consisted of our immediate families and a few close friends.

My father made a gallant effort to walk me across the living room and hand me off to his future son-in-law. He was undergoing radiation treatments for cancer and it was obvious he was not feeling well. The marriage was officiated by a judge chosen by my mother who had won a battle with my future mother-in-law. The fact that I was Jewish and Claude was Catholic was concerning to both mothers who believed deeply in their respective religions. My mother-in-law wanted a priest and a rabbi to officiate, but my mother refused to have a priest on the premises. They finally agreed on a judge. My mother had the last laugh—he was Jewish.

The reception was held at a French restaurant in downtown Pittsburgh—the food was outstanding. Claude's best man Lee gave the toast and recounted how we met at his tire store. It added a bit of humor and levity to our happy day. The Belgian chef came out of the kitchen in his chef's hat to introduce himself to my French in-laws. It was an entertaining spectacle. Our wedding cake had chocolate icing and was decorated with fresh yellow daisies. Nothing was conventional—just the way we liked it.

Our first acquisition as a married couple was a twenty-six-foot sailboat instead of a house which we kept in Kittery, Maine. We named it Snow Goose. We didn't tell our parents since we knew they would say we were crazy. Claude had learned to sail at Tufts and we both enjoyed being on the water. Sailing was our quiet time . . . a time to feel the wind in our faces, to smell the salt air, and to relax.

We tried to get pregnant about a year after we married, but for whatever reason I was unable to conceive. After going through humiliating and exhausting fertility testing and trials, we gave up and I resigned myself to a childless life.

Instead of making babies we spent our time traveling. We went to Europe, including Great Britain on multiple occasions, Haiti twice, the Bahamas, the West Indies, and a major month-long trip to Bora Bora, Fiji, New Zealand, and Australia.

My father died in 1977 and my mother in 1980. Sid died in 1986. Our marriage suffered greatly during those years. Losing Sid when he was only forty-nine years old after bypass surgery was the most devastating. I withdrew from the world and grieved for three long years. It was a sign of Claude's devotion to remain by my side during those difficult years. He carried the burden without complaint.

22

My Return to Rome with Claude

Molly had maintained contact with Gianni over the years. She began making annual pilgrimages to Italy, becoming a devoted student to learning proper Italian. She traveled with her language school to various parts of Italy to improve her knowledge and fluency of the language we both loved and held dear. She saw Gianni and Elena many times. They always questioned her about how I was doing, how "Claudio" was doing, and didn't understand why we didn't have any children yet. I sent occasional Christmas cards, but that was the extent of our contact until I decided to make the trip back.

In 1989 Claude and I decided to go to Italy on vacation. I hadn't returned since 1969. We planned to make a stop in Rome because I wanted to see Gianni. Claude knew about my past relationship. The anticipation of seeing him again after twenty years was stomach churning. How would he react? Would his wife be hospitable? How would I feel? How would Claude handle all the emotional turmoil I was anticipating?

I had been in touch with Gianni's wife Elena via email. She told me Gianni never learned how to use the computer so she would be the conduit for communication. She was welcoming, alarmingly so, and wrote to me as though I was a dear, old friend. It was disarming, especially for a traditional Italian woman who came from a small village in Umbria. She had been married for nineteen years and had three children to show for it. She probably figured she had won and what was there to fear from an old *fidanzata* (girlfriend).

Molly told me Elena would interrogate her about me when they got together. She was obviously curious. Molly said she was sure Gianni had made our relationship very clear to Elena. She knew I had been the love of his life and had accepted that fact. She seemed not to harbor jealousy toward me, but expressed genuine interest.

We set a time to meet. We were invited to Gianni's apartment for *pranzo*. When we arrived and I saw him waiting outside for us, I was overcome with emotion. I couldn't speak. I fought back tears. He smiled shyly. I awkwardly embraced him and felt a heavier body than I remembered, but he looked as though he had aged gracefully. He still had a full head of hair that hadn't yet turned gray. He seemed uncomfortable in my embrace and released me before I did, gently pushing me away. It probably brought back too many painful memories, too many unanswered questions.

Sadly, Signora Giulia had died several years before our return. Signor Arturo was carrying on her job as an exemplary cook by preparing lunch for us. He was as competent in the kitchen as his wife had been. He made a delicious pasta dish with porcini mushrooms. Italian cooks always took advantage of the freshest ingredients and porcini mushrooms were in season.

Claude appreciated a good meal given his French roots, and he cleaned his plate much as Gianni had done years before. He seemed to take the unusual circumstances in stride. He even admitted he thought Gianni was a nice guy. Claude had been hearing about him for years and finally had a chance to confront his nemesis face-to-face. It isn't every day your husband has lunch with your prior lover and remains married to you. Claude never questioned me about why I hadn't married Gianni. It wasn't a subject he chose to discuss. Gianni and I never had a moment alone except when he briefly showed me around his apartment. I noted that he and his wife had separate bedrooms.

Before we said goodbye, Signor Arturo made a point of taking me aside and asking me that dreaded question that Gianni had asked long ago, *"Perché ci hai lasciato?"* (Why did you leave us?) After all these years I still couldn't fully explain my actions to him.

Later that evening while I was in bed, I forced myself to think about it all over again and wondered why I had given Gianni such a shallow, brief explanation in 1969 that ended our relationship.

23

A Family and a Reunion

When I reached the ripe old age of forty-seven years old in 1991, I became obsessed with the idea of having a child call me Mama. I was determined to have a family, and when a friend adopted an adorable baby boy, I was sold—adoption was the answer. The process was arduous and debilitating, but we persevered. In July 1994 in Suzhou, China, I received the ultimate gift for my fiftieth birthday—the most beautiful, incredible tiny bundle of joy just thirteen months old. Lily was placed in my arms . . . I became a mother. There were tears of sheer happiness.

Lily looked shell-shocked. She kept her trusty thumb in her mouth and never cried, in fact there was no affect, no emotion—she didn't make a sound. Being a consummate worrier all my life, I immediately spoke to the pediatrician who accompanied our adoption group. She assured me everything was fine that Lily was hungry and exhausted from the bus trip from the orphanage. She told us to feed her, bathe her, and put her to sleep. When the pediatrician came to check on her later, she noted that we had put her diaper on backward. Parenting would be a learning curve.

A year and a half later we decided to do it all over again. We wanted another child. This time I stayed home with Lily while Claude made a valiant trip to China on his own to bring back Mimi. She was seven months old. It was clear from the moment she was put into his arms that this child would have a different personality. She gave him the most radiant smile and was completely animated vocally and physically. It was hard to contain her exuberance. Our family was now complete.

While Claude was in China, he called me every day for ten days. Our phone bill was over a thousand dollars! We agreed it might have been cheaper if I had gone with him. The phone company was very sympathetic after hearing our story and reduced the bill to a manageable amount.

Lily was two-and-a-half-years-old when Mimi joined our family. We had tried to prepare her for the arrival of a new baby sister and she was excited. She filled Mimi's room with some of her favorite toys. The reality was quite different. Once Mimi was ensconced in her room and was home for a few days, Lily asked me when she was going back to China. When I told her Mimi was here to stay, she marched into her room and retrieved all her toys and then summarily peed on Mimi's little chair. Her potty training took a major hit.

On another occasion I panicked when I walked into Mimi's room and found her hidden under a pile of crumpled up newspapers. Lily was not happy. It was an ongoing struggle particularly since Mimi was already crawling at record speed (backward). She was a dynamo and destroyed everything in her path including Lily's prized possessions. Somehow we managed it all even though it was trying at times.

We resigned ourselves to the new normal and that having children would change our lives forever. Everyone told us we looked and acted younger than our ages even though we were the oldest parents at every school PTO (Parents Teachers Organization) meeting. We advocated for our children throughout their schooling and tried to provide them with solid foundations in values and principles but always with a good dose of humor. We even welcomed Woody Pecker (a wooden penis) used as a prop in their graphic sex education classes. It made for hilarious dinner conversations. Nothing was off-limits. We were open and direct and fostered dialogue and communication at all levels. We laughed and cried with them. We tried to be the best parents we could, and maybe we had an advantage being older and wiser.

I've kept a journal since 1994 to document Lily and Mimi's childhoods, their development, achievements, trials, and tribulations. Traveling was put on hold, but not for long. Somehow we managed to eke out four trips to France, multiple vacations around New England, Cape Cod, New York City, Washington, D.C., North and South Carolina, and Florida with both of them.

2012 - Fiftieth High School Reunion

I had just gotten out of the shower when I heard the phone ring. "It's Susan. She wants to know if you're going to the reunion. Pick up!" Claude was downstairs in the kitchen. I hadn't heard from Susan in years. She was a figure from my past, a person who had once been my best friend and then we drifted apart and were practically strangers now. I hadn't really given the reunion much thought.

"Hi, Susan. Nice to hear from you. Yes, I did get the invitation but I hadn't actually considered going. Claude already told me he would feel left out, and I'm not keen on going by myself."

"You're kidding right? Since when don't you do things on your own? Giacomo isn't coming with me either. I seem to remember a free, independent spirit way back when."

"That was then, now is now."

After talking to Susan for at least an hour, we were laughing hysterically, recalling some of our more outrageous exploits. By the end of the conversation, she had convinced me to meet her in Pittsburgh in September for our fiftieth reunion. It got me thinking about a time that had remained dormant until now, even though it had been instrumental in changing my life forever. Since high school I had lost my parents and my brother Sid, seriously reducing the size of my immediate family to my brother David and my sister-in-law Ronnie, but I also gained a husband and two daughters. Soon our daughters would be living the years that had been critical in molding me into the woman I am now. Would they ever be curious about a fleeting glimpse into their mother's life? Maybe . . .

Memories began to flood my head as I made my way to the elevator headed to my fiftieth high school reunion without my husband, who had no interest in a reunion where he would be an outsider. Ron, my high school sweetheart, had flown in from California for the occasion. We had remained friends over the years, and we decided to brave the reunion together since our spouses were no-shows. He was waiting for me at the elevator door. As we started our ascent to the eighth floor, we both agreed high school had been a bitch. Now, fifty years after leaving its concrete walls, we were returning.

"Boy, they look old!" Ron scanned the ballroom in search of familiar faces. "There's no way we could possibly look like them!" He turned to me with a look of bewilderment. "I think we got off on the wrong floor. Did you notice a flier on the elevator wall about another reunion on the fourth? Maybe we should check it out just to be sure."

"Hi, Ron. Stan Rosenberg. Remember me? I sat behind you in senior English in Miss McDonald's class." A man with thinning gray hair stepped forward from the crowded room and extended a hand.

The jig was up. Ron winced in astonishment after shaking hands. We apprehensively entered the party room. There was a shocking sea of gray hair, some nicely polished bald heads, receding hairlines, and wrinkled brows and bodies—some with protruding stomachs hanging well over their expanded waistlines. There were obvious exceptions in the crowd like hair dyed a bronze-like orange, and nips and tucks here and there. Ron couldn't bring himself to lump us into that morass of Medicare recipients. Didn't he ever look in a mirror?

As the evening unfolded and the liquor began to flow, inhibitions and questions about why we had ever agreed to attend this reunion in the first place seemed to fall like confetti onto the shiny dance floor. Recapturing the last fifty years in one evening of reminiscing was impossible. I imagined many of us couldn't even remember what we did yesterday let alone fifty years ago. The events would be snippets, those important moments that might have changed the direction of our lives.

While speaking to several women who had been in the popular group, I was taken aback by their candor in recalling the anxiety they suffered. Jane a tall, willowy, curly, carrot top spoke up first.

"You know when I think back on those years, they weren't happy ones. I always felt I could be thrown out of the group on my ass if I made one wrong comment, or spoke to anyone they considered a jerk. It made it hard to concentrate on school work."

"Yeah, I know what you mean." Caroline, who used to be the prettiest girl in our grade, but was now chubby and shorter than I recalled chimed in. "It was constant pressure to be the most outstanding in everything but your grades. I had the latest fashions hanging in my closet, the most desirable shoes and trendy accessories. Everything had to have the seal of approval by the group. It was nerve-racking." Everyone nodded in agreement.

They expressed constant feelings of possible rejection, fearful they would be excluded from certain cliques and banished from the social pecking order of the day. One woman, a therapist, attributed her current profession to the difficulty she had experienced in high school. Another blamed her failed marriage on feeling pressured to marry a man who was in the popular group. There had been an element of general malaise in the student body that I was totally unaware of at the time.

Ron and I huddled in the corner figuring out who was who and making observational notes. "Get a load of Howard over there. He brought a cameraman with him to produce a video of the event. Who would have ever pictured him a big shot." Ron pointed his finger in Howard's direction.

Howard was a Hollywood producer who attended the event with a young ingenue with numerous body piercings and blonde hair down to her buttocks. She could have been his granddaughter, but was introduced as his live-in girlfriend. I remembered him as a nerd wearing heavy, black framed glasses with his pants hiked up to his armpits. Maybe he was experiencing a mid-life crisis since he had never dated in high school. He could now unabashedly enjoy his teenage years.

Then there was the hippie couple. They had never left the confines of the sixties commune . . . the sixty-eight-year-old woman sported waist long, frizzy, gray tresses, no makeup, flowers in her hair, and rows of beads around her neck. Her partner wore sandals, a flowered, partly unbuttoned shirt revealing a sagging hairy chest, and baggy pants. We were convinced they were stoned.

The president of the class of 1962, now a wizened, prune-like, little old man beyond recognition, made an impassioned speech about his life. He concluded his speech by reading off the names of classmates who had already kicked the bucket.

"Jonathan Feinstein, Carolyn King, Stanley Leopold . . ." The list was long enough to be organized alphabetically. Ron and I wanted to be entertained, not flooded with unhappy memories. Susan, who was the reason I was even at the reunion, joined the conversation. She had been my constant companion throughout my teenage years and into my twenties. "Sometimes I pick up my foot to see if there's an expiration date on the bottom. Everything has a shelf life." We all laughed. She still had her killer sense of humor.

The time to have fun was now. Susan's comment was not meant to be maudlin. It was a reminder to live out the rest of our lives in style while there was still time. Nora Ephron wrote a wonderful essay about turning sixty in *I Feel Bad About My Neck: And Other Thoughts on Being a Woman*. She fretted over some major questions.

> *Do you splurge or do you hoard? Do you live every day as if it's your last, or do you save your money on the chance you'll live twenty more years? Is life too short, or is it going to be too long?*

After pondering life's greatest questions Nora decided to do the splurging instead of the hoarding. So what if her bath oil was prohibitively expensive. Instead of one cap full, she filled the bathtub to the brim with the aromatic oil until it resembled an oil slick. Time is running out. Enjoy life's pleasures now.

24

The Sunshine State

When I returned from my reunion still basking in the glow of rekindled friendships and laughing until my sides ached, I began to reflect on the past and a time in my life that had almost been forgotten. It was a time of unadulterated fun and adventure, a time of coming of age with all its pleasures and pains. I reminded myself that there was still time to splurge and enjoy life before picking up my foot and seeing the expiration date on the bottom. Until then, grasp the brass ring on the merry-go-round and run with it.

In June 2013 Claude and I decided to move the family to Florida. My reunion was the catalyst which clinched the deal in our decision. Time was marching on and it was something we had thought about for years but had delayed until both girls graduated high school. Lily had graduated and was enrolled part-time at a community college trying to figure out what she wanted to do with her life. Mimi was about to start her senior year. We didn't want to wait another year—it was time. We both retired. We had had enough of New England winters. I concluded that over the years the gray, cold, sunless days of winter had taken a toll on my emotional state. I had descended into a perpetual depression that lasted through two seasons every year—late fall through winter.

It was one of our best decisions. My brother David and my sister-in-law Ronnie had moved to Florida. Their son Kevin and his wife and children were also living in Florida, as were one of Sid's sons, Cary, and his wife and children. We bought a house in Delray Beach approximately equidistant to everyone, so we were now surrounded by family and abundant sunshine. Claude developed a keen interest in nature photography and renewed his past prowess at surfing. I suppose you're only as old as you feel. I began writing again after being on hiatus for many years.

Both of our daughters adjusted well to the move and are happy, even though we were warned by friends and family that moving Mimi for her senior year of high school was a dire mistake. Lily enrolled in college and got a degree in graphic design and then reversed course and went back to college to major in health sciences. Mimi is in her first year of veterinary medicine following her dream to become a veterinarian. They are both on the road to success. There has been a vast improvement in my outlook on life. What could be better?

25

My Return to Rome without Claude

In 2014 Molly decided to rent an apartment in Rome for three months. Claude and I were planning a trip to France during the same time frame. It didn't take much prodding for Molly to convince me to spend two weeks in Rome with her and then meet Claude in Paris. It meant seeing Gianni again but under different circumstances. I would be alone.

Molly's apartment was in an upscale residential neighborhood far from Rome's tourist attractions. It was a well furnished penthouse with an extended terrace overlooking the city and the Vatican spire in the distance, a far cry from the humble apartments we had rented together in 1969. On Sunday we could actually hear the Pope's homily over the loudspeaker in St. Peter's Square. Molly called Gianni to invite him over after I had sufficiently recovered from jet lag.

"I'm getting butterflies. I don't know how I'm going to react. What if I start crying?"

"What if you do? Don't you think Gianni will understand?"

"I guess I'm still feeling guilty for what I put him through all those years ago. Maybe it's time to sit down and tell him why I really left."

"Is that going to change anything? Let's wait and see if he brings his wife before you get yourself all worked up."

When I heard the downstairs buzzer, I freaked out. My heart was pounding and I felt an anxiety attack creeping up on me. It brought back much of the angst I had experienced when I left Rome in 1969. Molly went down to let him in. He was alone. As he walked through the door, all I could remember was hugging him and being held tightly. His arms felt familiar, comforting. It was different than our last meeting in 1989. "*Come stai?* (How are you?) Sandy, Sandy." He kept repeating my name in his endearing way. He seemed genuinely happy to see me. He continued to hold me against his chest. I could feel his heart beating.

We sat down in the living room. I made Molly promise not to leave the room. My emotions were out of control, and I wasn't sure what would happen if we were alone. We talked for about two hours. We reminisced and laughed about funny things that happened during our time together. I remembered more than he did. Of course I had the letters my mother had saved, as well as the letters Gianni had written me.

The conversation turned more serious. He told us his marriage had eroded over the past eight years, and he and Elena went their separate ways, even though they lived in the same house. *I remember the separate bedrooms. Maybe his unhappiness is older than his admission.* He said she was jealous of his friendships and resented him leaving the house to spend time with his friends. When we asked if he had contemplated divorce, he said he couldn't afford it. Italian law made it difficult, and he would have to maintain two households to support her. Elena never had a profession and had stayed home to raise their three children, two of whom were still living at home. The more he talked about it, the more depressed he became. His face and eyes registered his unhappiness. I had seen that look before—when I left him in 1969. He was clearly suffering but was resigned to his fate, unable to walk away from his marriage. Would we have fared any better had we gotten married?

The next time I saw him he brought his wife. She had insisted on seeing Molly and probably wanted to see me again. The relaxed atmosphere at our last encounter was gone and Gianni was on guard. It didn't go well. Elena and Molly sat on one side of the room, and I sat on the couch with Gianni. She didn't waste any time in criticizing him and humiliating him in front of us. She addressed me directly and told me how lucky I was not to have married him, that I was too *brava* (good) for him. She complained about how inadequate he had been as a husband. We were speechless at her demeaning beatdown, uncomfortable with the whole tenor of the conversation. It was brutal. Gianni's body tensed, but he never uttered a word. He looked down at the floor and let her land blow after blow. We were relieved when they both left.

"I wasn't expecting that. How could she have dumped on him like that? She embarrassed him in front of us. It was awful! She wanted to draw blood."

"Yeah, I had no idea she felt that way. I've seen them many times over the years, but she never sounded angry like that before even in private conversations. Obviously things have gone downhill."

"I wonder what happened? I want to see him again before I leave and tell him how bad we feel for him. She really wanted to hurt him. I thought she was different from most other Italian wives—even magnanimous toward me when I met her in 1989. Boy was I wrong." It was distressing to me to think his wife had nothing but contempt for him. What had happened to their marriage? Had Gianni done something to deserve her rage?

I called Gianni later in the week to arrange another meeting. He agreed to stop over. When he rang the buzzer, Molly was in the bathroom. She told me to go down and open the door. I immediately panicked. It meant we would be alone in the two-person elevator. I was terrified. He seemed uneasy when he saw me, and it was difficult for our bodies not to touch standing in the small elevator side by side. The electricity in the air was palpable. *Is he feeling the same thing?* I didn't acknowledge what I was thinking, but Molly mentioned later that my face was flushed when I walked in.

"We're so sorry about your wife. She said terrible things," I said. We were sitting on the terrace under a blue sky, talking and trying to be supportive.

"I'm used to it. She does it all the time. It doesn't affect me anymore." Gianni looked at me intently. "It makes me sad to think I might never see you again," he said out of the blue. I was taken aback by his comment. I was not prepared for it.

"Why don't you come to the US and visit?" It was a silly thing to say, but I was flustered.

"It's too late for me. I've never flown and I don't speak English." When we said goodbye I told him we would get together again before I left for Paris.

"Molly, I really want to tell Gianni why I left. It's something long overdue."

"Are you sure he wants to hear it? He's going through a lot right now. Is it just that you're feeling guilty? He might not be able to handle it. It could make those old feelings come flooding back. Not helpful."

"I don't know. Maybe you're right. I want him to know the truth, but I don't want to make him feel worse."

"In this case the truth will not set him free, trust me. You didn't pick *him*. Listen, it was a long time ago. Why don't you just leave it alone?"

Instead of accepting Molly's sage advice, I called him a few days later and told him there was something important I needed to tell him and could he meet me somewhere alone. He agreed to meet me at a nearby café.

I didn't sleep at all the night before our meeting, rehearsing my Italian and what I was going to say. It didn't sound any better than it had years before. Would telling him we were culturally unsuited for each other and I didn't want to ruin his life sound any better, than I left him to go to graduate school? His life was already complicated trapped in an unhappy marriage. Unloading my guilt would only reopen an old wound—a painful time in our lives that was best left in the past. Molly was right.

The morning of our meeting he called and abruptly cancelled. I was disappointed and at the same time overwhelmingly relieved. He didn't offer an explanation. He clearly did not want to hear whatever I had to say. He may have realized finally that I could still hurt him—he didn't need that. We agreed to stay in touch. He told me to call him on Sunday mornings when he was usually out of the house and free to talk. We said our goodbyes. We will never have that conversation. I was leaving for Paris the following day, anxious to see Claude after an unforgettable two weeks in Rome.

Gianni will always own a tiny sliver of my heart. My periodic dreams of him after all these years are a testament to the effect he has had on my life.

Nothing will ever change that, but Claude owns my heart now.

Rome, 2017

Made in the USA
Middletown, DE
25 April 2019